TAXATION OF CROSS-BORDER PORTFOLIO INVESTMENT

Mutual Funds and Possible Tax Distortions

ORGANISATION FOR ECONOMIC CO-OPERATION AND DEVELOPMENT

Publié en français sous le titre :

LES INVESTISSEMENTS TRANSNATIONAUX DE PORTEFEUILLE FACE A L'IMPÔT

Organismes de placement collectif et distorsions fiscales

FOREWORD

The past decade has witnessed a significant increase in the volume of cross-border capital flows, and a pronounced shift in their composition towards portfolio investment. Much of this activity involves the use of mutual funds or "collective investment institutions" (CII) that invest on behalf of households who entrust savings with them, typically for fund management and possibly tax considerations. Given the importance of this area, OECD delegates commissioned the Secretariat to Working Party No.2 on Tax Policy Analysis and Tax Statistics of the Committee on Fiscal Affairs to collect, for a representative group of OECD countries, information on the interaction of home and host country tax rules applicable to cross-border portfolio investment, to determine the interaction of those rules, identify possible tax distortions, and put forward options open to governments to deal with such distortions. The results of this work are reported in the current publication.

This book identifies possible tax distortions to portfolio dividend flows in a number of cross-border investment cases. Net shareholder dividend tax rates are derived under different investment structures and under alternative capital market assumptions, and the results are compared with those obtained under the benchmark direct (non-intermediated) investment option. Withholding tax, foreign tax credit and tax integration considerations, as well as tax deferral opportunities, are shown to be important factors in determining possible tax distortions. The book offers a number of policy options which may be of value to OECD Member countries considering changes in their tax laws or practices in this area.

The book was prepared by Working Party No.2 of the OECD Committee on Fiscal Affairs. The project was led by W. Steven Clark of the OECD Fiscal Affairs Secretariat, with the assistance of Chiara Bronchi and guidance and input from Professor Richard Vann and Professor Jan Sodersten.

The Committee on Fiscal Affairs approved the report in January 1999 and agreed to its derestriction. It is published on the responsibility of the Secretary-General of the OECD.

TABLE OF CONTENTS

EXECUTIVE SUMMARY

Introduction

As part of a series of studies by Fiscal Affairs, OECD on the taxation of foreign source income, this report seeks to identify possible sources of distortion in the international taxation of "collective investment institutions" or CIIs, meaning publicly-marketed, widely-held investment funds investing in financial assets. A selection of OECD Member countries is studied, with the intention of indicating the nature of general international tax distortions specific to the area of CIIs.

The report examines both the domestic tax treatment of CIIs and the international tax treatment of cross-border portfolio investment through domestic CIIs and foreign CIIs, including 'offshore' CIIs. The taxation of non-intermediated (direct) portfolio investment in domestic and foreign shares is also analysed, and the results are used as benchmarks for the intermediated investment cases. This report does not recommend any general model for the taxation of CIIs or any special international tax regime for CIIs involving domestic law and tax treaties. Rather possible tax distortions are identified, and possible options considered, recognising the need for policy adjustments to be consistent with the general domestic tax regime for investment income adopted by a country.

The methodology employed in the report is similar to that used in recent OECD tax policy work such as *Taxing Profits in a Global Economy* and *Taxation and Household Saving*. Descriptions in standardised form have been obtained from a number of Member countries in relation to their domestic and international tax treatment of CIIs, which enables comparisons to be made among various possibilities for taxation. Further, net shareholder dividend tax rates are calculated under alternative capital market equilibrium assumptions for the core group of countries in the report to illustrate the possible variability in the taxation of domestic versus foreign portfolio dividend income.

Potential distortions caused by preferential tax treatment in some countries of capital gains relative to dividends, while covered in the descriptive text, are not analysed separately in the quantitative chapter given the already large set of tax rate comparisons to be made when addressing international tax considerations in relation to portfolio dividend income alone. Given the importance of retained profits, the absence of coverage of capital gains taxes limits the ability to draw conclusions about overall incentives and their likely impact on portfolio investment flows. Further, the case study analysis of dividend taxation is somewhat restricted to keep the exercise manageable. The calculations contained in the report, while illustrative and not capturing the full richness of the possible permutations under tax regimes -- in particular, not allowing for tax planning to remove distortions -- are nonetheless helpful in drawing out key tax distortions, neutrality conditions and possible policy approaches.

Recent developments in portfolio investment

The past two decades have witnessed fundamental changes in the volume, composition and direction of international portfolio investment flows. First, the annual *volume* of cross-border investment, both portfolio and non-portfolio (direct), rose sharply during the 1980s and into the 1990s. Second, a pronounced shift in the *composition* of capital flows occurred over the same period, with portfolio capital flows becoming increasingly important.

Much of observed cross-border portfolio investment activity involves the use of institutional investors -- mutual funds, pension funds and insurance companies -- that invest on behalf of households who entrust their savings with them, typically for fund management and possibly tax considerations. For example, U.K. institutional investors held over half of U.K. household financial assets in 1995, more than double the already significant figure of 23 per cent observed in 1980. While the growth of mutual funds in Europe has generally lagged that in the United States owing to the slower process of financial deregulation in the major continental countries, at mid-1995, total assets of domestic mutual funds resident in Europe have been estimated at $1.3 trillion, as compared to $2.3 trillion in the United States. Common driving forces have been at work in contributing to the expansion of these institutions: the opportunity of obtaining market-related returns (money market funds), the benefits of portfolio diversification (domestic and international funds), and cost considerations.

A notable trend in CII holdings, as with other institutional holdings, is an increased interest in cross-border investment. The percentage of foreign assets of equity mutual funds varies considerably across countries, with Italy and Belgium in 1995 showing figures of 55 and 50 per cent, Sweden at 21 per cent, France and Germany with roughly equal percentages of 34 per cent, and the U.K. somewhat higher at 42 per cent -- all significant figures. While there is little evidence to suggest that tax factors *per se* have strongly influenced foreign investment decisions, the magnitude of the amounts involved underscore the importance of tax rules governing this area.

While tax considerations may not factor prominently into foreign portfolio decisions generally, the same cannot be said of interest in CIIs located in tax havens and other low-tax jurisdictions (the so-called 'offshore' market) offering potential income tax deferral opportunities. Approximately 5,800 offshore investment funds are now managing in excess of an estimated (U.S.) $1 trillion in tax-free environments. A notable trend is a marked increase in the average asset size of more recently created funds. One fund alone established in 1996 was seeded with $ 32 billion in capital.

These developments show that, in quantitative terms, international tax considerations in relation to intermediated portfolio investment have become much more important than in the past. This growth underlies the need for ongoing development of tax policy rules to address a range of considerations that arise in the non-intermediated and intermediated portfolio investment cases. Indeed, there remain few industrial countries (if any) for which international tax considerations in this are not now a pressing issue.

Main findings of the report

After reviewing the basic tax rules in OECD countries governing the taxation of portfolio domestic and foreign-source dividend income earned directly by resident individuals in Chapter 2, the core part of the Report (Chapter 3) examines international tax considerations relevant to earning portfolio dividend income through a domestic versus a foreign CII. It first considers the general legal background of collective investment institutions. Next, the domestic taxation of such institutions (as of January 1, 1997) in seven selected OECD countries (Australia, Belgium, Germany, Japan, Sweden, the United Kingdom and the United States) is reviewed, at the level of the investment itself, at the level of the investment institution and at the level of the investor using a CII. It explains how most countries have tax rules specially for domestic CIIs which aim at ensuring that the tax burden on resident investors in a domestic CII is not greater than that which would have resulted from direct portfolio investment.

Chapter 3 then turns to international tax considerations, with a focus on investment in foreign shares through a domestic CII, investment in foreign shares through a foreign CII resident in the source country, through a foreign CII resident in a third country, and investment in foreign (or domestic) shares through an 'offshore' CII in a 'tax haven' country. Income tax, withholding tax and imputation relief considerations are discussed in each case.

For a number of reasons the international (combined host and home country) tax treatment of portfolio foreign investment in shares through domestic CIIs often differs from the treatment of portfolio foreign investment made directly. Similarly, investing through a foreign CII may result in a different overall tax burden as compared with direct portfolio investment. The main findings can be summarised as follows.

First, there may be problems in the operation of double tax relief (*i.e.*, foreign tax credit) mechanisms in the domestic CII case, to the disadvantage of this intermediated investment option. While often tax systems will prevent a mismatch of foreign withholding tax and foreign tax credit, in certain cases relief for foreign tax at source may not be available. Moreover, where tax credits are made available at the shareholder level, compliance and administrative problems in the claiming of the credit may arise.

Second, foreign funds may be characterised differently from domestic funds either because a different legal structure is used in a foreign country or because the special rules for transparent tax treatment that apply in the purely domestic case cannot be satisfied by foreign funds (*e.g.*, most simply because only a resident entity can obtain the special tax treatment). This second difference can cut both ways in terms of its effect on taxation of investment through a foreign CII as compared to direct investment. In some cases tax is higher in the foreign CII case because transparency is lost and the investor is denied credit for tax levied in the foreign country (*e.g.*, where tax is levied on the CII rather than the investor, the foreign tax credit mechanism will usually deny the portfolio investor an indirect credit for the CII-level tax).

On the other hand, to the extent that the foreign CII is not regarded as transparent in the residence country of the investor, it may be possible to roll up income in an 'offshore' CII and defer home country taxation. Taxation may even be removed where the investor realises investment income at the CII-level through the sale of unit interests in the CII and the resulting capital gains are not taxed. The offshore case generally provides the greatest advantage to the investor where there is no tax imposed on the investment income at source or at the CII level. This is the typical scenario with many off-shore funds, and some countries have therefore enacted legislation to take away or reduce tax advantages potentially gained by the investor.

Third, tax treaties often do not operate effectively in the case of CIIs to achieve their basic objectives of sharing taxing rights between source and residence countries, eliminating double taxation and (in certain cases at least) preventing double non-taxation. Again this issue can produce more or less taxation in the CII case as compared to the direct investment case. The source country may deny lower withholding tax rates in the CII case and the investor's country of residence may similarly refuse to credit the higher level of tax at source. Or the source country may apply a lower treaty rate of tax on the basis of residence of the CII (in a third country) while the investor resides in a country which would not be entitled to that lower rate, and moreover the investor may not be taxed on a current basis in his/her country of residence. It was this last case that attracted the most attention in a 1977 OECD study *The Taxation of Collective Investment Institutions* ('the 1977 OECD Study') and the International Fiscal Association report (1997 New Delhi Congress) *The Taxation of Investment Funds* ('the 1997 IFA Report.') It is not the purpose of this report to recommend changes in treaty provisions as this matter needs to be considered by Working Party No.1 of the OECD Committee on Fiscal Affairs, but approaches under current treaty provisions by some countries are noted.

Fourth, the operation of imputation systems whether under domestic law or tax treaties may also be different in the CII case. In particular, if a treaty provides for the extension of imputation benefits to (non-resident) individual investors (*i.e.*, investors resident in a given treaty country), but does not treat a CII in the treaty country transparently for this purpose, imputation benefits may be denied where the non-resident investors chooses to invest through a domestic CII. Note that this is a distinct problem from the general concerns that arise from the different ways in which most imputation systems treat resident versus non-resident investors. If distortions are produced as between resident and non-resident investors in the direct portfolio investment case, and are carried over into the non-resident CII context, then this is not a concern specifically relating to CIIs -- as the benchmark policy of an identical treatment of investment through CIIs and direct investment is achieved.

Chapter 4 presents net shareholder dividend tax rates derived under these alternative domestic and cross-border investment structures. The intermediated cases are benchmarked against the direct portfolio investment alternatives. A second set of net shareholder tax rate results is considered which allows for adjustments to pre-personal tax rates of return caused by possible capitalisation of dividend taxes including imputation relief (if any), which rests on a different assumption regarding the operation of capital markets. The results presented in this chapter underscore many of the considerations raised in Chapters 2 and 3, while adding some additional insights. The simplest results show that if all shares pay the same pre-tax rate of return, then investors in countries with imputation systems would tend to favour investing in domestic shares directly, rather than in foreign shares. At the same time, individuals resident in countries with classical tax systems would be drawn to foreign host countries offering them foreign tax credits.

Results are also presented which reflect the general tax policy adopted in most countries of attempting to achieve neutrality for portfolio investment in domestic shares whether made directly or via a *domestic CII*. When considering investments in foreign shares through a domestic CII, neutrality with the benchmark case is shown to be dependent on treaty withholding tax rate reductions and foreign tax credits being passed on. Host country integration relief, if available to domestic investors in the direct portfolio investment case, would also have to pass through to investors in a domestic CII. In effect, the domestic CII must be treated as a transparent entity.

In the *foreign CII* case, neutrality is shown to require that income tax not apply at the foreign CII level, and foreign portfolio dividends routed through a foreign CII be tagged with the same level of integration relief as attached to portfolio dividends received directly from the host country. In the three-country foreign CII case, the main distortion identified is shown to be the absence of foreign tax credit mechanisms to relieve tax withheld on portfolio dividends at source, which gets stuck at the CII level. However, it is also shown that these potential disadvantages associated with the use of a foreign CII may be offset if the CII is resident in a jurisdiction that does not tax CIIs or impose a distribution requirement, allowing for home country tax deferral.

The second set of results also reflects the importance of the preceding considerations, but adds a different perspective by admitting the possibility that integration relief may encourage corporate-level investment, and not just savings, by getting shifted back and allowing a reduction in the cost of capital. The first set of results shows integration credits as having the effect of attracting investors able to access those credits, while leaving other investors generally indifferent. The second set of results instead shows integration credits as having the effect of leaving investors able to access those credits generally indifferent between choosing those shares or an alternative investment, while leaving other investors discouraged from purchasing those shares.

It may be that where imputation relief is provided, its actual effects lie somewhere between the two sets of results, with that relief only partially capitalised into share prices. This however implies distortions on both sides of the coin -- with investors able to claim imputation relief in respect of given shares encouraged to purchase them (although less so than indicated by the results in Table 4.1), while those without access to the credit generally discouraged from purchasing those shares (again, less so than indicated by the second set of results in Table 4.3.) The results depend on the assumptions of the model and are therefore tentative. As more evidence becomes available on the impact of imputation relief on capital markets, countries may wish to revisit this area, with a view to further examining the advantages of an imputation system versus a dual income tax system, or a classical system with a final flat dividend tax rate.

Policy options

The Report identifies four potential areas of policy concern and offers five policy options that countries could consider to address these areas, bearing in mind the specific context and features of their tax systems (for example, taxpayer identification and information collection systems.) The first concerns income tax deferral possibilities when using offshore CIIs, and how these might be dealt with. The second focuses on withholding tax rate differentials that might arise when using foreign or domestic CIIs, and reviews some past and recent analysis of how this area might be addressed. The third and fourth deal with imputation tax relief and draws on the findings of Chapter 4 in addressing possible policy considerations that under certain assumptions may argue in favour of (and under alternative assumptions, caution against) the provision of imputation relief to non-resident shareholders investing through a foreign or domestic CII. The fifth considers possible foreign tax credit complications and suggests that these be dealt with bearing in mind both transparency and compliance considerations.

A. *Addressing income tax deferral possibilities*

Using a foreign CII to make foreign portfolio investment raises the possibility of an additional layer of non-creditable tax at the CII level. However, as noted in Chapter 3, countries that tax the income of resident CIIs typically impose a zero/low effective tax rate, while others exempt CIIs from income taxation altogether. Thus, in most cases, income tax at the CII level, which for a non-resident portfolio investor in the CII would be a non-creditable tax, constitutes no great problem. In fact, as the present Report notes, the residence country of the CII may not attach a distribution requirement to CII income tax relief, implying income tax savings through deferral opportunities for investors in the CII -- savings that are not available when investing directly in the underlying shares (or through a domestic CII in the country of residence of the investor.)

A potential deferral advantage arises because countries typically do not impose domestic tax on the investment income or capital gains of foreign entities. Moreover, such income is typically not subject to income tax in the CII's country of residence. Income tax or more specifically domestic income tax on earnings at the CII level therefore may be deferred until the investor receives distributions from the CII or disposes of his/her interest in the CII, absent special rules to tax investors in the CII on their pro-rata share of that income as its accrues (*i.e.*, on an accrual basis.)

Tables 4.1 and 4.3 illustrate the effect of income tax deferral possibilities, which lower the net dividend tax rate on foreign (and domestic) shares held through an offshore 'roll-up' CII that reinvests earnings at the CII level. The potential tax savings can operate to encourage individuals to invest in portfolio equities through offshore CIIs, rather than through domestic CIIs or directly where investment returns are taxed on a current basis. This distortion may be viewed by tax policy makers as inappropriate, posing revenue loss, efficiency and equity concerns.

Such concerns have led a number of OECD countries, including Australia, Canada, New Zealand and the United States, to adopt anti-deferral rules in the portfolio investment area, sometimes referred to as passive foreign investment fund (PFIF) rules. Although the specific PFIF rules differ from one country to the next, they share a common goal of eliminating domestic income tax deferral benefits otherwise available when investing in offshore CIIs. In addition, PFIF rules can address domestic tax avoidance tied to the conversion of dividends into capital gains subject in some countries to a preferential tax rate. The successful operation of PFIF rules of course requires the appropriate infrastructure for collecting taxpayer information.

An alternative approach for eliminating income tax deferral advantages and attendant distortions tied to the use of offshore CIIs would be for all countries to impose income tax at some minimum significant rate (*e.g.*, 25 per cent) on resident CIIs, which could be creditable against withholding tax on CII distributions. However, such an approach might be viewed as difficult and too radical a departure from existing tax treatment designed to ensure transparency in the resident CII resident investor situation. Moreover, given the virtual certainty that not all countries could be convinced of such a structure, tax deferral opportunities would continue through the use of CIIs resident in those countries. This would appear to leave the PFIF-approach as the more appropriate policy direction.

Policy Option 1: *Countries that do not have anti-deferral passive foreign investment fund (PFIF) rules may consider adopting such rules as a means to curtail domestic tax base erosion, and to address efficiency and equity concerns linked to the avoidance of domestic tax on passive investment income earned via offshore CIIs.*

B. Addressing withholding tax differential possibilities

The possibility of different source country withholding on direct versus intermediated investment may arise where a domestic investor uses a *domestic CII* to earn foreign source income.

In this situation, the withholding tax rate applied to foreign portfolio dividends paid to a domestic CII might be higher than that applied if the dividends were received directly, tending to discourage the domestic CII option.

Similarly, the use of a *foreign CII* raises the possibility of withholding at source on portfolio dividends at a rate different from that applied if dividends were received directly (or through a domestic CII.) This generally does *not* occur where the distributing (source) company is resident in the same country as the foreign CII, as most countries apply the same non-resident withholding tax rate to portfolio dividends whether paid abroad directly by a resident (source) company or through a resident CII (with the withholding occurring either at source or at the CII level.)

However, the withholding tax rate at source on a distribution to a CII in a third country may be higher than that applied to a dividend paid directly to a domestic investor, tending to discourage portfolio investment through the foreign CII. This situation could arise where the source and CII countries have concluded a tax treaty that provides for a reduced withholding rate for portfolio dividends paid (directly) to *individuals* resident in the CII country, but not for portfolio dividends paid to CIIs. Moreover, investing through a foreign CII generally will be tax discouraged on account of withholding tax considerations alone even where the withholding tax rate at source is the same in the foreign CII and direct investment cases, owing to foreign tax credit limitations under the foreign CII option.

Alternatively, the withholding tax rate at source on a distribution to a foreign CII might be lower than that applied to a dividend paid directly to a domestic investor and, despite such tax being non-creditable, may result in an overall tax saving when choosing the foreign CII, tending to encourage this option. Indeed, individual investors may 'treaty shop' for a CII resident in a foreign country that has a broad treaty network providing resident CIIs with reduced source country withholding tax. For this reason, a given source country may be unwilling to apply a treaty rate to dividend payments to a non-resident CII if it perceives that interests in the CII held by investors resident in other (non-treaty) countries are significant.

Germany's treaty practice is to follow the *proportionality approach*, which limits withholding tax relief based on the treaty between the source country (Germany) and the CII residence country to the proportion of (individual) investors in the CII that are resident in the country of residence of the CII. The relief (in the form of a greater cash receipt) goes to the CII which then allocates it among its investors as it sees fit. This approach seems to be premised on the view that the treaty operates at the level of the investor, but that for practical reasons treaty relief can only operate at the level of the CII.

The 1977 OECD Study and the 1997 IFA Report propose that CIIs should be entitled to treaty benefits in their country of residence whatever their legal form, subject to certain conditions. The IFA report recognises that entitling CIIs to treaty benefits may open the way to treaty shopping, and gives a simple example of how limitation of benefits might be effected in such situations (virtually identical to the solution considered in the 1977 OECD Study) with the aim of achieving neutrality with the direct portfolio investment case, including the denial of treaty benefits where the CII does not meet a proportionality test. Unfortunately, the proposal presents some pitfalls, including a requirement of uniform tax treaties between the countries considered and withholding tax at the CII level.

Measured against the array of international tax impediments associated with the use of CIIs in certain cases, the triangular case (where the source country, country of residence of the CII, and country of residence of the investor are different) may not be particularly problematic, at least currently. However, given the likelihood of increased internationalisation and growth in the CII area, work should continue to resolve this issue. Given that similar problems arise in the context of other forms of institutional investment, this work should run parallel with those efforts.

Policy Option 2: *Countries follow projects underway by Working Party No 1 on Double Taxation of the Committee on Fiscal Affairs concerning the treatment of transparent entities and pension funds under tax treaties, and consider the findings and conclusions of reports on those projects before considering possible treaty approaches to address differential withholding tax treatment in the CII case. This would permit consideration of a similar or tailored approach to a similar problem which arises in the context of other transparent entities and pension funds.*

C. Addressing differential imputation relief possibilities

As discussed in Chapter 2, a country may provide its resident shareholders with integration relief in respect of corporate income tax imposed on resident firms, with the objective of lowering the cost of capital and thereby encouraging real investment and economic growth, and/or with the objective of encouraging domestic savings incentives. As considered in Chapter 4, where the intention is to lower the cost of capital for resident companies, the same (source) country may grant integration relief to non-resident direct portfolio shareholders as well, while recognising that part of the relief may be taxed away by the investor's home country tax system, resulting in a partial transfer of revenues from the source country to the home country of foreign investors.

Taking the taxation of direct foreign portfolio investment case as a policy benchmark, integration relief attached to dividends paid directly to non-resident portfolio investors in treaty countries should also be granted -- on pure neutrality grounds and if possible -- where the dividends are routed instead through a CII resident in the source country (the two-country case.) However, before taking a policy position, it is important to consider the incidence of imputation relief and the economic effects of extending such relief to non-resident portfolio investors. Where integration relief is provided and gets 'shifted-back', resulting in a lowering of the cost of capital, the extension of integration relief to non-resident portfolio shareholders on inbound direct and intermediated portfolio investments may be necessary if the host country desires that this investor group not be discouraged from investing in portfolio shares issued by firms in the host country, favouring domestic (home country) or other foreign shares instead. Concerns could arise, for example, where foreign capital is needed to finance domestic investment projects.

Alternatively, integration relief may not get shifted back and reduce the cost of funds of resident firms. Where this is the case, host country imputation relief may operate to distort portfolio savings decisions and cross-border portfolio flows by encouraging non-resident individuals to invest in host country shares, purely for tax reasons, directly or via a host country CII where integration relief passes through. This outcome may be viewed as unsatisfactory by both host and home countries. For the host country, if imputation relief does not result in a lowering of the cost of capital (*i.e.*, a lowering of shareholder required rates of return) for companies resident there, implying little or no boost to real investment activity, the revenue loss from granting windfall integration relief to non-resident shareholders might be viewed as unwarranted. Furthermore, the residence (home) country of portfolio individuals investing in foreign shares offering imputation credits may be concerned that the attraction of domestic taxpayers to foreign shares paying excess rates of return, supported by integration relief, might make the collection of domestic tax revenues more difficult, given the increased problems in obtaining information on foreign investment income. Where imputation relief is found to have mostly windfall effects, attracting savings from abroad, while having a negligible impact on the cost of capital to firms, it may be appropriate for host countries to deny such relief to non-resident shareholders in direct *and* intermediated investment cases. While recognising the general policy goal of most tax systems of not providing windfall gains, and the fact that possible windfall gains in relation to integration relief are not limited to intermediated investment cases, the following policy options may be considered.

Policy Option 3: *Countries that maintain an imputation system and extend imputation relief to non-resident individuals on direct portfolio investments may consider providing the same relief when those individuals invest through a CII resident in the host country, and where such relief is believed not to provide purely windfall effects. Where imputation relief is believed to provide purely windfall effects, consideration might be given to not granting such relief to non-resident investors unilaterally, and to refrain from granting such relief when negotiating/renegotiating tax treaties.*

Policy Option 4: *Countries that maintain an imputation system and extend on a bilateral treaty basis imputation relief to non-resident individuals on direct portfolio investments, may consider providing the same relief when those individuals invest through a domestic CII (resident in the investor country) where such relief is believed not to provide purely windfall effects. Further, countries that extend imputation relief to non-resident CIIs may consider restricting this relief to account for possible treaty shopping abuses. One approach might be to apply the proportionality approach, and limit imputation relief to the proportion of individual investors in the CII that are resident in the CII country.*

D. Addressing possible foreign tax credit concerns

A further issue in relation to the use by domestic investors of domestic CIIs through which to earn foreign dividend income concerns the possibility that a foreign tax credit in respect of withholding tax at source may be in question.

From a compliance perspective, it might be argued that foreign tax credit claims in respect of foreign withholding tax on investment income paid to domestic CIIs should be taken at the CII level. However, for this approach to be viable, there must be tax at the CII level, whether in the form of income tax or withholding tax (as in the case of Japan), or for CII distributions to be dealt with under an integration system which effectively ignores the foreign source of the income generating the distribution (the U.K. system comes fairly close to this paradigm.)

Treating tax at the CII level as final may be objected to where progressive taxation of such income is sought. The alternative of providing individual investors with a tax credit in respect of income tax paid by domestic CIIs on foreign source income, net of foreign tax credits, may also be seen as unacceptable to countries that have not adopted a domestic integration system. Moreover, in countries where CIIs are not subject to tax, as a means of achieving transparency, introducing tax at the CII level may prove difficult.

From the neutrality perspective of seeking to achieve the same outcome for intermediated investment via CIIs as for direct portfolio investments in foreign securities, the appropriate solution would seem to be the provision of foreign tax credits at the investor level. This approach permits progressive taxation, and by not requiring the imposition of tax at the CII level for foreign tax credit claiming purposes, by-passes the potential problem of introducing an additional (non-creditable) tax wedge at the CII level that would not arise on a direct portfolio investment.

Providing foreign tax credits at the shareholder level raises difficulties for foreign unitholders of domestic CIIs who generally will not be able to access a foreign tax credit in respect of withholding tax imposed by the source country.

Policy Option 5: *Until it is demonstrated that the triangular case is very common, a simpler solution to a potential foreign tax credit problem may be that countries seek within the context of their domestic regimes for CIIs to produce an outcome consistent with transparency, but with the compliance burden falling mainly at the CII level.. If foreign tax credit claims are to occur at the individual investor level, consideration may be given to changes to simplify the operation of the system, as in the U.S. and U.K. systems.*

Chapter 1

INTERNATIONAL TAXATION OF PORTFOLIO INVESTMENT AND COLLECTIVE INVESTMENT INSTITUTIONS

An Overview of the Issues

1.1 Introduction

As part of a series of studies on the taxation of foreign source income, Working Party No. 2 (WP2) of the Committee on Fiscal Affairs has examined the taxation of collective investment institutions in an international setting. Collective investment institutions are understood for this purpose in a broad sense to include the kinds of funds that exist in all developed countries to facilitate collective investment and are usually taxed on a transparent basis (mutual funds, unit trusts and the like) as well as more specialised funds for which there are usually detailed and often concessional tax rules, of which the two common examples are pension funds and life insurance.

The present report is confined to the general rather than the more specialised vehicles for collective investment, though where the line is drawn is to a degree artificial, as some countries have specific and concessional tax rules for a broad range of collective investments. The report deals with publicly-marketed, widely-held investment funds and with funds mainly investing in financial assets (shares, bonds, certain kinds of derivatives.) It does not cover private vehicles used by wealthy individuals to organise their investment activities (except to the extent that the same vehicles are used for publicly-marketed collective investments) or funds that specialise in investment in immovable property (real estate) or commodities, for which some countries have special regimes. For the purpose of the report, the term 'collective investment institution' and the abbreviation 'CII' are understood in this narrower sense (which in fact is commonly used). For similar reasons, not every OECD Member country is studied; rather a selection has been made which should indicate the general nature of any international tax distortions specific to the area of CIIs.

The report examines both the domestic tax treatment of CIIs and the international tax treatment of cross-border portfolio investment through domestic CIIs, foreign CIIs and 'offshore' CIIs, in order to allow an assessment of any specific international tax distortions. The taxation of direct (non-intermediated) portfolio investment in domestic and foreign shares is also analysed, and the results are used as benchmarks in the intermediated investment cases. Unlike the 1977 OECD study *The Taxation of Collective Investment Institutions* ('the 1977 OECD Study'), this report does not recommend any general model for the taxation of CIIs or any special international tax regime for CIIs involving domestic law and tax treaties. As demonstrated in the recent OECD report on the *Taxation and Household Saving*, the taxation of investment income generally, let alone the taxation of investment income earned through CIIs, is too diverse across countries to make that a practical project.

Rather this report seeks to identify sources of distortion in the international tax treatment of CIIs, and to the extent possible, considers what actions or steps to address them could be considered by individual countries. The policy actions reviewed here are limited in the sense that they need to be consistent with the country's general domestic tax regime for investment income. They could be effected either by way of changes in domestic law or by utilising mechanisms in existing bilateral tax treaties.

No changes to the OECD Model Tax Convention on Income and Capital are contemplated. Working Party No. 1 on Double Taxation of the Committee on Fiscal Affairs has two projects underway concerning transparent entities and pension funds under tax treaties which may impact on issues considered in the present report. This report is limited in the treaty area to noting some current problems, practices and tax impediments (distortions) in relation to the international taxation of CIIs.

The methodology employed in the report is similar to that used in recent OECD tax policy work such as *Taxing Profits in a Global Economy* and *Taxation and Household Saving*. Descriptions in standardised form have been obtained from a number of Member countries in relation to their domestic and international tax treatment of CIIs, which enables comparisons to be made among various possibilities for taxation. Further, net shareholder dividend tax rates have been calculated under alternative capital market equilibrium assumptions for the core group of countries in the report to illustrate the variability in the taxation of domestic versus foreign portfolio dividend income earned directly, earned through a domestic CII or through a foreign CII, and the corresponding potential for economic distortion caused by the international tax system.

In particular, the report derives net shareholder dividend tax rates when investing in *domestic portfolio shares* through a *domestic CII* and compares these to the rates observed when investing directly in those shares, with the direct (non-intermediated) portfolio investment case taken as the benchmark. The report also derives net shareholder dividend tax rates when investing in *foreign portfolio shares* through a *domestic CII*, using in this case the direct foreign portfolio investment structure as the benchmark. The use of a *foreign CII* is considered next, and two cases are distinguished -- one where the CII is resident in the foreign source country, and another where the CII is resident in a third country (other than the source country), which includes the 'offshore' (or tax haven) investment structure. Pre-personal tax (after-corporate tax) rates of return at source are initially taken to be fixed and equal across all investment cases. The assumption of identical pre-personal income tax rates of return on all securities simplifies the analysis. The results are also a special case of a second set of net dividend tax rate calculations which are derived under the assumption that pre-tax rates of return are set at the 'marginal' shareholder level.

Potential distortions caused by preferential tax treatment in some countries of capital gains relative to dividends, while covered in the descriptive text, are not analysed separately in the quantitative chapter (Chapter 4) given the already large set of tax rate comparisons to be made when addressing international tax considerations in relation to portfolio dividend income alone. Given the importance of retained profits, the absence of coverage of capital gains taxes limits the ability to draw conclusions about overall incentives and their likely impact on portfolio investment flows. Indeed, even the case study analysis of dividend taxation must be partially restricted to keep the exercise manageable.

The calculations contained in the report, while illustrative and not capturing the full richness of the possible permutations under tax regimes -- in particular, not allowing for tax planning to remove distortions -- are nonetheless helpful in drawing out key tax distortions, neutrality conditions and possible policy approaches. As emphasised above, the view taken in the report is that scope for action is relatively circumscribed. The recommendations provided in the final chapter are accordingly limited.

1.2 Recent developments in portfolio investment

The past two decades have witnessed fundamental changes in the volume, composition and direction of international portfolio investment flows. There are many factors which can account for the observed trends, including successive waves of deregulation of financial markets, computer technology development and application, expansion of telecommunications, and financial innovation including the now widespread application of derivative financial instruments which often do not give rise to measured capital flows.

Deregulation has taken a multiplicity of forms. The most common has been the elimination of controls on capital movements, most notably in the form of foreign exchange controls. But there have also been more subtle changes in this respect such as the lifting of 'prudential' rules that limit the share of foreign investments undertaken by certain categories of financial intermediaries -- notably pension funds and insurance companies. The globalisation of capital markets has also been boosted by changes in practices governing market operations, including tax factors. Market participants now routinely use standardised contracts (ISDA master agreement). Characteristics of securities (in the Euromarkets) have also been standardised. Further, market dealers have ensured that payments flows are more secure -- for example by clearing and settling securities transactions through centralised institutions such as CEDEL and Euroclear, or by agreeing to netting of counterpart exposures. In many countries, transactions taxes have been gradually lowered, thereby reducing significantly the costs of short-term investments.

A. The increased importance of cross-border portfolio investment

As a first step towards tracing fundamental changes in the volume and composition of capital flows which have taken place over the last two decades, consider Charts 1.1 and 1.2, which show changes in the composition of gross capital outflows and inflows, respectively, aggregated over all industrial countries (as defined by the International Monetary Fund.)[1] Several developments are noteworthy. First, the annual *volume* of cross-border investment, both portfolio and non-portfolio (direct), rose sharply during the 1980s and into the 1990s.

Second, a pronounced shift in the *composition* of capital flows occurred over the same period. Gross *direct* capital outflows increased nearly ten-fold, from an average of roughly (U.S.) $34 billion over the period 1975-1979 to $318 billion by 1996. This growth, while strong, pales in comparison to that observed for cross-border portfolio investment, with annual gross *portfolio* capital outflows increasing from roughly $12 billion over the period 1975-1979 to $583 billion by 1996. In percentage terms, the share of portfolio investment in total capital outflows increased from roughly 25 per cent in 1975-1979 to in excess of 65 per cent by 1996.

Chart 1.1

$U.S. billion

Changes in Composition of Gross Capital Outflows, 1975-1996

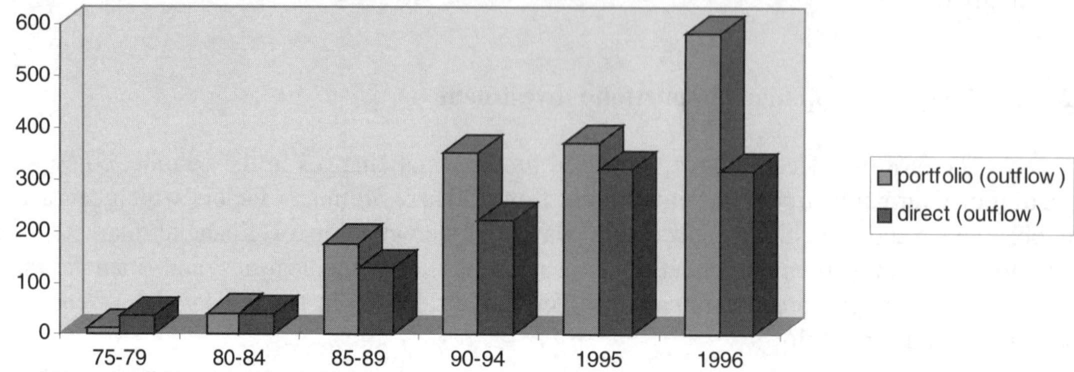

Source: International Monetary Fund 1997

Third, reported *portfolio capital outflows* from industrial countries in recent years are markedly lower than reported *portfolio capital inflows*. As illustrated in Charts 1.1 and 1.2, reported portfolio capital inflows are roughly one-third larger than reported capital outflows, suggesting that a significant percentage of portfolio inflows are being financed 'offshore', outside of the industrial country group, or a significant percentage of portfolio outflows are not being reported, or both.

Chart 1.2

$U.S. billion

Changes in the Composition of Gross Capital Inflows, 1975-1996

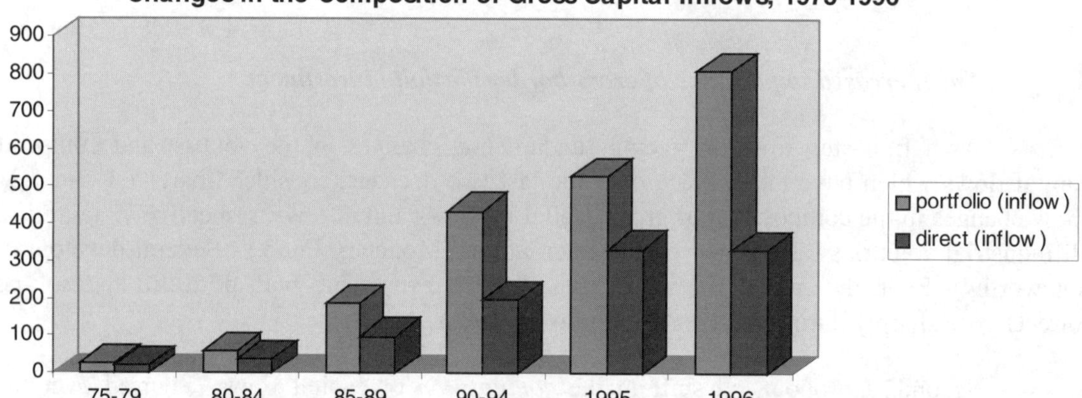

Source: International Monetary Fund 1997

These trends in capital flows have at least two important implications. First, in quantitative terms, international tax considerations, both in relation to portfolio and non-portfolio investment, will have become much more important, given the growth in cross-border investment activity. Indeed, there remain few industrial countries (if any) for which international tax considerations are not now a pressing issue. Second, the relative importance of portfolio investment has escalated dramatically. This growth underlies the need for ongoing development and adoption of tax policy rules to address a range of considerations that arise in the non-intermediated and intermediated portfolio investment cases.

B. The growth and internationalisation of institutional savings

Much, if not most, of observed cross-border portfolio investment activity involves the use of institutional investors -- mutual funds, pension funds and insurance companies -- that invest on behalf of households who entrust their savings with them, typically for fund management and possibly tax considerations. Data reveal that individuals are investing increasing percentages of their savings with such entities whose asset base has grown rapidly, to staggering levels in some countries, making them significant players in the portfolio investment area (often with correspondingly significant influence in portfolio capital markets.)

Data shown in Chart 1.3 confirm that U.K. institutional investors held over half of U.K. household financial assets in 1995, more than double the already significant figure of 23 per cent observed in 1980. Similar growth has been observed in the U.S. and Germany, where institutional investors roughly doubled their importance over the same period, with (resident) household financial assets under management increasing from roughly 20 to about 40 per cent in each country. Institutional investors in France caught up with their U.S., U.K. and German counterparts by 1995, also managing in that year 40 per cent of household financial assets, up dramatically from the 11 per cent figure posted in 1980. (Figures for Germany and Italy, which are not given full coverage in this report, are shown for comparative purposes.)

Chart 1.3
The Growth of Institutional Investors
-- financial assets as percentage of total household financial assets --

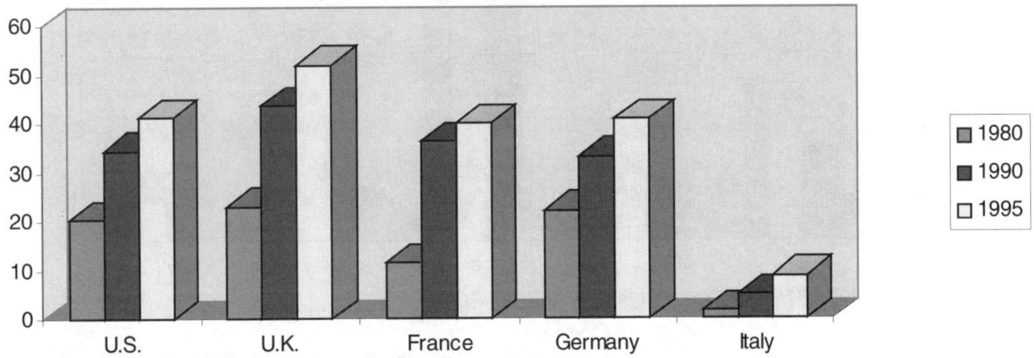

Source: Bank for International Settlements and national sources

Part of this growth can be explained by increasing pressures on public pension schemes, with people turning to private pension plans to cover their retirement needs. Pension saving is likely to accelerate in coming years, now that countries such as France, Italy and Germany have set up the appropriate institutional frameworks for those schemes.[2] The growth can also be explained in part by the special tax status granted to institutional investors. In many countries pension funds are allowed to roll-up income tax-free. Insurance companies also typically enjoy a tax-privileged position, in many cases through tax deductions for premium payments and tax deferral for the investment income earned on reserves. CIIs are also often granted special tax relief, as discussed later in this report.

i) *A focus on Collective Investment Institutions (CIIs)*

Chart 1.4 shows the changing composition of household savings accounted for by domestic CIIs (included along with pension funds and insurance companies in Chart 1.3.) Mutual funds, which existed for several decades in the United States, did not take off until money market mutual funds were launched in the early 1980s to get around the limitations imposed by Regulation Q and other restrictions. By 1995, over 12 per cent of household financial assets were managed by domestic CIIs, a six-fold increase from the low 2 per cent figure posted in 1980.

In France, domestic CIIs held over 21 per cent of household financial assets in 1995, while the figure for the U.K. in that year was 6 per cent. The growth of mutual funds in Europe has generally lagged that in the United States owing to the slower process of financial deregulation in the major continental countries. At mid-1995, total assets of domestic mutual funds resident in Europe have been estimated at $1.3 trillion compared to $2.3 trillion in the United States. Common driving forces, however, have been at work in contributing to the expansion of these institutions: the opportunity of obtaining market-related returns (money market funds), the benefits of portfolio diversification (domestic and international funds), and cost considerations (relative to individual accounts).

Chart 1.4
The Growth of Collective Investment Institutions
-- financial assets as percentage of total household financial assets --

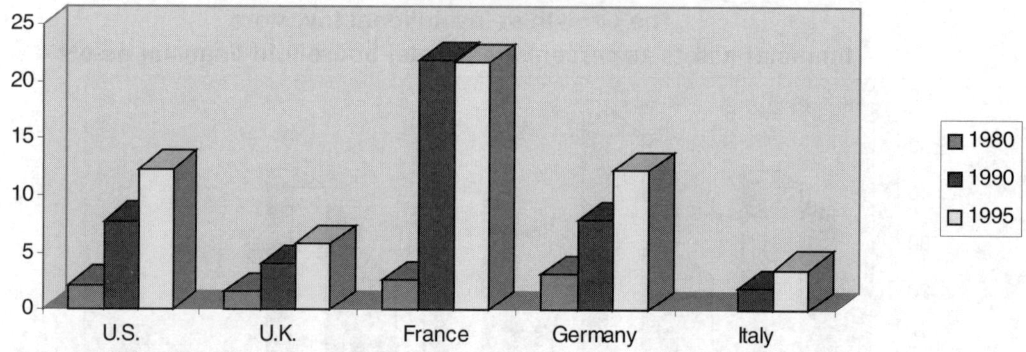

Source: Bank for International Settlements and national sources

A notable trend in CII holdings, as with other institutional holdings, is an increased interest in cross-border investment, captured in the gross cross-border portfolio investment flow data shown in Charts 1.1 and 1.2.[3] This interest is illustrated in Chart 1.5 which shows, for a number of countries the percentage of total assets of resident (equity) mutual funds managed by 'domestic funds' (specialising in domestic shares), 'foreign funds' (specialising in foreign shares), and 'international funds' (with a mix of domestic and foreign shares.) In the U.S., over 85 per cent of total assets were managed by domestic funds in 1997, implying a strong domestic focus by U.S. equity mutual funds. In Sweden, the U.K. and France, domestic funds managed 72 per cent, 63 per cent and 59 per cent respectively of total assets. In Germany and Italy, about one-half of resident equity mutual fund assets consisted predominantly of domestic shares managed by domestic funds, with the other half consisting of a mix of domestic and foreign shares. In Belgium, 51 per cent and 8 per cent of total assets were managed by foreign funds and international funds respectively.

Chart 1.5
Percentage Domestic vs Foreign vs International CIIs (1997)

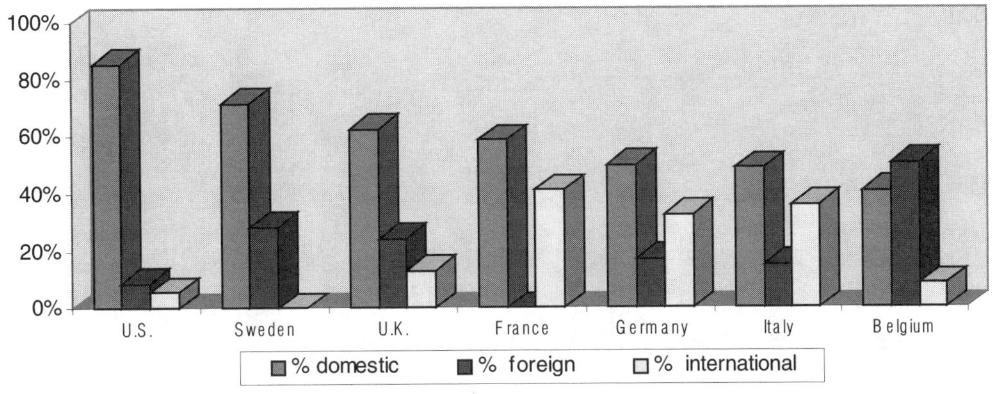

Source: European Federation of Investment Funds and Companies, Annual Statistics.

Foreign diversification of investments has been driven, at least in part, by numerous studies, analyses and performance reports showing the benefits of internationally diversified investment in terms of reduced risks and higher returns. The closer integration of financial markets in the past decade has also had a major impact. While tax considerations may have played a role in the case of certain specific types of investment, in general there is little evidence to suggest that tax factors have strongly favoured foreign portfolio investment. The same cannot be said of interest in CIIs located in tax havens and other low-tax jurisdictions (the so-called 'offshore' market) offering potential income tax deferral opportunities, to which the discussion now turns.

ii) Increasing interest in 'Offshore' CIIs

A final trend to note is in the offshore fund area, with offshore investment funds now managing in excess of an estimated (U.S.) $1 trillion in tax-free environments. Chart 1.6 considers growth in the number of offshore funds, which stood at just over 450 in 1986. By 1988, this figure doubled to roughly 900 funds. Four years later, over 2,500 offshore funds had been created. This figure again more than doubled to in excess of 5,800 funds by 1996. As of the first-half of 1997, total *reported* assets under management by these funds was close to $600 billion. This total does not include assets of over 200 funds created in 1996-97, many of which are very large and account for the overall estimated total of $ 1 trillion in offshore portfolio investment.

A notable trend is a marked increase in the average asset size of more recently created funds (*i.e.*, more recently created funds tend to manage much larger stocks of capital than do older funds.) One fund alone established in 1996 was seeded with $ 32 billion in capital.

Chart 1.6
The Growth in Offshore 'Roll-up' CIIs, 1988-1997

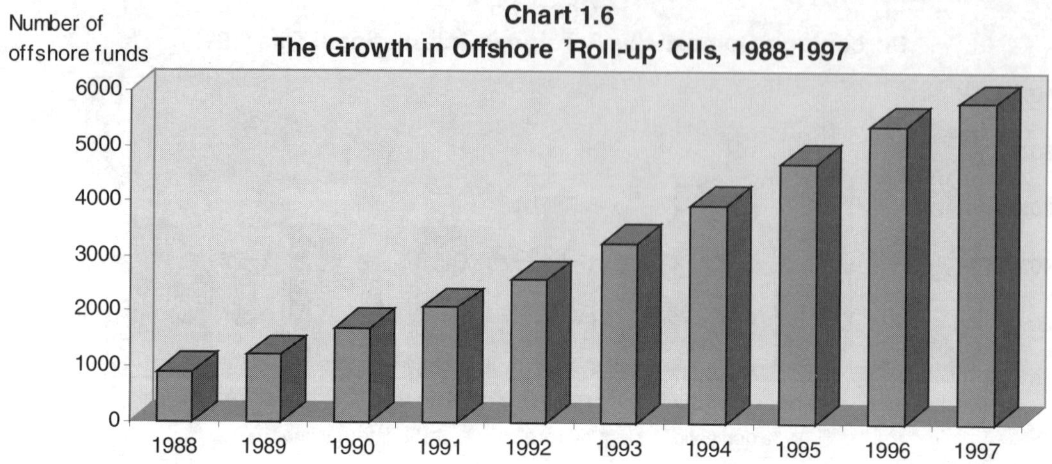

Source: Micropal Ltd.

1.3 Prior studies into non-neutralities in the international taxation of CIIs

Tax considerations raised by the complexities introduced by portfolio investment through a CII have been the subject of considerable study. Stemming from previous OECD work in the area of CIIs leading to the 1972 OECD *Standard Rules for the Operations of Institutions for Collective Investment* and Resolutions of the Congresses of the International Fiscal Association (IFA) at Athens in 1962 and Washington DC in 1971, the OECD worked on taxation issues through an ad hoc group of the Committee on Fiscal Affairs from 1970 to 1977. In keeping with developments in Europe at that time, such as the 1975 proposed EC Directive on Corporate Taxation designed to introduce a level of uniformity in domestic tax systems for companies and shareholders, the 1977 OECD Study attempted to provide a comprehensive solution for domestic law and bilateral tax treaties to deal with international tax problems for CIIs. The study was not adopted as a recommendation by the OECD Council because the proposals were regarded as going well beyond what was feasible, and so met a fate similar to that of the 1975 EC Directive. It would appear to be generally accepted that overnight harmonisation of tax regimes or major parts of them is unlikely. At the same time it is necessary to identify specific problems in relation to the existing framework of international taxation of CIIs and to suggest solutions to them.

The 1997 IFA Congress in New Delhi returned to the topic of CIIs. The IFA has taken an interest in investment funds since the earliest days, including problems posed by international investment via CIIs. The Athens and Washington Congresses of 1962 and 1971 argued in favour of similar treatment of investors whether they invested directly or through a CII. They also sought to extend this treatment to international tax situations though unilateral and treaty provisions. The 1997 IFA Congress produced a set of specific recommendations which bear close resemblance to the conclusions of the 1977 OECD Study.

Both the 1977 OECD Study and the 1997 IFA Report focus on treaty problems raised in the triangular situation (CII, investor, and income source each located in a different country.) The general problem in this area relates to the potential loss an investor could face when investing through a CII that is not granted treaty withholding tax relief that would be available on a direct portfolio investment. In short, where a CII possesses legal personality, it qualifies in principle for a reduction of withholding tax under a convention between the CII state and the source state. The remainder of the withholding tax would usually be offset against the tax payable by the CII. However, because the CII usually pays little or no tax, such offsetting is impossible, while the investor in the CII cannot offset the tax because he/she is not directly the beneficiary of the income. If the CII does not possess legal personality, it is generally not subject to tax and therefore cannot ask for reduction of withholding tax under a tax treaty. In theory, the CII participant could invoke the tax treaty but this is impractical and therefore in practice does not happen, with the result that double taxation occurs.

The 1977 OECD Study and the 1997 IFA Report propose similar structures to alleviate problems posed by the triangular structure (these are considered in the final chapter of the present report.) However, it can be argued that the triangular case is not the most pressing issue and that greater focus should be on the more limited and common problem cases. Furthermore, the 1977 OECD Study and the 1997 IFA Report tend to downplay the tax evasion issues raised by 'offshore' CIIs, whereas this issue is considered in some detail in this report and its policy observations and considerations.

The problems of the international taxation of CIIs have been around for many years which prompts the question why little further study has occurred since the 1970s. As the IFA Report hints at on a number of occasions (such as references to avoidance techniques adopted by CIIs to overcome withholding taxes by sales of income streams), the reason why the matter has not become an issue of urgency in many countries is that CIIs have adapted themselves to the existing international tax environment. As such adaptation is, however, based on tax planning on the side of CIIs it may be that the outcome is less taxation than in the case of direct portfolio investment, rather than the policy ideal of the same level of taxation. The present report seeks to address both aspects of the problem.

1.4 Structure of report

The structure of this Report, which consists of five chapters, is as follows. Chapter 2 reviews the basic tax rules in OECD countries governing the taxation of portfolio foreign-source dividend income earned directly by resident individuals. For comparative purposes, rules applicable to the taxation of portfolio domestic-source dividend income are also summarised. In order to provide a framework for illustrating similarities and differences in tax treatment between countries, a numerical example considering investors operating from a small number of countries is provided. The example calculates net shareholder dividend tax rates that apply under the tax rules in each country.

Chapter 3, the core part of the Report, examines international tax considerations relevant to earning portfolio dividend income through a domestic versus a foreign CII. It first considers the general legal background of collective investment institutions. Next, the domestic taxation of such institutions (as of January 1, 1997) in seven selected OECD countries (Australia, Belgium, Germany, Japan, Sweden, the United Kingdom and the United States) is reviewed, at the level of the investment itself, at the level of the investment institution and at the level of the investor using a CII. It explains how most countries have tax rules specially for domestic CIIs which aim at ensuring that the tax burden on resident investors in a domestic CII is not greater than that which would have resulted from direct portfolio investment. Chapter 3 then turns to international tax considerations, with a focus on investment in foreign shares through a domestic CII, investment in foreign shares through a foreign CII resident in the source country, through a foreign CII resident in a third country, and investment in foreign (or domestic) shares through an 'offshore' CII in a 'tax haven' country. Income tax, withholding tax and imputation relief considerations are discussed in each case

Chapter 4 presents net shareholder dividend tax rates derived under these alternative domestic and cross-border investment structures. As in Chapter 2, the net shareholder dividend tax rates measure the 'all-in' rate of tax on one currency unit of distributed income, taking into account the interaction of applicable statutory provisions that apply at source, at the level of the CII, and at the level of the investor. The intermediated cases are benchmarked against the direct portfolio investment alternatives. A second set of net shareholder tax rate results is considered which allows for adjustments to pre-personal tax rates of return caused by possible capitalisation of dividend taxes including imputation relief (if any), which rests on a different assumption regarding the operation of capital markets. This extension allows for the possibility that net shareholder dividend tax rates may differ from those presented earlier in cases where the tax treatment of returns to the domestic shareholder differs from that applicable to a 'marginal' shareholder group which influences required rates of return and equity prices. This part will appeal mostly to readers interested in linkages between this Report and marginal effective tax rate analysis. This part does not need to be read by the general reader, as the main considerations brought to the analysis by admitting this case are taken up in the summary section of Chapter 4 and in the concluding Chapter 5.

Chapter 5 brings together the major elements from the preceding discussion and seeks to draw conclusions that seem to be valid across all or most countries as to the current international tax treatment of direct portfolio investors and CIIs. This final chapter offers several policy options which may be of practical value to OECD Member countries and do not require substantial revisions of either current domestic law or existing tax treaties.

NOTES

1. 'Industrial' countries, as defined by the IMF, consist of 22 OECD countries.

2. Pension fund assets in Europe stood at roughly $1.85 trillion in 1994, compared to $3.75 trillion in the United States (Hurley et al., 1995). About one-half of European pension assets were accounted for by the United Kingdom and the Netherlands alone.

3. Foreign diversification by pension funds has also been marked. The share of foreign investments in total assets of U.S. pension funds is estimated to have grown from less than 2 per cent in 1990 to 10 per cent by 1996, at roughly $500 billion. The internationalisation of institutional holdings has advanced further in Europe. In the U.K., the Netherlands and Belgium, the percentage of pension fund assets invested in foreign shares and bonds amounts to over 30 per cent, 27 per cent and 50 per cent, respectively.

Chapter 2

INDIVIDUAL DIRECT PORTFOLIO INVESTMENT

2.1 Introduction

The central purpose of this chapter is to set out the basic tax rules in OECD countries governing the taxation of portfolio *domestic*-source and *foreign*-source dividend income *earned directly* (this is the case where a shareholder directly owns shares) and to illustrate the main differences in this area among tax systems. As noted in Chapter 1, considerations linked to the taxation of capital gains in the CII context are covered only briefly in the descriptive text in Chapter 3, and not at all in the quantitative sections, given the already large set of effective tax rate comparisons relevant to the international taxation of portfolio dividend income alone.

In the domestic direct portfolio investment case, a key tax considerations is whether some form of double taxation relief is granted to shareholders. Normally, in all OECD countries, Greece being an exception, dividend income is taxed in the hands of shareholders. Some countries grant shareholders an imputation or integration tax credit in respect of the underlying domestic corporate income tax (or more generally a dividend tax credit which may or may not be linked to the amount of corporate-level tax paid on a dividend) which reduces the tax burden on dividend income and raises the net return to the investment.

In the foreign direct portfolio investment case, additional tax considerations arise. Dividends received from a foreign source may be subject upon distribution to a second layer of tax in that foreign country (with the first layer being underlying corporate income tax.) This non-resident withholding tax on foreign source income cannot always be fully offset against the income tax which a shareholder is due in his/her home country. Where a country provides its residents with a *foreign tax deduction*, only partial relief is given. Where a *foreign tax credit* is available, limitations may apply such that foreign withholding tax cannot be offset in full, although this is less likely for shareholders taxed at the top rate. Furthermore, in the case of foreign portfolio dividend income, relief for underlying corporate income tax typically is not provided by the home country, and may not be provided by the foreign source country either.

A second purpose of this chapter is to explore how taxation might influence an individual investor's decision whether to invest in foreign shares or domestic shares of equivalent risk. In the absence of taxation, an investor would in general be indifferent between both investment opportunities as each would pay the same rate of return equal to a given 'world' interest rate set in international capital markets (under the assumption of perfect capital mobility, and absent transaction costs). The introduction of taxes can distort the savings decision to the extent that shareholders are subject to differential taxation on returns from foreign and domestic shares.

Tax considerations relating to direct portfolio investments are also relevant to the discussion in the following chapters of the tax treatment of income from investments through a collective investment institution (CII). The direct portfolio investment case will be considered as a benchmark for assessing tax distortions that may be at play when considering the option of intermediated portfolio investment.

Section (2.2) reviews the general tax treatment of portfolio domestic-source dividend income in OECD countries. Section (2.3) presents worked examples measuring net shareholder tax rates on portfolio domestic-source dividend income for Australia, Belgium, Sweden, the U.K. and the U.S. Section (2.4) then reviews the tax treatment of portfolio foreign source dividend income, while section (2.5) extends the numerical analysis to this case. Section (2.6) summarises the main findings.

2.2 Tax treatment of direct portfolio domestic-source dividend income

In a given market, individual savings through portfolio investments depend *inter alia* on the amount of tax paid on dividends on the route from the company to the ultimate, individual investor. Usually, personal income taxation introduces a positive wedge between the (after-corporate) tax return to capital and the net (of personal income tax) return to savings. Depending on the size of this *net shareholder tax rate*, individuals may be more or less stimulated to increase their savings and/or to channel them towards alternative investments.

CHART I
Direct (non-intermediated) Domestic Investment

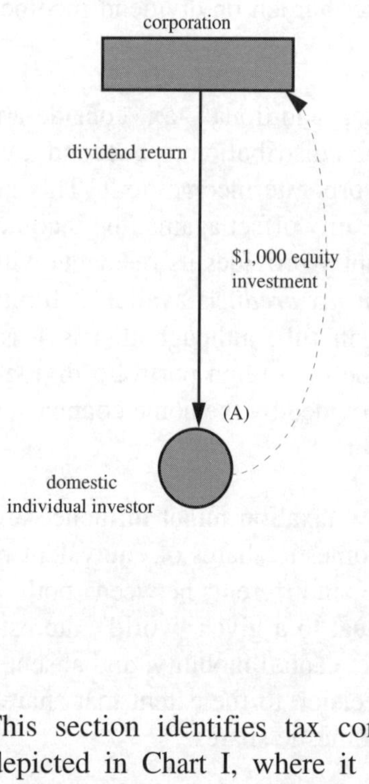

Possible Tax Considerations in Direct Domestic Investment Case

• source (home) country integration relief (A)

	classical tax system	*integration tax system*
after-corporate tax (pre-personal tax) rate of return (R)	R=10%	R=10%
equity investment	1,000	1,000
pre-personal tax return (distributed)	D=100	D=100
personal income tax (PIT):		
integration relief (*home country*)	none	full (or partial)
dividend gross-up	none	D(c)=50 (with CIT@33.33%, c=0.50)
dividend inclusion	D=100	D(1+c)=150
dividend tax credit	na	D(c)=50
PIT (@40%)	Dm=40	D((1+c)m-c)=10
after-PIT return	D(1-m)=60	D(1+c)(1-m)=90

This section identifies tax considerations relevant to the simple domestic investment structure depicted in Chart I, where it is assumed that an individual investor holds shares in a domestic company and receives a dividend at the end of the investment period. Often, dividends are subject to double taxation: a company distributes dividends after the payment of corporate taxes, subsequently the same return is subject to personal income tax in the hands of the domestic shareholder. However, some forms of relief may be granted, at the company or at the shareholder level, in order to reduce or eliminate the double taxation of dividends. Tax considerations are grouped under three headings: corporate income tax considerations, personal income tax considerations and imputation tax relief considerations.

A. *Corporate income tax considerations*

All OECD countries levy taxes on the profit of corporations. One rationale for imposing such a tax is that corporate income taxes collect payment for public goods and services enjoyed by corporations (*e.g.*, infrastructures) and other benefits (*e.g.*, limited shareholder liability) from residing in the host (taxing) country. A second rationale is that corporate income tax can be used to impose tax on economic rents earned on location-specific or on scarce factors of production.[1] Finally, another relevant reason is that such a tax can be required in order to effectively tax, on a current basis, individual shareholders (resident and non-resident) on income from capital that is retained at the corporate level. In this case, personal income tax deferral opportunities can be reduced.[2]

When tax systems attach a withholding function to the corporate income tax, they usually provide some degree of integration between corporate and personal taxes to reduce or eliminate double taxation of dividends. This relief can take the form of a *deduction* from the personal income tax base of the underlying corporate income tax, of an *exemption* of dividend income from the personal income tax or of a *tax credit* to set off against personal income tax liability.

B. *Personal income tax considerations*

Broadly speaking, there are three basic approaches to the taxation of capital income accruing to individuals resident in OECD countries. These approaches are shown in column (1) of Table 2.1 which summarises the basic treatment of profits distributed by a domestic company to a resident shareholder.[3] The first approach is based on a comprehensive definition of income, with income from capital taxed as ordinary income (*e.g.*, Australia, Canada, Germany) and taxes are generally levied at a progressive rate.

The second approach subjects income from capital to final withholding tax, which can differ according to the source of income (bank deposits, government bonds, dividends). These regimes have been implemented in the past to direct savings towards specific financial instruments. At present, there is much greater uniformity of rates. The personal income tax system of some countries (Austria, Belgium, Italy, Japan and Portugal) has optional regimes for capital income whereby taxpayers are allowed to choose between a flat rate final withholding tax in lieu of being taxed at progressive rates (and setting-off the withholding tax against personal income liability). Generally, the flat rate levied on dividends is lower than the top personal income tax rate and equates to the flat rate levied on other capital income.

Finally, the Nordic countries' dual income tax (DIT) stands between these two systems. Denmark, Finland, Norway and Sweden divide the income of individuals into two broad categories: personal income and income from capital respectively.[4] The former is taxed under the personal income tax system (usually at progressive rates), the latter is generally subject to a single flat rate of tax.

Table 2.1 **Domestic portfolio dividend income (as of January 1, 1997)**

Country	Type of personal tax system	Type of corporate tax system	Tax credit as % of dividend	Dividend imputation credit as % of underlying corporate tax *
	(1)	(2)	(3)	(4)
Australia	IT	FI	9/16	100
Austria	25 O	CL	n.a.	n.a.
Belgium	15 O*	CL	n.a.	n.a.
Canada	IT	PC	16.67	n.a.
Czech Rep.	25F	PD	n.a.	n.a.
Denmark	25/40 IC*	CL	n.a.	n.a.
Finland	IC(28C)	FI	7/18	100
France	IT	FI	1/2	100
Germany	IT(G)/IT(25 C)	FI/SR	3/7	100
Greece	EX*	ZR	n.a.	n.a.
Hungary	20 F, 27 F*	CL	n.a.	n.a.
Iceland	10F	CL	n.a.	n.a.
Ireland	IT	PI	23/77*	70
Italy	12.5 F/IT (10C)	PI	9/16	67.67
Japan	35 F, 20 O, IT(20 C)*	PC	1/4	53.33
Korea	IT(G),IT(15C),E(X)	PC	3/17	48.15
Luxembourg	IT(25C)*	CL	n.a.	n.a.
Mexico	IT(34C)	FI	17/33	100
Netherlands	IT(25C)*	CL	n.a.	n.a.
New Zealand	IT(33 C)	FI	1/2	100
Norway	IC(G)*	FI	7/18	100
Poland	20F	CL	n.a.	n.a.
Portugal	25 O	PC	1/3	63.13
Spain	IT(G),IT(25 C),EX*	PC	40	2/5
Sweden	30IC	CL*	n.a.	n.a.
Switzerland	IT(35C)	CL	n.a.	n.a.
Turkey	IT(10C/20C)*	PC	33.33	n.a.
U.K.	IT*	PI	1/4	60.6
U.S.	IT(G)	CL	n.a.	n.a.

Key to abbreviations used in Table 2.1

IT(G): Dividend is received gross and taxed as ordinary income; **IT(10 C):** There is a 10% withholding tax (or dividend imputation credit), which is always creditable against ordinary income tax liability; **10 F:** The 10% withholding tax (or non-refundable dividend imputation credit) is final in all cases; **10 O:** The 10% withholding tax (or dividend imputation credit) is either final or creditable against income tax liability, at the taxpayer's option; **EX:** Dividend is exempted from tax; **IC:** Treated as capital income; **CL:** Classical system; **FI:** Full imputation credit; **PI:** Partial imputation credit; **PD:** Partial deduction of dividends paid; **PC:** Partial credit for domestic shareholder; **ZR:** Zero rate of tax on dividends received; **SR:** Split rate (lower tax on distributed income).

NOTES TO TABLE 2.1

Column (1) shows the amount of withholding tax or tax credit as a percentage of the taxable amount (*i.e.*, for the U.K., 20% being the tax credit of 25 divided by the taxable amount of 125: the dividend of 100 plus tax credit of 25).

Column (4) shows dividend relief as a percentage of underlying corporate tax being the sum of central government corporate tax plus sub-central government corporate tax (if any).

Belgium: 15% for dividends from shares issued after 1.1.1994, 25.75% for dividends from other shares.

Denmark: The 40% rate applies to dividend income exceeding DKr 34,000.

Germany: A gross dividend of 100 is subject to corporate income tax on distributions of 30. On the remaining 70 there is a withholding tax on dividend income of 25%, so that 52.5 is paid out to the shareholder. Both corporate income tax and withholding tax are credited against the personal income tax liability, where the base includes the gross dividend.

Hungary: The regulations on taxation of dividends received by private persons were amended on I January 1997. According to the new rules, tax on the dividends shall be determined as follows:

a) the value falling on the private person in question from the part of the equity of the business association reduced by the valuation reserve shall be calculated in proportion to the pecuniary stake (share, business quota, property note etc.) of the private person entitled to dividend;

b) the part of the amount indicated in paragraph a) shall be calculated in accordance with double the basic rate of interest of the central bank valid on the first day of the year of establishment of the dividend;

c) the rate of tax shall be 20% on the part of the amount paid to the private person on grounds of dividend and not exceeding the amount determined in paragraph b), while the rate of the tax on the further part shall be 27%.

Ireland: * There is a separate credit rate attaching to dividends in respect of companies availing of manufacturing relief.

Japan: Dividends are subject to a withholding tax of 20% (15% for national tax and 5% for local tax - as inhabitant tax) on distribution. For a dividend of Y50,000 or below the taxpayer can opt to pay the withholding tax as final tax. For a one-payment dividend of Y 250,000 (dividend income must be under the ceiling of Y500,000, per year) or below the taxpayer can opt for a final withholding tax at 35%. For amounts over Y500,000 per year, dividend payments are subject to the personal income tax.

Dividends received	Tax treatment
less than 50,000 Y	20O
between 100 000 and 500 000 Y	35F or 20C
above 500,000 Y	20C

Luxembourg: Dividends distributed by a taxable company resident in Luxembourg are 50% exempt.

Netherlands: First 1 000 NGL of dividend is exempted. Dividends are subject to a 25% dividend withholding tax. From January 1st 1997 dividends received on stocks that are part of a substantial participation and don't fall under the first tax bracket are taxed with 25%. In that case, the dividend income exemption is not applicable.

Norway: There is a full imputation system regarding dividends from Norwegian companies distributed to shareholders. As the aggregate rate of the company income tax at 28% will be equal to the rate of tax applying to capital income of individuals, the imputation systems implies that no income tax will be due on dividends received.

Spain: Dividends exempt up to 29 000 PTAs in 1997.

Sweden: From 1997, part of dividends on unquoted shares are tax exempt.

Turkey: Creditable withholding tax: 10% on dividends from publicly held corporations; 20% on dividends from others.

U.K.: Basic rate of tax on dividends is 20%, satisfied by the tax credit. Basic and lower rate taxpayers will have no more tax to pay on their dividends.

C. *Imputation relief considerations*

All OECD countries provide resident individual shareholders with some degree of domestic economic double taxation relief. By reducing or eliminating the double taxation of distributed income, these systems may operate into two directions. On one side, it may stimulate investments by lowering the after-corporate tax rate of return that a company must pay to shareholders; on the other it may, for a given after-corporate tax rate of return, encourage domestic savings by providing shareholders with a return higher than the rate of return on alternative investments bonds (which are not subject to dividend relief). The degree to which integration measures encourage investment or saving or a combination of the two can depend on a number of factors, including the design features of the integration system and the tax-characteristics of the existing/new shareholders that supply capital at the margin.

In Table 2.1, column (2) summarises the corporate tax system in each OECD country, while columns (3) and (4) show two different parameters which give a measure of the degree of double economic taxation relief.[5]

Corporate tax systems may be classified according to the degree of integration between corporate and individual taxes on dividends. Two broad categories are usually distinguished: classical systems and integration systems. The frame in Chart I illustrates the operation of both categories.

i) Classical systems

Luxembourg, the Netherlands, Switzerland, and the USA operate a pure classical system. In classical systems, business income is subject to taxation first at corporate level, and distributions, after corporate income tax, are subject to tax in full at personal income tax rates.[6] It follows that this system limits dividend relief to a deduction of the corporate income tax underlying dividend received by shareholders.

Hungary, Poland and Sweden also apply a variant of the classical system. However, this variant differs from the 'pure' system because dividends do not form part of the personal income tax base but are taxed at a single flat rate which is usually lower than the top personal income tax rate.

Austria and Belgium allow individual taxpayers to choose between the two systems, at 1 January 1997.

ii) Integration systems

Domestic integration systems can be differentiated on the basis of whether they *partially* or *fully* relieve corporate tax at the *company* level or at the *shareholder* level. There are two methods to reduce double economic taxation of dividends at the company level: the *dividend deduction system* and the *split-rate system.* Under the former system, which is applied by the Czech Republic, dividends are deducted from the corporate tax base, under the latter (applied only in Germany) the reduction is made through a lower corporate tax rate on distributed income.

Integration systems providing relief at the shareholder level can be differentiated according to whether they exempt distributed corporate income from personal tax (*exemption system*) or whether they include distributed income in the shareholder's taxable income but provide him/her with an imputation (or dividend) tax credit to partially or fully offset corporate-level tax (*imputation system*). Within the latter group, some systems adopt a *variable* imputation tax credit where the amount of credit depends on the actual amount of underlying corporate income tax paid on the distributed income (*e.g.*, Australia). Others provide a *fixed* imputation tax credit based on a fixed corporate tax rate (*e.g.*, Canada, Finland, France, Italy and the United Kingdom).

In countries that do provide resident shareholders with tax relief in respect of domestic corporate-level tax on dividends, such tax relief is typically in the form of a *tax credit*. Column (3) of Table 2.1 shows the rate of the credit which is expressed here as a percentage of the after-corporate tax dividend. In countries which apply the classical system or the zero rate system the credit rate is zero by definition. Having been provided with a full or partial offset to corporate-level tax actually or implicitly paid, shareholders are then subject to tax at their personal income tax rate on a pre-corporate tax measure of distributed income ('grossed-up' dividends).

Column (4) of Table 2.1. presents the dividend imputation credit rate which measures the degree of integration between corporate and personal taxes. This parameter shows the corporate rate imputed to the dividends before personal taxation and it is measured as a percentage relief from underlying corporate tax.[7] Of course, when the full imputation system is applied, the imputation rate equals the corporate tax rate and the dividend imputation credit is equal to 100. At present, only Australia, Finland, France, Germany, Mexico, New Zealand and Norway impute the full corporate tax rate to dividends paid to domestic shareholders. Most other countries allow only for partial imputation which does not fully eliminate double economic taxation.

In fixed dividend tax credit systems (as well as in certain variable credit systems), some countries have mechanisms in place to ensure that corporate-level tax, consistent with the fixed dividend tax credit, has in fact been imposed (*e.g.*, France, Ireland, Italy, United Kingdom.)[8] In comparison, other countries (*e.g.*, Canada) provide their resident individual shareholders with a tax credit equal to some fixed percentage of domestic source dividend income received, without reference to the actual amount of regular corporate tax paid, and without a creditable corporate distributions tax in place that ensures that at the corporate level tax has been imposed at a rate corresponding to the dividend tax credit provided to individual shareholders.

2.3 Net shareholder tax rates on direct portfolio domestic-source dividend income

Table 2.2. works out a simple numerical example, for five representative countries (Australia, Belgium, Sweden, the United Kingdom and the United States). The exercise shows the net shareholder tax rate on domestic dividend income distributed by a *resident* firm, to a *resident* top rate shareholder.

The corporation in which the resident portfolio investor holds shares is assumed to earn an after-corporate tax rate of return on capital of 10 per cent, and to distribute its after-tax earnings in full Thus a 1 000 dollar (or other currency unit) investment in shares by the investor yields a 100 dividend each period. The net tax rate (in percentage terms) paid by the shareholder on domestic source dividends (row 11 in Table 2.2) is calculated as the difference between the dividend of 100 paid by the firm (row 1) and the net return to the investor (row 10). Differences across countries are due to different personal income statutory tax rates and to different degrees of integration relief between personal and corporate taxes.[9]

Table 2.2 **Taxation of Portfolio Domestic-Source Dividend Income (PDSDI)**

Row		AU	B	S	U.K.	US
1	**Dividend paid by corporation**	100	100	100	100	100
2	**Tax system**	FI	CL	CL	PI	CL
3	**Tax credit rate (%)**	56.25	0	0	25	0
4	**Dividend plus gross-up (if any)**	156.25	100	100	125	100
5	**Cash receipt**	**100**	**100**	**100**	**100**	**100**
6	**IT rate (%)**[(1)]	48.5	15	30	40	46.6
7	**IT liability (= row 4 x row 6)**	75.78	15	30	50	46.6
8	**Less tax credit**	56.25	n.a.	n.a.	25	n.a.
9	**Tax due**	19.53	15	30	25	46.6
10	**Net return**	**80.47**	**85**	**70**	**75**	**53.4**
11	***Net shareholder tax rate (%)* = (row 1 - row 10)**	**19.53**	**15**	**30**	**25**	**46.6**

AU = Australia, B = Belgium, S = Sweden, U.K. = United Kingdom. US = United States.
CL = Classical system, FI = Full imputation, PI = Partial imputation.

(1) The personal income tax rate for Australia, the U.K. and the U.S. is the top marginal personal income tax rate. Belgian investors have the option of paying a final withholding tax at the rate of 15 per cent on domestic shares issued, since 1994 (preferable to taxation of income at top rate of 60.4 per cent.) The Swedish rate is a flat rate on dividend income (local taxes do not apply). The AU rate includes additional *universal medical insurance*. The Belgian personal income tax rate includes surcharges and local taxes. Finally, the U.S. rate includes State and local taxes and some social security contributions.

In countries which allow the option between personal income tax and a final withholding tax, the net shareholder tax rate is always lower for a top rate shareholder when opting for final withholding tax. Although the Belgian tax system is of the classical type (*i.e.*, does not allow tax relief for the underlying corporate tax), high-income investors seem to be the least affected by the tax system. Indeed, the option of final withholding tax at 15 per cent on a conventional dividend of 100 imposes a much lower net shareholder tax rate on dividends than the regular personal income tax rate (top rate of 60.4 per cent). This is also the case in Sweden with its dual income tax system which taxes dividends as income from capital at a 30 per cent flat rate (far below the top marginal rate of 60.6 per cent for personal income tax).

In Australia and the U.K., a conventional dividend paid by a company to resident shareholders carries an (indirect) tax credit for underlying corporate income tax. In both countries the shareholder tax liability is calculated on the grossed-up dividend. Even though the Australian top income tax rate is higher than the U.K. rate, the full imputation system applied in Australia compensates for the difference, yielding a lower personal net shareholder tax rate.

Generally, the highest net shareholder tax rate on portfolio domestic source dividend income is levied in countries where a pure classical system applies and where the personal income tax system is based on a progressive system (with high top rates). For example, in the United States the high (relatively to the other countries in the example) net shareholder tax rate is a combination of double economic taxation of dividends (full dividends received form the tax base of the personal income tax and do not receive any tax relief for underlying corporate taxes) and a relatively high top statutory personal income tax rate (including sub-central government income taxes).

2.4 Tax treatment of direct portfolio foreign-source dividend income

Often, tax systems treat portfolio *foreign*-source dividend income (PFSDI) in a different way than portfolio *domestic*-source dividend income. Chart II considers the case of foreign direct portfolio investment. First of all, upon distribution to non-resident shareholders, dividends may be subject to withholding tax in the source country (where the distributing company is resident). Second, the country of residence of the individual shareholder may provide a tax relief (*foreign tax credit*) for the withholding tax at source, but limitations may apply. Foreign tax credits may offset foreign withholding taxes in full or only partially. Finally, countries generally do not provide resident portfolio shareholders with tax relief (an *indirect foreign tax credit*) for foreign corporate income tax underlying a foreign dividend receipt. However, in certain situations host countries may provide such relief. This section discusses these tax considerations under three headings: withholding tax considerations, foreign tax credit considerations and integration relief considerations.

CHART II
Direct (non-intermediated) Foreign Investment

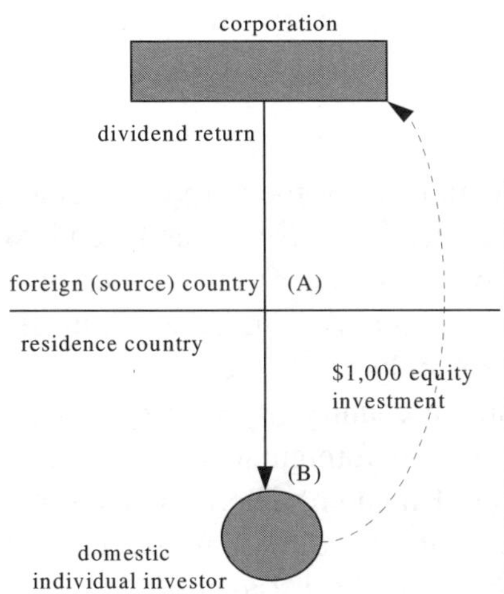

Possible Tax Considerations in Direct Foreign Investment Case

- source country withholding tax (A)
- foreign tax credit limitations (B)
- source (host) country integration relief (A)

	classical tax treatment	*integration treatment*
pre-personal tax return at R=10% (distributed)	D=100	D=100
integration relief *(host country)*	none	D(c*)=50 (with c*=0.5)
distribution	D=100	D(1+c*)=150
non-resident withholding tax (at rate w=0.15)	Dw=15	D(1+c*)w=22.5
personal income tax (PIT):		
dividend received	D(1-w)=85	D(1+c*)(1-w)=127.5
dividend inclusion	D=100	D(1+c*)=150
foreign tax credit (at rate ω=min(w,m'))	Dω=15	D(1+c*)ω=22.5
PIT (@40%)	D(m-ω)=25	D(1+c*)(m-ω) =0.042
after-PIT return	D(1-w-m+ω)=60	D(1+c*)(1-w-m+ω)=90

A. Withholding tax considerations

Nearly all source countries (*i.e.*, the country where the dividend income has originated) levy a withholding tax on dividends distributed to non-resident shareholders. In the *non-treaty* case, the withholding tax rate is usually higher than the rate provided by the *treaty* case. Most OECD countries have entered bilateral agreements which provide for lower withholding tax rates on dividends distributed to shareholders resident in member countries. The most common treaty rate for PFSDI is 15 per cent. However, some countries apply a lower treaty rate. For example, Sweden levies a 5 per cent withholding tax on dividends distributed to U.K. shareholders (see Table 2.6 below).

U.K. tax authorities, being an exception among OECD countries, do not levy withholding taxes on the payment of dividends, either abroad or at home. This country does, however, abate the payment of the imputation tax credit to a non-resident under the provisions of a double tax treaty.

B. Foreign tax credit considerations

None of the OECD countries provides its resident individual shareholders with *tax relief* in respect of the actual or some notional amount of underlying *foreign corporate income tax* on foreign-source dividend income earned directly. Instead, home countries provide individual shareholders with a *foreign tax deduction*, as foreign-source portfolio dividends are typically included in the shareholder's taxable income net of host country income tax, without any further home country relief in respect of foreign corporate income tax paid by the company located in a foreign tax jurisdiction.[10]

Most OECD countries do, however, provide their resident individual shareholders with a *foreign tax credit* (*e.g.*, France, Italy, Portugal, United Kingdom, United States) in respect of *foreign withholding tax* imposed on foreign source dividend income, as this withholding tax is considered to be a direct tax on the shareholder. In some countries, such relief is provided unilaterally by domestic statute (*e.g.*, Canada, Denmark, Germany, Greece, Italy, the Netherlands (in the case of withholding at source by developing countries), the United Kingdom), whereas in other countries foreign tax credit relief (*i.e.*, a tax credit against domestic tax otherwise payable, in respect of foreign withholding tax) is available only in respect of distributions received from treaty countries, or by special decree.

The foreign tax credit claim may be subject to limitations. For the purpose of determining these limitations, in some countries (*e.g.*, Austria, Canada, Finland, the Netherlands, and Norway) PFSDI is pooled together with other passive investment income, as well as other types of income, derived from the same foreign country (*income pooling by country*). In other countries (*e.g.*, Australia, the United States), PFSDI is instead pooled together only with other amounts of passive investment income, but without reference to the (source) foreign country (*pooling by income type*). Some countries (*e.g.*, Spain, Switzerland) instead pool all types of foreign source income from all foreign countries.[11] Others (*e.g.*, Italy, France, Portugal, United Kingdom) determine the limit on the foreign tax credit claim in respect of PFSDI, as well as the limit on the foreign tax credit claim in respect of other amounts of foreign source income, on an *item-by-item* basis (*no pooling*).

The maximum foreign tax credit that can be claimed in respect of creditable amounts of foreign tax associated with a given pool, or in some countries a given item, of foreign source income is typically constrained to be the lesser of (i) the total amount of creditable foreign tax in that pool (with carry-over provisions in some countries -- Australia, the Netherlands) or in respect of that item, and (ii) the amount of domestic tax otherwise payable on foreign-source income in that pool or in respect of that item.

It is possible that the foreign tax credit available at the margin on a unit of PFSDI falls short of the amount of creditable foreign withholding tax imposed on that unit.[12] In some countries (*e.g.*, Canada, the Netherlands) where a taxpayer is unable to fully utilise a foreign tax credit, *foreign tax deduction* -- where the foreign withholding tax is simply deducted from dividend payments received -- is an available option. In certain cases, claiming a foreign tax deduction in respect of foreign withholding tax may be more desirable than the option of a foreign tax credit for withholding tax. If, for example, taxpayers are not allowed to carry-forward or carry-back excess (unused) foreign tax credits, or if the taxpayer does not expect to be able to utilise excess foreign tax credits over the allowed carry-forward period, it may be preferable to claim a foreign tax deduction in order to carry the relief forward under loss carry-forward provisions. Or the taxpayer may find it simpler to claim a foreign tax deduction and avoid the complications involved in foreign tax credit calculations.

C. Imputation relief considerations

While some OECD country tax systems provide resident individual taxpayers with some degree of double taxation relief in respect of domestic underlying corporate income tax on portfolio *domestic* source dividend income, such relief is denied by the home country in the case of portfolio *foreign* source dividend income. This would suggest that, on the basis of tax considerations alone, domestic shareholders in such countries would generally prefer to invest in domestic shares rather than foreign shares paying the same pre-personal tax rate of return, even if they are able to fully offset foreign withholding tax using foreign tax credits.

This is not always the case though, especially where the source country extends the benefits of integration to non-resident shareholders unilaterally or by tax treaty. For instance, France has a bilateral agreement with Sweden, the United Kingdom and the United States (row 2 in Tables 2.5 -- 2.7 below) by which dividend income distributed to an investor resident in one of these countries is entitled to the *avoir fiscal* (*i.e.*, tax credit of one-half of the distribution) for the underlying French corporate tax, just as French residents are.

In general, the non-resident shareholder pays a withholding tax on the dividend grossed-up for the tax credit granted by the source country -- which usually equals the tax credit provided to resident individuals who invest in domestic shares -- and later the home country grants a *tax credit* for the foreign withholding tax and levies tax on the foreign grossed-up dividend. In this instance, the integration relief provided to dividends distributed to non-resident investors may create a bias in favour of shares held in companies resident in an imputation country.

2.5 Net shareholder tax rates on direct portfolio foreign-source dividend income

This section extends the numerical example presented in table 2.2 of section 2.3 to illustrate the tax rules governing the taxation of PFSDI. Tables 2.3 -- 2.7 shown at the end of this chapter report outcomes for the same five representative countries (Australia, Belgium, Sweden, the United Kingdom and the United States). The example assumes that an individual saver may invest in any of the five countries above and in four other OECD countries (France, Germany, Italy and Luxembourg). The pre-personal tax rate of return to the investment is the same in every country. As in the domestic investment case, the paying company distributes a conventional dividend (net of foreign corporate taxes) of 100 currency units (row 1 in Tables 2.3 -- 2.7).[13] However, in the foreign case the shareholder receives a cash payment (row 5) gross of tax credit (if any is granted by the source country) and net of foreign withholding tax (rows 2-4). In the home country, he may claim the foreign tax credit and will be subject to personal income tax on the grossed-up amount.

The net (of all taxes) return from dividend income (row 9) is equal to cash receipts (row 5) less the tax due (net of imputation credit or foreign tax credit) by the shareholder in the home country (row 8). Inversely, the net shareholder tax rate on savings is calculated as the difference between the dividend paid by the foreign corporation (row 1) and the net return from the foreign investment (row 9).

In most source countries, dividend income is subject to the withholding tax which (as explained above), can be claimed against domestic tax liability in the country of residence (row 7). This applies in all representative countries except for Belgium where the foreign withholding tax is deducted from the tax base of domestic personal income tax.

Indeed, Belgium -- which is a classical country -- treats foreign-source dividend income in a different way all together. Belgian tax authorities do not give a credit for foreign withholding taxes, but allow their deduction from the personal income tax base. Therefore, different withholding taxes across countries do affect the size of the *net shareholder tax rate* on foreign source dividend income. Table 2.4 shows that there is an equal incentive to invest in Belgium and in the U.K. -- where net shareholder tax rates are lower and identical -- because the latter country does not levy any withholding tax on dividend payments and the tax liability is the same whether the source of income is domestic or located in the U.K. None of the remaining source countries grants some form of dividend relief to Belgian shareholders while foreign withholding taxes can only be deducted from the domestic income tax base and not claimed against income tax liability as it is the case in the other four representative countries.

Differences in *net shareholder tax rates* on foreign-source dividend income within the remaining four representative countries can be attributed mainly to whether the source country attaches integration relief to dividend distributions to foreign portfolio shareholders and on the extent of the integration relief for the underlying corporate tax.[14]

For instance, the U.K. tax system (Table 2.6) favours domestic portfolio investments versus foreign portfolio investments in countries which have a classical system (Belgium, Luxembourg, Sweden and the United States) or which do not grant the U.K. resident investor a dividend relief for the underlying foreign corporate tax (Australia). This is no surprising result. The U.K. resident shareholder receives the same pre-personal tax PFSDI and is subject to the same tax rate on this income (40 per cent) irrespective of the source countries, with the only difference that at home he can offset the imputation tax credit (25 per cent of dividend) against his income tax liability and therefore raise the after-tax return on his domestic portfolio investments.

However, the U.K. tax system is seen as diverting savings from domestic portfolio investments into France and Italy which both extend dividend relief for the underlying corporate tax to U.K. investors. British savers who invest in new shares in France (Table 2.6, column 6) and in Italy (Table 2.6, column 8) receive the dividend grossed-up for the credit -- *avoir fiscal* and *credito di imposta*, respectively -- and pay a foreign withholding tax of 15 per cent on the grossed-up dividend. On repatriation, U.K. tax law grants a *tax credit* for the foreign withholding tax and imposes tax on the foreign grossed-up dividend. In this case, U.K. resident shareholders can offset, against their income tax liability, a higher imputation credit whether they invest in France (50 per cent of dividend) or Italy (56.25 per cent of dividend) and therefore raise the after-tax return above the domestic one (see Table 2.6). The net shareholder tax rate which results from investing in these two countries is lower than in the other six foreign countries which do not give a tax relief for the underlying corporate tax to U.K. portfolio investors. Still, the outcome is not necessarily identical. The difference between the net shareholder tax rate for investments in French and Italian shares is due to different domestic corporate tax rates and therefore different imputation credit rates endorsed by the two countries.

In Australia, the combination of tax systems is seen to provide strong incentives to invest savings in domestic equities (the net shareholder tax rate on foreign source dividend income (Table 2.3, row 10) is higher than the domestic net shareholder tax rate). This outcome is drawn out, once again, by the fact that the pre-personal tax return on investments in new equity and the income tax rate is the same for Australian savers wherever they invest, but they are entitled to a dividend relief only at home and in the U.K. where the after-tax rate of return becomes higher than in any other country. However, the U.K credit is not as generous as the domestic one leaving unaffected the bias in favour of domestic investments.

In the United States and in Sweden -- which are classical countries -- net shareholder tax rates are the same, irrespective of whether the investment is in domestic shares or in shares issued in countries which apply the classical system to portfolio dividend income or in imputation countries which do not grant dividend relief to U.S. and Swedish shareholders (*e.g.*, Australia and Italy). Once again, the non-neutrality across countries derives from the practice of some imputation countries of extending the full dividend relief, offered to resident individuals, to U.S. and Swedish portfolio investors.

Swedish shareholders are shown to receive an extremely favourable tax treatment on investments in French companies (Table 2.5, column 6). The tax system operates as a subsidy to the Swedish investor yielding a negative net shareholder tax rate (row 10 in Table 2.5). Indeed, the French withholding tax of 15 per cent is set off in full against the foreign credit granted by the resident country leaving the Swedish shareholder with a dividend relief (*avoir fiscal*) which more than compensates the domestic income tax liability. Investments in British companies are also subject to a lower net shareholder tax rate (still positive though) than at home or in countries which do not grant a dividend relief to Swedish shareholders.

Table 2.7 shows that tax considerations would divert non-intermediated U.S. portfolio savings primarily into France -- where the imputation credit is the highest, the net shareholder tax rate is therefore the lowest. The U.K. is shown to be the second most attractive destination for U.S. shareholders investing directly, followed by Germany.

In conclusion, tax incentives to allocate savings to a foreign country rather then at home hinge upon whether and to what extent investors are granted some form of dividend relief in the source country. This is under the assumption that the pre-personal tax return on portfolio investment equals the market interest rate for all countries no matter what the tax treatment of domestic and foreign source dividend income is in each single country. However, if the tax system in the source country (domestic or foreign) grants an imputation credit for underlying corporate tax, the infra-marginal saver is biased in favour of new share investments because their after-tax return rises above the after-tax return on investments in bonds.[15] Moreover, the higher the imputation credit, the higher the after-tax return on equity.

2.6 Summary

A general result of the preceding analysis is that, in the context of direct portfolio investment, tax non-neutralities for shareholders (*i.e.*, differences in *net shareholder tax rates* across countries) generally are not driven by different withholding taxation at source (as shareholders, particularly those subject to top personal income tax rates, typically can offset these taxes using foreign tax credit) -- but rather are mainly explained by whether or not portfolio investors are granted relief for underlying corporate income tax on dividends, the level of that relief, and how that relief varies across source countries. This result depends critically on the assumption of equal after-corporate tax rates of return across investment cases.

Under the framework adopted in this chapter, an individual investor receives the same pre-personal tax return on savings irrespective of the country of residence of the company in which he/she holds shares. Identical treatment for tax purposes is automatically accomplished for savers resident in classical countries who invest into either classical countries or countries which do not extend dividend relief to non-resident shareholders, (*e.g.*, a U.S. saver who invests in Luxembourg). In this case, the net return to savings is the same and the shareholder is indifferent between holding shares in a domestic company or in a foreign company.

Differences in tax treatment of dividend income may arise instead, when savers are granted a credit for the underlying corporate tax either at home or abroad. Usually tax incentives to individual shareholders are biased in favour of domestic investments if they receive a tax relief on dividend income only from the home country tax authorities (*e.g.*, Australian shareholders find domestic shares the most attractive in our example). However, if imputation countries grant foreign investors a dividend relief higher than the dividend relief (if any) allowed in the home country (*e.g.*, France grants a higher relief to U.K. savers), savers are encouraged to invest in foreign imputation countries.

Under the assumption that shareholder-level taxation does not impact on pre-personal tax rates (relaxed in Chapter 4), differences in savings tax rates do not factor into the allocation of physical capital, as firms are assumed to earn the same after-corporate tax rate of return in all cases (implying inefficiencies in the allocation of productive capital, assuming differences in effective tax rates at the corporate level.) Different taxation of savings may however influence portfolio investment by influencing the after-tax return on savings, which may result in tax distortion in the allocation of savings across countries.

Table 2.3 **Taxation of PDSDI and PFSDI received via direct portfolio investment**
Portfolio investment by an individual resident in Australia into

Row		**AU (1)**	**B (2)**	**S (3)**	**U.K. (4)**	**US (5)**	**F (6)**	**G (7)**	**It (8)**	**L (9)**
1	Dividend paid by corporation	**100**	100	100	100	100	100	100	100	100
2	Tax credit from source country	**56.25**	0	0	25	0	0	0	0	0
3	Dividend plus gross-up (if any)	**156.25**	100	100	125	100	100	100	100	100
4	Foreign withholding tax	**n.a.**	15	15	18.75 (15%)	15	15	15	15	30
5	**Cash receipt**	**100**	**85**	**85**	**106.25**	**85**	**85**	**85**	**85**	**70**
6	Income tax (48.5% of row 3)	**75.78**	48.5	48.5	60.62	48.5	48.5	48.5	48.5	48.5
7	less domestic/foreign tax credit	**56.25**	15	15	18.75	15	15	15	15	30
8	tax due	**19.53**	33.5	33.5	41.87	33.5	33.5	33.5	33.5	18.5
9	**Net return**	**80.47**	**51.5**	**51.5**	**64.38**	**51.5**	**51.5**	**51.5**	**51.5**	**51.5**
10	**Net shareholder tax rate = row 1 - row 9**	**19.53**	**48.5**	**48.5**	**35.62**	**48.5**	**48.5**	**48.5**	**48.5**	**48.5**

AU = Australia, B = Belgium, S = Sweden, U.K. = United Kingdom, US = United States; F = France, G = Germany, It = Italy, L = Luxembourg.

Table 2.4 **Taxation of PDSDI and PFSDI received via direct portfolio investment**
Portfolio investment by an individual resident in Belgium into

Row		AU (1)	B (2)	S (3)	U.K (4)	US (5)	F (6)	G (7)	It (8)	L (9)
1	Dividend paid by corporation	100	**100**	100	100	100	100	100	100	100
2	Tax credit from source country	n.a.	**n.a.**	n.a.	0	n.a.	n.a.	n.a.	n.a.	n.a.
3	Dividend plus gross-up (if any)	100	**100.**	100	100	100	100	100	100	100
4	Foreign withholding tax	0	**n.a.**	15	0	15	15	15	15	15
5	**Cash receipt**	**100**	**100**	**85**	**100**	**85**	**85**	**85**	**85**	**85**
6	Domestic withholding tax (15%/25% of row 5)[1]	25	**15**	21.25	**25**	21.25	21.25	21.25	21.25	21.25
7	less domestic/foreign tax credit	n.a.	**n.a.**	n.a.	**n.a.**	n.a.	n.a.	n.a.	n.a.	n.a.
8	tax due	25	**15**	21.25	**25**	21.25	21.25	21.25	21.25	21.25
9	**Net return**	**75**	**85**	**63.75**	**75**	**63.75**	**63.75**	**63.75**	**63.75**	**63.75**
10	**Net shareholder tax rate = row 1 - row 9**	**25**	**15**	**36.25**	**25**	**36.25**	**36.25**	**36.25**	**36.25**	**36.25**

AU = Australia, B = Belgium, S = Sweden, U.K. = United Kingdom, US = United States; F = France, G = Germany, It = Italy, L = Luxembourg.

1 The withholding tax (flat personal tax on dividend income) is 25 per cent on foreign source dividends, and computed on dividend income net of the foreign non-creditable withholding tax.

Table 2.5 **Taxation of PDSDI and PFSDI received via direct portfolio investment**
Portfolio investment by an individual resident in Sweden into

Row		AU (1)	B (2)	S (3)	U.K. (4)	US (5)	F (6)	G (7)	It (8)	L (9)
1	Dividend paid by corporation	100	100	**100**	100	100	100	100	100	100
2	Tax credit from source country	n.a.	n.a.	**n.a.**	25	n.a.	50	n.a.	n.a.	n.a.
3	Dividend plus gross-up (if any)	100	100	**100.**	125	100	150	100	100	100
4	Foreign withholding tax	0	15	**n.a.**	18.75 (15%)	15	22.5 (15%)	15 (15%)	15	15
5	**Cash receipt**	**100**	**85**	**100**	**106.25**	**85**	**127.5**	**85**	**85**	**85**
6	Income tax (30% of row 3)	30	30	**30**	37.5	30	45	30	30	30
7	less domestic/foreign tax credit	0	15	**n.a.**	18.75	15	22.5	15	15	15
8	tax due	30	15	**30**	18.75	15	22.5*	15	15	15
9	**Net return**	**70**	**70**	**70**	**87.5**	**70**	**105**	**70**	**70**	**70**
10	**Net shareholder tax rate = row 1 - row 9**	**30**	**30**	**30**	**18.75**	**30**	**-5**	**30**	**30**	**30**

AU = Australia, B = Belgium, S = Sweden, U.K. = United Kingdom, US = United States; F = France, G = Germany, It = Italy, L = Luxembourg.

Table 2.6 **Taxation of PDSDI and PFSDI received via direct portfolio investment**
Portfolio investment by an individual resident in the United Kingdom into

Row		AU (1)	B (2)	S (3)	U.K. (4)	US (5)	F (6)	G (7)	It (8)	L (9)
1	Dividend paid by corporation	100	100	100	**100**	100	100	100	100	100
2	Tax credit from source country	0	0	0	**25**	0	50	0	56.25	0
3	Dividend plus gross-up (if any)	100	100	n.a.	**125**	100	150	100	156.25	100
4	Foreign withholding tax	0	15	5 (5%)	**n.a.**	15	22.5 (15%)	15	23.44 (15%)	15
5	**Cash receipt**	**100**	**85**	**95**	**100**	**85**	**127.5**	**85**	**132.81**	**85**
6	Income tax (40% of row 3)	40	40	40	**50**	40	60	40	62.5	40
7	Less domestic/foreign tax credit	0	15	5	**25**	15	22.5	15	23.44	15
8	Tax due	40	25	35	**25**	25	37.5	25	39.05	25
9	**Net return**	**60**	**60**	**60**	**75**	**60**	**90**	**60**	**93.75**	**60**
10	**Net shareholder tax rate = row 1 - row 9(%)**	**40**	**40**	**40**	**25**	**40**	**10**	**40**	**6.25**	**40**

AU = Australia, B = Belgium, S = Sweden, U.K. = United Kingdom, US = United States; F = France, G = Germany, It = Italy, L = Luxembourg.

Table 2.7 **Taxation of PDSDI and PFSDI received via direct portfolio investment**
Portfolio investment by an individual resident in the United States into

Row		AU (1)	B (2)	S (3)	U.K. (4)	US (5)	F (6)	G (7)	It (8)	L (9)
1	Dividend paid by corporation	100	100	100	100	**100**	100	100	100	100
2	Tax credit from source country	0	0	0	25	**n.a.**	50	0	0	0
3	Dividend plus gross-up (if any)	100	100	100	125	**100**	150	100	100	100
4	Foreign withholding tax	0	15	15	18.75 (15%)	**n.a.**	22.5 (15%)	15 (15%)	15	15
5	**Cash receipt**	**100**	**85**	**85**	**106.25**	**100**	**127.5**	**85**	**85**	**85**
6	Income tax (46.6% of row 3)	46.6	46.6	46.6	58.25	**46.6**	69.9	46.6	46.6	46.6
7	less domestic/foreign tax credit	0	15	15	18.75	**n.a.**	22.5	15	15	15
8	tax due	46.6	31.6	31.6	39.5	**46.6**	47.4	31.6	31.6	31.6
9	**Net return**	**53.4**	**53.4**	**53.4**	**66.75**	**53.4**	**80.1**	**53.4**	**53.4**	**53.4**
10	**Net shareholder tax rate = row 1 - row 9**	**46.6**	**46.6**	**46.6**	**33.25**	**46.6**	**19.9**	**46.6**	**46.6**	**46.6**

AU = Australia, B = Belgium, S = Sweden, U.K. = United Kingdom, US = United States; F = France, G = Germany, It = Italy, L = Luxembourg.

NOTES

1. Taxing economic rents is generally an efficient means of raising revenues. Theory suggests that the investment and financing decisions of business should not be affected by taxes in the presence of economic rents. Taxing economic rents may also be viewed as equitable on the grounds that all residents of a given (host) country should derive benefits from the exploitation of scarce factors of production, and not just shareholders.

2. Note that capital income in the form of dividend (and interest) income paid to residents may be taxed on a current basis at the individual shareholder level, without necessarily calling for corporate-level tax on such income. However, retained earnings pose a problem as most tax systems tax capital gains earned by individuals on a realisation basis. This would allow shareholders to shelter, in the absence of corporate taxation, equity income from taxation by retaining/investing corporate-level earnings, as opposed to distributing the income and subjecting it to personal-level dividend taxation.

3. Table 2.1 reflects the systems applied by OECD countries as of January 1, 1997 and covers only those taxes which are levied by central government.

4. Denmark splits individual income into three categories: *personal income, income form capital* and *income from shares.* The aggregate of personal income and income from capital less deductions is termed *taxable income. Income from shares* is taxed separately.

5. This analysis applies to investors who hold unqualified quota.

6 However, the Netherlands exempts the first 1000 NGL for individuals and the first 2000 NGL for married couples.

7. Letting u* denote the *imputation credit rate*, and u denote the *corporate income tax rate*, the degree of dividend imputation credit relief may be measured as u*/u.

8. These systems can be distinguished from those that provide integration relief for retained as well as distributed income. This class would include 'flow-through' (i.e. partnership-type) systems that waive corporate-level tax but tax individual shareholders at personal rates on their allocable share of corporate income. An alternative 'full' integration approach, one considered in the US Treasury's 1992 integration study, would be to retain corporate-level tax, and tax individual shareholders on their allocable share of corporate income as it is earned, with a credit for corporate taxes paid.

9. Note that higher degrees of integration relief can also reflect higher rates of underlying corporate tax.

10. Yet, certain OECD countries provide (usually by tax treaty, in other instances by domestic law) a tax credit to non-resident shareholders. See examples in Tables 2.3 -- 2.7 below.

11. Spain changed its foreign tax credit regime for corporations in 1996.

12. In those countries where PFSDI is pooled together with other amounts of foreign source-income subject to creditable foreign income tax (e.g., withholding tax) at varying rates, it is also possible that the foreign tax credit available at the margin on a unit of PFSDI exceeds the amount of creditable foreign withholding tax imposed on that unit.

13 Under this framework, the after corporate-tax return that a company must earn to attract savings is the same across countries. It follows that whether and to what extent dividend relief is granted to portfolio investors does not affect company investment decisions but influences the allocation of savings across countries.

14. Note that all the countries considered here, with the exception of Belgium, give a *foreign tax credit* for foreign withholding taxes and levy personal income tax on dividend grossed-up for the foreign tax credit. In these countries, different withholding taxes across countries do not affect the level of the net shareholder tax rate.

15. Note that in the case of Belgium, the choice between domestic new equity and British new shares is neutral because the relief takes place at the withholding tax level. The U.K. does not levy any withholding tax on dividend payments to Belgium.

Chapter 3

DOMESTIC VS FOREIGN COLLECTIVE INVESTMENT INSTITUTIONS AND INTERNATIONAL TAX CONSIDERATIONS

3.1 Introduction

For a number of reasons the international (combined host and home country) tax treatment of portfolio foreign investment in shares through domestic CIIs often differs from the treatment of portfolio foreign investment made directly. Similarly, investing through a foreign CII may result in a different overall tax burden as compared with direct portfolio investment.

First, there may be problems in the operation of double tax relief (*i.e.*, foreign tax credit) mechanisms in the domestic CII case, to the disadvantage of this intermediated investment option. While often tax systems will prevent a mismatch of foreign withholding tax and foreign tax credit, in certain cases relief for foreign tax at source may not be available. Moreover, where tax credits are made available at the shareholder level, compliance and administrative problems in the claiming of the credit may arise.

Second, foreign funds may be characterised differently from domestic funds either because a different legal structure is used in a foreign country or because the special rules for transparent tax treatment that apply in the purely domestic case cannot be satisfied by foreign funds (*e.g.*, most simply because only a resident entity can obtain the special tax treatment). This second difference can cut both ways in terms of its effect on taxation of investment through a foreign CII as compared to direct investment. In some cases tax is higher in the foreign CII case because transparency is lost and the investor is denied credit for tax levied in the foreign country (*e.g.*, where tax is levied on the CII rather than the investor, the foreign tax credit mechanism will usually deny the portfolio investor an indirect credit for the CII-level tax).

On the other hand, to the extent that the foreign CII is not regarded as transparent in the residence country of the investor, it may be possible to roll up income in an 'offshore' CII and defer home country taxation. Taxation may even be removed where the investor realises investment income at the CII-level through the sale of unit interests in the CII and the resulting capital gains are not taxed. The offshore case generally provides the greatest advantage to the investor where there is no tax imposed on the investment income at source or at the CII level. This is the typical scenario with many off-shore funds, and some countries have therefore enacted legislation to take away or reduce tax advantages potentially gained by the investor.

Third, tax treaties often do not operate effectively in the case of CIIs to achieve their basic objectives of sharing taxing rights between source and residence countries, eliminating double taxation and (in certain cases at least) preventing double non-taxation. Again this issue can produce more or less taxation in the CII case as compared to the direct investment case. The source country may deny lower withholding tax rates in the CII case and the investor's country of residence may similarly refuse to credit the higher level of tax at source. Or the source country may apply a lower treaty rate of tax on the basis of residence of the CII (in a third country) while the investor resides in a country which would not be entitled to that lower rate, and moreover the investor may not be taxed on a current basis in his/her country of residence. It was this last case that attracted the most attention in the 1977 OECD Study and the 1997 IFA Report. It is not the purpose of this report to recommend changes in treaty provisions as this matter needs to be considered by Working Party No.1 of the OECD Committee on Fiscal Affairs, but approaches under current treaty provisions by some countries are noted.

Fourth, the operation of imputation systems whether under domestic law or tax treaties may also be different in the CII case. In particular, if a treaty provides for the extension of imputation benefits to (non-resident) individual investors (*i.e.*, investors resident in a given treaty country), but does not treat a CII in the treaty country transparently for this purpose, imputation benefits may be denied where the non-resident investors chooses to invest through a domestic CII. Note that this is a distinct problem from the general concerns that arise from the different ways in which most imputation systems treat resident versus non-resident investors. If distortions are produced as between resident and non-resident investors in the direct portfolio investment case, and are carried over into the non-resident CII context, then this is not a concern specifically relating to CIIs -- as the benchmark policy of an identical treatment of investment through CIIs and direct investment is achieved.

3.2 Possible cases

With three tax variables -- the source of the income, the residence of the CII and the residence of the investor -- eight cases can be identified from any country's perspective, summarised as follows.

	Source	CII residence	Investor residence
1	domestic	domestic	domestic
2	domestic	domestic	foreign
3	domestic	foreign	domestic
4	domestic	foreign	foreign
5	foreign	domestic	domestic
6	foreign	foreign	domestic
7	foreign	domestic	foreign
8	foreign	foreign	foreign

The first pure domestic case is examined below in section 3.3 The last case can be eliminated as being completely foreign from the domestic/home country's perspective. Rather than focus on all six remaining cross-border cases, the Report focuses on the three most common cases, namely Cases 4, 5 and 6, and even within these the discussion can be further limited by recognising that Case 4 is analogous to Case 5, with the domestic country (*i.e.*, the country of residence of the domestic investor) being alternatively the host country (Case 4) and the home country (Case 5.)

Case 5 represents the typical outbound portfolio investment case (at least in the past), where individuals invest through a domestic CII (resident in the same country as the investor) due to regulatory and other factors that lead to domestic marketing of investments through domestic CIIs. Case 4 represents the typical inbound case, again where the investor and the CII are resident in the same country (although the case also covers the situation where the CII and the investor are resident in different countries.) The potential tax distortions that arise in Case 4 are similar to those in Case 5. Thus these two cases can be considered alongside one another. While the tax distortions raised in each case are similar, the tax policy issues of potential concern to a given domestic country arising from these distortions will differ depending upon whether it is the host/source country (Case 4) or the home country of the individual investor (Case 5.)

The rapidly growing exception to the typical outbound investment case (Case 5 with the investor and CII resident in the same country) is given by Case 6, where an investor uses a foreign fund, often for tax benefits. This case, like Case 2, covers the situation where the CII, attracting non-resident investors, is based in a country where the CII industry is large and mainly invests in local securities. That part of the US mutual fund industry which invests in US shares and bonds and attracts foreign investors would be a typical example of this type of case. Case 2 involves the mirror image of Case 6, and the exception to the typical inbound investment case, with a foreign investor choosing to invest in domestic shares (foreign shares from the non-resident investor's perspective) through a CII resident in the source country, rather than through a CII resident in his/her home country. The international tax distortions that arise in Case 2 are akin to those identified in Case 6, and thus Case 2 may be considered alongside Case 6 in this Report. As noted below, the international tax implications of Case 6 (and Case 2) where the source and CII-residence countries are the same, often produce a tax bias in favour of an investor choosing a CII resident in the same country as the investor for entering foreign stock markets.

Case 6 also encompasses the possibility that the foreign CII-residence country and the source country (*i.e.*, the country in which the income is sourced or originates) are separate countries, which will often be the case. Where the income is subject to substantial tax in the foreign-source country and/or the country of residence of the CII, possibilities of increased taxation in the foreign intermediated investment case arise. The more common situation under this heading is the off-shore fund case, where the income suffers little or no tax at source or at the CII level and tax on the investor is deferred because the income is rolled-up in the offshore fund.

Case 3, which involves domestic investors doubling back through the CII to their same (home) jurisdiction, could also involve off-shore funds viewed from the country of residence of the investor and, though possible outside the off-shore fund context, especially in the EU, is probably still not common. It does not receive any separate treatment in the discussion which follows. Similarly, Case 7 is probably not common outside the off-shore fund area and so is not examined separately.

It would be possible to further multiply the number of cases by allowing for the situation where, rather than assuming that dividend income is sourced at the place of residence of the distributing company, the income is sourced in another country. Given that this extension would not add significantly to the analysis, it is not considered. That is not to say that tax consequences may not arise where a company's income is sourced outside its country of residence, especially where the company is resident in a country with an imputation system, but those consequences generally relate to imputation systems and raise similar issues as those identified in relation to investing in companies directly or through a CII.

The Report, both in the remainder of this chapter and separately in Chapter 5, considers in some detail imputation relief in the international situation and considers conditions under which there may be a bias as between investment through a CII (domestic or foreign) and investment directly in a company subject to an imputation system. The Report also considers the interesting issue of the possible incidence and economic impact of integration relief, and the implications for extending integration relief in the CII case. The discussion leads to a broader set of considerations regarding the instances in which imputation relief may have its desired effects, with the Report taking the tax treatment of portfolio investment in the direct (non-intermediated) investment situation as the benchmark case.

Section (3.3) reviews a range of domestic tax considerations in the pure domestic CII case, with additional information in Appendix II. Section (3.4) then turns to the domestic CII case with foreign source income, and section (3.5) the foreign CII case, with summary information provided in Appendix III. Section (3.6) summarises main findings. The following Chapter 4 provides a comparison of net shareholder tax rates under alternative intermediated investment structures and compares these with the benchmark case.

3.3 Domestic CIIs and domestic tax considerations

This section considers the general legal background of collective investment institutions (CIIs) and the domestic taxation of CIIs within the selected countries analysed in this report. The legal and regulatory requirements in the countries studied are explained because they turn out to be important to the domestic and international position of CIIs in ways to be explained below. The domestic tax treatment of CIIs is then explained, looking first at the taxation of underlying domestic investments made by CIIs, then at the taxation of the CII itself, and finally at the taxation of domestic investors in the CII. The investment structure is depicted in Chart III-1.

CHART III-1
Intermediated Domestic Investment (Domestic CII)

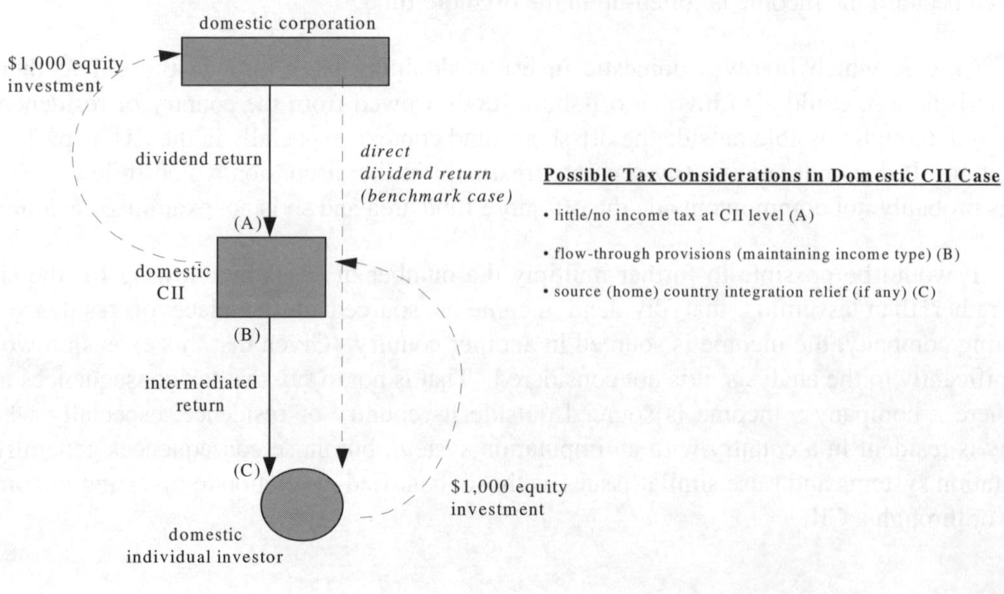

Normally, in most countries, the policy objective concerning the taxation of CIIs is to achieve transparent taxation for CIIs. In other words, the outcome is intended to be the same as if the investor directly acquired the underlying investment. The mechanisms by which this result is achieved vary from country to country, which also turns out to have significance in the international context. In some countries, various kinds of CIIs are used to encourage individual investment through concessional tax regimes, and in most countries there seem to be some advantages in investing through domestic CIIs.

A set of illustrative shareholder after-tax returns when investing in domestic shares through a domestic CII are calculated for the countries examined in this report. Rather than considering these results in isolation, they are presented in Chapter 4 with other cases, so as to permit a comparison of outcomes.

Legal form and regulation

Table AII.1 (in Appendix II) summarises a number of issues concerning the legal form and regulation of CIIs in the five countries examined here in detail (Australia, Belgium, Sweden, U.K. and U.S.), and for two other countries (Germany, Japan) to allow further comparison. The following points can be drawn out from Table AII.1. The legal form used for CIIs varies within countries and across countries involving variously companies, partnerships, trusts and contractual arrangements. For example, both trusts and companies are used in the U.K. and the U.S., while in Sweden corporate and contractual forms are found. Within countries, this does not matter greatly for tax and other purposes as, via regulatory or tax regimes, special rules apply to closely control the nature and functions of CIIs. As is explained below, internationally the variety of legal constructs and entities leads to entity classification problems.

The regulatory and associated tax regimes for CIIs often have quite specific domestic histories (as for the bond and dividend funds in Japan). In some cases an existing form was adopted for use as a CII (*e.g.*, the unit trust in Australia), while in others the development of the CII industry has been driven by the qualifying rules for special tax treatment (whether to achieve transparency or to obtain tax concessions). In all countries studied, there is now extensive non-tax regulation of CIIs designed to achieve protection of investors, in the form of disclosure, licensing and prudential regimes. Recently, in line with policies aimed at deregulation and removal of domestic barriers to globalisation, some countries have begun to wind back the extent of domestic regulation of CIIs.

Taxation

To compare investment directly by an individual or via a CII, it is necessary to consider the total tax position for the underlying investment, the CII itself, and the investor in the CII.

A. *Underlying domestic investment*

Table AII.2 summarises the underlying taxation regime for investment in shares and bonds in the countries covered by this report. Part of the difficulties in the CII area stem from the quite different regimes used domestically to tax the underlying investment. Some countries, like Sweden, operate special regimes for capital income which differ generally from the taxation of other income, some countries have imputation systems, others not, while some countries have special regimes for interest.

While the overall outcome in most countries is to obtain the same result for investment directly by individuals and through CIIs, these special rules, together with the fact that the CII is treated in some respects as a company for tax purposes, often flow back to the taxation of the underlying investment, especially on the withholding front. Because CIIs themselves can act as withholding agents, in some cases the responsibility for withholding is moved from the payer of the income on the underlying investment to the CII, as in Japan. The different withholding treatment is sometimes mixed with the tax treatment of the CII through the general nature of the CII for tax purposes. For example, if withholding tax on investment income is only levied on payments to individuals, the fact that the CII is treated in some respects as a company, at least for tax purposes, may mean that payments to it are not subject to withholding tax, while payments by the CII to individuals are subject to withholding tax.

B. Domestic CII

Table AII.3 summarises the taxation regime for CIIs in the countries covered by this report. As noted there, the investment fund is usually a tax subject but, by a variety of mechanisms, is not generally subject to tax except as a withholding agent or proxy for its members or as a sanction for not following the rules for achieving transparency. In some countries, exemption from tax at the CII level depends on distribution of income to members (U.S.). In other countries removal of tax at the CII level does not depend on distribution (Germany). Where tax is levied on the fund it is often in the form of a rough proxy tax for a tax on investors in the CII (unitholders) with no further tax at the member level (Belgium). Tax at the CII level often takes the form of a withholding, though in some countries where the type of income concerned is subject to flat rate taxation in the hands of individuals, the withholding is formally or effectively final (Japan).

The 1997 IFA Report identified five generic models for taxation of the CII which may be paraphrased as follows:

a) The CII is disregarded for tax purposes, *i.e.*, tax effects occur at the level of the investor and the CII is merely a conduit by which the individual derives the income (which may be compared to the way in which partnership income is treated in many countries).

b) The CII is recognised for tax purposes and is potentially subject to tax, but it is in fact exempt from tax, usually because it fulfils certain tax criteria specifically designed for CIIs.

c) The CII is recognised for tax purposes and is subject to tax at normal rates, but usually the tax is nil or close to nil because of the way the tax base is constructed (usually featuring a deduction for distributions, often again subject to criteria specifically designed for CIIs.

d) The CII is recognised for tax purposes and is subject to tax, but at special rates often close to zero, often again subject to criteria specifically designed for CIIs.

e) The CII is recognised for tax purposes and subject to tax at normal rates on a normal tax base, with full integration of the tax on the CII and tax on the investor in the CII (e.g., by way of exemption for the investor or by full imputation).

While many of the countries studied can be fitted into one or another of these categories (Belgium in (a), the U.S. in (c)), the main point for the present is to note the variety of formal ways at the level of the CII through which the same substantive result is sought to be achieved - that the tax is the same as where the investment is made directly rather than via the CII.

C. Domestic investor

Table AII.4 summarises the taxation regime for investors in CIIs in the countries covered by this report. Generally, the investor is at least nominally the person liable to the tax on income derived through the CII. In some countries the income is included in the tax return of the investor along with other income and taxed under a global income tax. In other countries, withholding in one form or another occurs at the CII level which effectively discharges the investor's tax liability. Various devices are used to identify the nature of the income received in cases where that matters (*e.g.*, dividends, interest or capital gains subject to different tax rates, dividends attracting imputation credits). Where the investor in the CII is a small individual investor these mechanisms can create compliance problems, but these problems are small compared to those created by the international tax system.

In some cases the investor ends up with a tax advantaged position compared to investing directly, rather than with simple transparency. The schemes in the U.K. in particular allow deferral of capital gains tax until withdrawal from the CII, *i.e.*, the CII is exempt from tax on its capital gains.

The varying ways in which countries' systems differ in relation to taxation of underlying income, the different devices used to achieve transparent taxation and the ways in which withholding mechanisms are used or not in the combined taxation of the underlying income, the CII and the investor in the CII all imply that it is likely to be difficult to achieve harmonisation of domestic countries' tax systems for CIIs. **As this report is focused on the international issues, no recommendations or detailed comments are made with respect to the domestic tax treatment of CIIs and their investments and investors.** It should be noted, however, that the OECD 1977 Study regarded it as necessary to achieve a certain harmony among domestic regimes for international problems to be solved. Likewise the 1997 IFA Report, in recommending a similar outcome to the OECD 1977 Study, assumes a certain degree of similarity in domestic tax regimes. The issue of whether progress can be made on the international front without impinging on domestic regimes is discussed in what follows.

3.4 Tax considerations in the foreign source income / domestic CII / domestic investor case

This section considers the typical outbound intermediated portfolio investment case involving the use of a domestic CII, depicted below in Chart III-2. The purpose of the present discussion is to identify tax distortions or considerations relevant to this investment structure that might operate to encourage or discourage its use, relative to the direct foreign portfolio investment option, taken as the benchmark. These considerations are grouped under three headings: income tax considerations, withholding tax considerations, and imputation tax relief considerations. Chart III-2 is intended as a reference point that may be helpful to the reader in recounting the relevant factors in this case, to be compared with those arising in the other portfolio investment structures analysed in this Report.

A. ***Income tax considerations***

The main income tax considerations in this case are (i) no or low (non-creditable) income tax at the CII level; and (ii) income flow-through provisions to maintain the character of income where this matters at the individual investor level.

i) No/low CII-level income tax

Investing in shares through a domestic CII raises the possibility of CII-level income tax which could discourage this investment option if such tax were non-creditable at the portfolio investor level. However, as reviewed below, most countries waive domestic tax on foreign source income realised and distributed by domestic CIIs, or impose CII-level income tax but relieve this tax at the individual investor level through their imputation system.

CHART III-2
Foreign Investment -- Direct versus Domestic CII

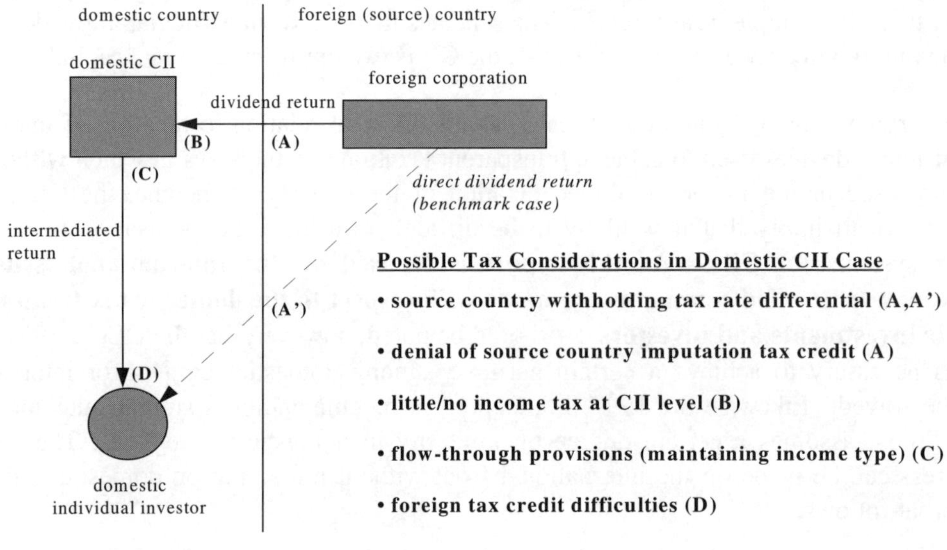

As noted earlier, domestic CIIs are disregarded in certain countries for tax purposes (similar treatment to partnership income in many countries, with tax effects occurring at the level of the investor.) In this 'pure' conduit case, there is generally no prospect of income tax at the CII level which could operate to discourage investment through this domestic intermediary investment channel.

Other countries, while recognising CIIs for tax purposes, either exempt such entities from tax, impose tax at normal rates on a minimal tax base, or impose CII-level tax at rates close to zero. Typically, such treatment is conditional upon the CII satisfying certain tax criteria specifically designed for CIIs -- in particular, a requirement that the CII distribute all/most of its income. As indicated in Tables 4.5 and 4.6, CIIs resident in Australia, Belgium, Sweden and the U.S. generally are not subject to tax on distributed foreign source investment income.

Still other countries recognise CIIs for tax purposes, and subject them to tax at normal rates on a normal tax base, but provide for full integration of CII-level tax with tax at the individual investor level by way of exemption or full imputation. For example, foreign source dividend income earned by AUTs in the U.K. is subject to income tax and to Advance Corporation Tax (ACT) upon distribution (set-off against net CII-level income tax), with a personal tax credit at the individual investor level.[1]

The various rules providing for either effectively little/no income tax at the domestic CII level, or for the integration of such tax with income tax at the investor level, means that a domestic individual's option of investing through a domestic CII generally will not be discouraged relative to the alternative of investing directly in foreign shares.

ii) *Income flow-through provisions*

Various devices are used to identify the character (*i.e.*, type) of return received/realised at the domestic CII level in situations where the distinction matters. In particular, foreign source dividends, interest or capital gains subject to different tax treatment in the hands of individual investors typically will be pooled or tracked separately at the CII level, and passed on to unitholders as separately identified flows of income. Such separation will matter, for example, where (host country) imputation tax credits attach to foreign dividends, or where foreign capital gains are subject to preferential tax rates.

B. *Withholding tax considerations*

The two main withholding tax considerations in the context of earning foreign source dividend income where the investor and CII are resident in the same country are (i) the possibility of different withholding tax rates applied at source to dividend income paid to a resident (domestic) CII, as compared to dividend income paid directly to a resident investor; and (ii) foreign tax credit complications that may limit a resident investor's ability to obtain relief for foreign portfolio dividend withholding tax when investing through a domestic CII.

i) *Possibility of different withholding tax rates*

In the *non-treaty case* where the foreign source country and the home country of the domestic investor have not concluded a tax treaty, the possibility of different withholding tax rates being imposed in the direct versus domestic CII cases generally does not arise, as source countries generally impose the same non-treaty (statutory) withholding tax rate on portfolio dividends paid to a non-treaty country, one that does not turn on the particular nature of the investor (*i.e.*, individual versus corporation/trust.)

However, in the *treaty case*, a reduced portfolio dividend withholding tax rate applied to dividends paid directly to a domestic investor, as set by tax treaty between the foreign source country and the residence country of the domestic investor, may or may not apply where a domestic CII is used. In certain cases, the domestic CII may be regarded as a treaty subject so that the treaty withholding tax rate that would apply in the direct portfolio investment case could apply equally.

In other treaty cases, the domestic CII may not be regarded by the foreign source country as a treaty subject and a treaty withholding tax rate reduction may not be provided. Where individual investors in a CII (and not the CII itself) are regarded by the source country as the beneficial owners of income paid to the CII, the relevant treaties are those between the source country and the residence country of each of the investors, with the country of residence of the CII being irrelevant (although the same, in this case, as the country of residence of a domestic investor.)[2] As discussed below, access to a treaty-reduced withholding tax rate is unlikely in this case.

One approach would be for the CII to calculate treaty benefits separately for each investor in the CII and for the source country to apply different withholding tax rates to different parts of the dividend income paid to the CII, on the basis of this information. The information requirements and compliance problems associated with this approach would appear to make its operation simply impossible to carry out. The alternative is for the host country to first withhold at its non-treaty rate, leaving it up to the individual investor to apply for a treaty reduction. However, the compliance costs involved at the shareholder level with this option may be viewed by individual investors as too high relative to the relief obtained. If investors do <u>not</u> apply, the result is that the treaty-reduced withholding tax rate applicable when investing in foreign portfolio shares directly is lost when investing through a domestic CII not regarded as a treaty subject by the foreign host/source country.

A Note on Tax Treaty Access to Reduced Withholding Tax on Investment Income

Under typical tax treaty provisions, up to four key considerations have to be satisfied before a tax treaty can operate to reduce withholding tax on dividend (and interest) income. The taxpayer claiming the treaty benefit has to be in terms of the relevant tax treaty a person, and a resident, beneficially entitled to the income and not disqualified by general or specific rules directed at treaty shopping or treaty abuse. Each of these can present problems in the case of income derived through a CII.

A CII may not be regarded as a person or as a resident for treaty purposes because it is not a separate legal person (*e.g.*, where a simple contractual arrangement is used) and not subject to tax due to the transparent tax treatment of the CII, as in many countries. Even if a CII qualifies as a person and a resident (as at least some of the entities used in the countries studied will do, such as US mutual funds), it may not be regarded as the beneficial owner of the income, either on the basis of legal form (*e.g.*, where a trust structure is used) or on the basis of its economic substance (*i.e.*, it is simply a conduit for the investor.) If the CII is regarded as passing the beneficial owner test, it may yet be disqualified on treaty shopping or abuse grounds where investors in the CII, resident in a third country, would not be entitled to similar treaty benefits under a treaty between that third country and the source country of the income.

The preceding would suggest that tax treaties should recognise CIIs resident in a given contracting country as treaty subjects. However, a consistency problem exists with operating tax treaties at the CII level (*i.e.*, applying the withholding tax rate applicable to distributions from the source country to individuals resident in the CII country), which rests on the fact that a CII is essentially a conduit (as recognised by most domestic tax regimes for CIIs) and may attract individual investors resident in other (third) countries not party to a bi-lateral tax treaty between the source country and the CII country (*i.e.*, the country in which the CII is resident.) By disregarding the residence of the investors in the CII, as generally occurs where the CII is taken to be the treaty subject, third-country investors may gain access to reduced withholding tax rates that would not apply on their direct portfolio investments in the source country, thus encouraging treaty shopping. As a result, the overall outcome in terms of tax may not be the same as would be observed where portfolio investments in the source country were made directly.

If the foreign CII is regarded as a treaty subject, the treaty determined rate could be either the general treaty rate for portfolio dividends (*i.e.*, the rate applicable to dividends distributed to *individuals* resident in the CII-residence country, giving the general (full) treaty rate reduction), or alternatively one providing only partial treaty relief with the applied rate exceeding the general treaty rate but below the statutory rate for portfolio dividends. The provision of only partial treaty relief reflects a practice followed by certain countries (*e.g.*, Germany) of restricting source country treaty benefits in the case of portfolio dividends paid to a non-resident (foreign) CII. Rather than giving the full treaty rate reduction for portfolio dividends paid to non-resident CIIs, the rate reduction is limited to the percentage of unit interests in the CII that are interests of individuals resident in the CII treaty country, in recognition of the fact that all investors in the CII may not be resident in the CII country, raising treaty shopping concerns.

ii) Foreign tax credit complications

In the intermediated investment case, the claiming of a foreign tax credit in respect of withholding tax at source on investment income will be in question. This problem arises even in exemption countries, as the exemption systems are generally not operative for foreign portfolio income (especially if a reduction in tax at source has occurred under a tax treaty.)

Often, in cases like the one under consideration where the CII and the investor in the CII are resident in the same country, the CII tax regime will prevent a mismatch of tax and tax credit, so that relief from foreign withholding tax is obtained, as in the direct portfolio investment case. In some systems, foreign tax credits may be claimed at the investor level, as in the case of Australia. In the U.K., the use of the corporate tax regime at the level of the CII together with the system of foreign income dividends (FIDs) effectively achieves pass-through of the foreign tax to the investor. In Japan, the credit is available at the CII-level for credit against the withholding tax on distributions to investors (problems may arise where the foreign tax exceeds the 20 per cent withholding rate, as the withholding tax in Japan is effectively final for individual investors.)

However, in certain other cases, foreign tax credit relief may not be available -- for example, where the credit is available to the CII and not to individual unitholders, but the CII effectively is not taxed (being subject to transparent tax treatment) and thus has little or no tax liability against which to claim the foreign tax credit. In Sweden this problem may arise in mainly non-treaty cases. In the U.S., individual investors are denied foreign tax credits unless a majority of the CII's investments are in foreign securities (investor level tax calculations are simplified in this case by treating all of the income from the CII as foreign source income.)

Even in the first-noted case, where the foreign tax credit can pass through to the investor, compliance and administrative problems are likely to arise in that small investors are unlikely to be able to cope with the complexity of the foreign tax credit system in a number of countries (*e.g.*, Australia.) High compliance cost to the investor may make the effort of claiming the foreign tax credit unworthwhile, especially where the foreign income constitutes only a small proportion of the CII's income. This consideration no doubt explains at least in part the U.S. position of providing investors with foreign tax credits only where a majority of the CII's investment is in foreign securities.

C. Imputation relief considerations

In general, countries that provide resident individual investors with an imputation or dividend tax credit giving relief from underlying corporate income tax on distributed income received from a resident company, deny such relief to non-resident investors. However, a number of countries with imputation systems (*e.g.*, France, Italy, U.K.) have concluded tax treaties that extend full or partial imputation relief to non-resident individual shareholders. Under such arrangements, the host country provides individuals resident in a foreign (treaty) country with a cash refund for all or part of the host-country corporate income tax underlying a dividend distribution, and typically 'claws back' part of that relief by imposing withholding tax on dividends measured gross of the cash refund.[3] Certain other countries provide integration relief under domestic law by eliminating non-resident withholding tax, as in the Australian example.

Where withholding tax is waived on portfolio dividends under domestic law as a means of delivering integration relief and the exemption does not vary by the nature of the investor (*e.g.*, Australia), the choice over direct versus intermediated investment generally would not be biased as a result of this tax consideration, as foreign tax credit complications in this case would not be at issue. Where foreign withholding tax would otherwise be fully creditable at the investor level in the direct portfolio investment case, and also in the intermediated investment case where the CII is treated as a conduit with foreign tax credit claims at the investor level (*e.g.*, the basic U.S. system), elimination of withholding tax would alter the sharing of tax revenues between host and home countries (with foreign tax credits reduced dollar for dollar with the withholding tax reduction) without influencing investor rates of return. The (gross) dividend would in both cases be subject to a combined host and home country overall tax rate equal to the investor's marginal personal tax rate (with or without withholding tax.)

Where instead the investor would otherwise be in an excess foreign tax credit position (with the foreign withholding tax rate being the effective tax rate at the margin), the absence of this tax generally would imply, in this situation as well, taxation of (gross) foreign dividends at the same rate (*i.e.*, the investor's marginal personal tax rate) in both the domestic intermediated and direct investment cases. Moreover, if foreign tax credit relief in respect of foreign withholding tax (if imposed) is unavailable when investing through a domestic CII, the elimination of this tax would remove a potential distortion and thus improve neutrality.

Similarly, where foreign tax credits are taken at the CII level and net CII-level tax is creditable against individual tax (*e.g.*, the U.K. AUT-system), the absence of foreign withholding tax at source would mean lower host country tax revenues, increased net CII-level tax, with increased imputation tax credits at the investor level, but again with the overall result of taxation of the (gross) dividend at a combined host and home country tax rate equal to the investor's marginal personal tax rate. Lastly, where foreign withholding tax is credited against final withholding tax at the CII level (*e.g.*, the Japanese system), home country tax revenues would increase at the expense of host country revenues, and returns to investors generally would not be affected.

Considering now the situation where a given foreign host country has agreed, under a tax treaty, to provide integration relief to domestic individual investors (non-resident portfolio investors from the host country's perspective) and grant a cash refund for underlying corporate income tax, such relief may be lost if the individual invests in shares using a domestic CII. In particular, where portfolio dividend income sourced in the foreign host country is paid to (routed through) a domestic CII, and a treaty between the home country and the foreign host country stipulates that the host country attach a refund to dividends paid to domestic *individual* shareholders, a key issue that arises is whether the domestic CII is deemed by the source (host) country to be a separate legal person or not.[4]

If the CII is treated on a transparent basis and individual investors are viewed to be the beneficial owners of income derived by the domestic CII, then integration benefits may pass through as in the direct investment case.[5] In this case a potential tax distortion is avoided. Under the Australia-U.K. tax treaty, for example, an Australian unit trust is regarded as purely transparent for this purpose, enabling individual investors access to imputation treaty benefits on portfolio dividends from the U.K. If, on the other hand, the CII is regarded as a separate legal person, it may not be entitled to imputation benefits given that it is not an *individual* investor. On this basis, a domestic investor may be encouraged to invest directly in foreign shares rather than use a domestic CII.

3.5 Tax considerations in the foreign source income / foreign CII / domestic investor case

This section analyses the outbound intermediated portfolio investment case involving the use of a foreign CII. The 'two-country case' is examined, where the foreign source country and the CII country (the country in which the foreign CII is resident) are the same. Also considered is the 'three-country case' where the CII is resident in a different (third) country than the foreign source country. The purpose once again is to identify tax considerations that might encourage or discourage the use of foreign CIIs relative to the benchmark direct foreign portfolio investment case.

The two-country case

When considering portfolio investment through a foreign CII, one possible case is where the CII is resident in the same country as the company generating the foreign source income. This two-country case (with the second country being the (home) country of the domestic investor) is depicted below in Chart III-3, which lists a range of tax considerations that could potentially influence a domestic investor's choice over earning portfolio foreign source dividend income directly or through a foreign CII.

CHART III-3
Foreign Investment -- Direct versus Foreign CII
(two-country case)

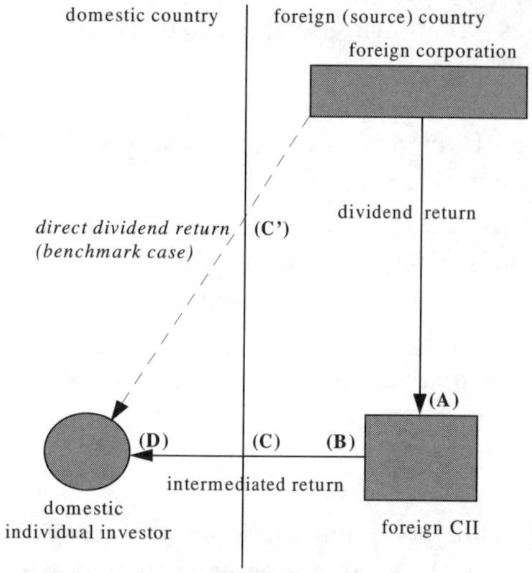

Possible Tax Considerations in Foreign CII Case

- **non-creditable income tax on CII (A)**
- **income conversion (dividends to gains) (B)**
- **source country withholding tax rate differential (C,C')**
- **flow-through of host country imputation tax credit (if any) (C,C')**
- **home country domestic tax deferral (D)**

The three-country case

Another possible structure involving the use of a foreign CII is one where the foreign CII is resident in a different (third) country than the foreign source country. This so-called 'triangular' structure characterises the tax haven or 'offshore' portfolio investment case. It raises treaty-shopping issues and potential concerns, under certain conditions relating to source and CII-residence country tax rules. This three-country case is shown in Chart III-4.

CHART III-4
Foreign Investment -- Direct versus Foreign CII
(three-country case)

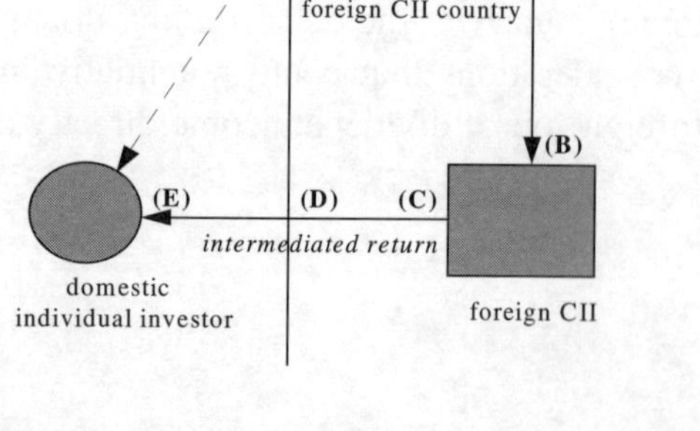

Possible Tax Considerations in Foreign CII Case

- **source county withholding tax rate differential (A, A')**
- **non-creditable withholding tax (A)**
- **differential host country imputation tax credit (if any) (A, A')**
- **non-creditable income tax on CII (B)**
- **income conversion (dividends to gains) (C)**
- **additional withholding tax (D)**
- **home country domestic tax deferral (E)**

A. *Income tax considerations*

The main income tax considerations in the context of earning foreign source dividend income through a foreign CII are (i) the possibility of non-creditable income tax at the CII level, which would tend to discourage investment through this channel, (ii) the possible deferral or elimination of domestic tax on foreign source income accumulating in offshore investment funds, tending to encourage their use; and (iii) the possible conversion of foreign dividend income into foreign source capital gains which may be taxed preferentially in the home country of the domestic investor relative to dividend income earned directly, which also could encourage the use of foreign CIIs. The offshore investment incentive generally is greatest where no/low foreign tax is imposed on the income of a foreign CII,[6] the home country does not have in place or cannot effectively implement anti-deferral rules to tax on a current basis the foreign source income of resident individuals, and the home country preferentially treats foreign capital gains.

i) Possibility of additional income tax (CII level)

Certain countries impose income tax on the investment earnings of resident CIIs. This creates an additional tax wedge on investment returns to non-resident portfolio investors in CIIs, relative to the direct portfolio investment option, given that (even in exemption countries) portfolio shareholders are generally not provided with an indirect foreign tax credit (FTC) in respect of underlying foreign income tax in determining their home country tax on foreign source dividend income (*i.e.*, non-transparent tax treatment.) This can be contrasted to the case of a domestic CII, where transparent tax treatment afforded by domestic law will usually prevent any tax paid by the CII being stuck at the CII level.

ii) Possibility of home country tax deferral/elimination

Certain countries impose low/zero income tax on investment earnings of resident CIIs. One can distinguish three cases:

a) a foreign CII resident in an offshore 'tax haven' country that imposes low/zero income tax;

b) a foreign CII resident in a 'high-tax' country (*i.e.*, one that generally imposes income tax at significant rates) that waives CII-level tax *without* a distribution requirement; and

c) a foreign CII resident in a 'high-tax' country that waives CII-level tax *with/subject to* a distribution requirement.

Given the typically limited range of real investment opportunities in tax haven countries, case a) generally involves three countries, with the foreign income sourced in a different country than the residence country of the CII. In cases b) and c), the foreign income may be sourced in the same country as the CII, or in another (third) country. The case b) situation, which can generate results similar to that observed in case a), may occur where the residence country of the CII seeks transparency and chooses to effect this by not taxing the CII. Such a regime will provide for income tax deferral generally only if there is no distribution requirement attaching to the non-taxation of the CII, as assumed in case b) Case c) represents the typical CII tax regime in most OECD countries.

Where case a) or b) occurs, shareholder-level income tax on foreign investment income may be deferred or even removed where the investment income is 'rolled-up' (retained) in the foreign CII, itself free of income tax. The tax advantage will be realised if the home country does not or is unable to tax offshore 'rolled-up' earnings on a current (accrual) basis. This situation would arise where the home country's tax system does not contain passive foreign investment fund (PFIF)-type rules to tax resident individual investors on their attributed earnings of a foreign CII on a current basis. Or it may be that such rules are in place but cannot be enforced due, for example, to a lack of information exchange, or because resident investors are able to avoid the application of such rules through tax-planning techniques.

In case c) where tax at the CII level is eliminated subject to a given distribution requirement, tax deferral opportunities are generally removed. However, depending on the specific rules governing the distribution requirement (*e.g.*, the minimum percentage amount of CII-earnings that must be distributed in order that income tax at the CII-level be waived), some scope for avoiding home country taxation may be available. In the U.S., for example, a regulated investment company (RIC) generally will not be subject to tax on its earnings provided, among other things, that 90 per cent or more of the fund's income is distributed to shareholders. Lower distribution thresholds would provide for home country tax deferral opportunities on a larger percentage of foreign investment income.

iii) *Advantageous income conversion possibilities (dividend income into capital gains)*

A domestic income tax advantage (relative to the benchmark direct portfolio investment case) may also arise where the character (*i.e.*, type) of foreign dividend income is converted when realised through a CII (constituting another form of 'non-transparency.') This potential benefit rests on the fact that returns at the CII-level may be realised at the individual investor level through dividend distributions by the CII, or through capital gains on the buy-back/redemption of investor interests in the CII or the sale of interests to a third-party investor, where the price in each case reflects the asset backing in the CII. Where dividend (or interest) income at the CII level is realised at the investor level as a capital gain through the disposition of individual interests in the CII, a tax preferred result may occur to the extent that foreign capital gains are taxed in the home country preferentially as compared to foreign dividend (or interest) income. Investments in offshore funds would be most attractive relative to the benchmark case where there exist both income conversion and home country deferral possibilities.

iv) *Disadvantageous income conversion possibilities (capital gains into dividend income)*

While not the particular focus of this Report (which concentrates on dividend-producing investments), it should be noted that the interposition of a foreign CII can also generate disadvantageous home country income tax results. This result can arise where the foreign CII realises capital gains and distributes these amounts to individual unitholders. A negative tax result will occur if capital gains on the disposition of foreign securities (realised at the individual level if held directly) are taxed preferentially in the home country (*e.g.*, are not taxed, as is the case in a number of countries) as compared with foreign dividend income.

For this reason, CIIs investing in growth stocks, or more generally securities offering investors potential returns in the form of capital gains rather than dividends, would generally seek to avoid the conversion of gains by not distributing earnings to unitholders. In particular, the CII might be expected to provide for redemption of unit interests, or more generally for making a market at a price reflecting asset backing in the CII, to allow unitholders to obtain their tax preferred result.

B. Withholding tax considerations

In analysing relevant withholding tax considerations, it is useful to distinguish the two-country case from the three-country case. In the two-country case, the main withholding tax consideration is the possibility of converting dividend income into tax-preferred capital gains. In the three-country case, the main withholding tax considerations are those tied to treaty shopping arrangements, and those linked to routing portfolio investment through CIIs located in tax-havens (to be considered separately.) As noted below, withholding tax issues tied to treaty shopping are raised in a 1977 OECD study *The Taxation of Collective Investment Institutions* ('the 1977 OECD Study'), and more recently in a 1997 report by the International Fiscal Association, *The Taxation of Investment Funds* ('the 1997 IFA Report.') This report summarises the main issues, and highlights the problems raised.

The two-country case (foreign income source and CII resident in the same foreign country)

In the two-country case, where the CII is resident in the foreign source country, the main withholding tax consideration in relation to the earning of foreign dividend income is the possibility of accessing reduced withholding tax through the conversion of such income into capital gains. This relief adds to the potential attractiveness of 'roll-up' funds resident in countries (*e.g.*, Japan) that do not attach an earnings distribution requirement to the non-taxation of CIIs and thus, in addition to providing tax-deferral opportunities, facilitate such income conversion. Moreover, as noted above, foreign capital gains may be treated preferentially relative to foreign dividend income in the home country. Where dividend income earned by a foreign CII is not converted (*i.e.*, is passed on to investors by way of dividend distribution), generally no withholding tax advantages (or disadvantages) arise relative to the benchmark foreign direct portfolio investment case as in both cases the same statutory (or treaty) withholding tax rate applicable to portfolio dividends from the source (CII-residence) country would apply.

i) Advantageous income conversion possibilities (attracting reduced withholding tax)

The possibility of converting dividend income into capital gains subject to reduced withholding tax can arise with a 'distributor' fund which distributes all or most of its earnings (typically to avoid CII-level income tax.) Income conversion in this case generally would be limited to current period earnings and would involve the disposition of interests in the foreign CII just prior to the distribution of current earnings to unitholders. However, income conversion possibilities are greatest in 'non-distributor' or 'roll-up' funds which may be found not just in 'tax havens' but also, as noted earlier, in certain 'high-tax' countries that do not attach a distribution requirement to the non-taxation of resident CIIs, while providing same-country real investment opportunities (*i.e.*, the two-country investment case.) Withholding tax relief tied to the conversion of dividend income into capital gains may encourage the use of such funds, which may be already attractive due to home country tax deferral possibilities and the application (if at all) of reduced home country tax rates on capital gains rather than dividends, as noted above.

Reduced withholding tax accompanying income conversion may apply in non-treaty and treaty situations. In the *non-treaty case*, a source country may waive withholding tax on capital gains derived by non-resident shareholders, or alternatively may levy withholding tax on capital gains realised by foreign investors but may not have administrative rules in place to effectively collect such a tax.[7] In the *treaty case*, the treatment depends on how the CII is regarded for treaty purposes. If the CII is regarded by the source country in which it is resident as a company for treaty purposes,[8] so that the treaty is deemed to apply directly between the CII and the non-resident individual investor in the CII, then the disposition of his/her interests in the CII typically would be treated as a tax-exempt capital gain.[9] Under this scenario, the foreign CII offers withholding tax advantages relative to the direct portfolio investment case.

If, however, the CII is not regarded as a company under the treaty, but is instead regarded as a transparent entity (a conduit) that is not a treaty subject, implying that the treaty applies directly between the distributing (source) company and the non-resident investor, then the character of the dividend income would not change for treaty purposes and would be subject in principle to portfolio dividend withholding tax. Imposition of dividend withholding tax on capital gains realised on the disposition by an individual investor of his/her interest in the foreign CII may be feasible in practice where the disposition is by way of *redemption* (share buy-back), by shifting the withholding obligation to the CII which should have the necessary information for the application of the relevant portfolio dividend withholding rate. Imposing dividend withholding tax on capital gains on the sale of interests in the CII to a *third* party investor would be administratively more difficult.

However, if the disposition is treated as dividend income and dividend withholding tax is collected, and if the country of residence of the investor agrees on the classification of the foreign CII as a purely transparent entity enabling the investor to claim a foreign tax credit under the treaty in respect of the tax withheld, and if the investor is able to calculate the foreign tax credit claim, then the outcome would be the same in the foreign CII case as in the direct portfolio investment treaty case. This situation may be described as the *pure transparency* case. Where withholding tax cannot be imposed, investing in the foreign CII can result in a tax-preferred result relative to the benchmark direct portfolio investment case.

The preceding result assumes that the countries of residence of the investor and the foreign CII agree on the classification of the CII (as a company or transparent entity.) It will not be uncommon, however, for the countries to disagree on this matter. Where, for example, the source country views the CII as a conduit and imposes withholding tax at source, while the home country views the foreign CII as a company and denies a foreign tax credit, the use of the foreign CII would tend to be discouraged.

ii) Disadvantageous income conversion possibilities (attracting increased withholding tax)

Again, while not the focus of this Report, it should be noted that depending on the type of foreign source income being earned, the use of a foreign CII may give rise in certain cases to disadvantageous withholding tax results. This result can arise where, rather than earning dividend income, the foreign CII earns interest income or realises capital gains and these amounts are distributed as dividend income to individual unitholders. Where the foreign CII is regarded by the source country as a company and resident for treaty purposes, distributions by it will be regarded as dividends and subject to the dividend article accordingly. Even where the residence country of the CII achieves transparent taxation of the CII, the distributions will be taxable under the treaty in the hands of the non-resident investor in the CII at (usually) 15 per cent, the tax being withheld by the CII. In other words, for treaty purposes, interest income or capital gains realised by the foreign CII will be converted to dividend income, leading usually to a higher rate of tax than would apply if the investor derived interest (where treaties normally provide for a 10 per cent tax) or capital gain (usually tax exempt.)

Thus the investor may be doubly disadvantaged if the CII is subject to income tax in its own right (which is not creditable under normal treaty provisions in the hands of the individual investor), and if tax-preferred interest income or capital gains are converted to dividends.[10] Note however that where the CII is not regarded by the source country as a company, and is instead deemed to be a transparent entity, the treaty is taken to apply directly between the source company and the non-resident investor, with the result that the character of the income does not change and treaty benefits are obtained, so that the outcome generally remains the same as would be observed in the direct portfolio investment case.[11]

The three-country case (foreign income source and foreign CII resident in different countries)

In the three-country (triangular) case where the foreign CII is resident in a different (third) country than the foreign source country, the main withholding tax considerations in the context of earning foreign dividend income are: (i) the possibility of different withholding tax at source compared with the benchmark (direct portfolio investment) option, with generally more restrictive opportunities for foreign tax credit relief in respect of source country withholding tax in the triangular situation; (ii) the possible imposition by the CII country (*i.e.*, the country in which the CII is resident) of additional withholding tax on dividend distributions by the CII; and (iii) income conversion possibilities to avoid application of this (additional) withholding tax on dividends distributed by the foreign CII.

In examining tax distortions arising from the possible application of withholding tax at source on portfolio dividend income, and the possible application of withholding tax at the CII level in the triangular case, the key considerations are the relative levels of applicable withholding tax rates in the direct versus intermediated investment cases, and secondly, the constraints that apply in claiming foreign tax credits in respect of these taxes.

i) Possibility of different withholding tax rates

In the direct investment case, the applicable withholding tax rate would be the source country's statutory withholding rate for portfolio dividends (generally positive, zero in some country cases) in the absence of a treaty between the source country and the (home) residence country of the domestic investor. Alternatively, if a tax treaty exists, the general treaty rate for portfolio dividends would apply.

Similarly, in the triangular case, the applicable source country tax rate would be its statutory withholding tax rate in the absence of a treaty between the source country and the CII country. Where a treaty exists with the CII country, the source country's statutory rate or a treaty negotiated rate would be imposed. If the source country does not regard the CII as a treaty subject, then generally the statutory rate would apply. Where a treaty exists between the source country and the home country of the domestic investor, the investor could apply to the source country for application of a treaty rate (*i.e.*, apply for a withholding tax refund), but in practice this generally would not be observed due to the transactions costs involved. If the foreign CII is regarded as a treaty subject, the general treaty rate for portfolio dividends or alternatively one providing partial treaty relief (addressing treaty shopping concerns) might be applied.

In the triangular investment structure, dividend income potentially subject to withholding tax at source that is received by a foreign CII and then *distributed* to a domestic investor (a non-resident investor to the CII) may be subject to another (second) layer of withholding tax imposed by the CII country. In the non-treaty situation, tax would be withheld at the CII country's statutory withholding rate applicable to portfolio dividends. Alternatively, if a tax treaty exists between the CII country and the (home) residence country of the domestic investor, the general treaty rate for portfolio dividends would apply. In general, the portfolio withholding tax would be creditable at the unitholder level, being a direct tax on that investor.

ii) Foreign tax credit restrictions (source country withholding tax)

The net impact of different withholding taxation under these various cases also depends critically on the available foreign tax crediting mechanisms. Withholding tax at source (if any) in the benchmark case would be fully or partly creditable at the individual unitholder level in most cases. Similarly, withholding tax imposed by the country of residence of a foreign CII on dividends routed through it and paid to domestic investors (non-resident investors from the CII country's perspective) would also be fully or partly creditable at the individual unitholder level. In contrast, while the domestic tax regime of the CII country may provide for a matching of tax and credit at the individual investor level for investors resident in that country, withholding tax at source in the triangular structure generally would not be creditable at the *non-resident* individual investor level. Moreover, source country withholding tax cannot be credited against CII-level income tax if the CII itself is not subject to tax, as is typically the situation under tax regimes for domestic CIIs designed to achieve transparency. This leaves the final possibility of crediting source country withholding tax against tax withheld at the CII level on its distributions. The net effect of these various considerations is taken up below.

Consider first that in order for a domestic shareholder to derive foreign tax credit (FTC) relief in respect of source-country withholding tax in the triangular structure, generally one of the following three candidate crediting mechanisms would have to be in effect:

option (a): FTC claim at the CII level against CII-level income tax

option (b): FTC claim at the domestic investor/unitholder level, or

option (c): FTC claim at the CII level against tax withheld at the CII level.

Option (a) requires that the CII be subject to corporate income tax. If, in fact, the CII is treated as a company and is subject to income tax, such as in the case of AUTs in the U.K., then the crediting of source country withholding tax against CII-level income tax would involve the substitution of one tax that is non-creditable at the non-resident individual investor level (source country withholding tax) for another tax that is also non-creditable at the individual investor level (CII-level income tax.) This result, which follows from the fact that portfolio shareholders typically are granted only direct (as opposed to indirect) foreign tax credit relief, would therefore not alleviate the unrelieved foreign tax.

Option (b) providing foreign tax credits at the individual level for source country withholding tax in the intermediated investment case generally would not be feasible at a reasonable administrative and compliance cost.[12] Furthermore, even assuming that investors could be provided with the information necessary to compute the foreign tax credit available to them in respect of tax on investment income earned at the foreign CII level, the domestic authorities of the home country may not regard the foreign CII as a transparent entity and therefore may be unwilling to permit a foreign tax credit in this case.

Option (c) allowing source country withholding tax to be credited against withholding tax levied at the CII level on distributions by the CII also generally would not solve the problem of withholding tax being stuck at the CII level, discouraging its use. This is because such crediting would reduce CII-level withholding tax (a creditable tax at the investor level), rather than source country withholding tax which is not creditable at the investor level (absent special provisions that would explicitly recognises CIIs as flow-through entities and provide for credits at the unitholder level for source country withholding tax.)

Possible cases and tax distortions

The fact that in practice source country withholding tax may be effectively 'stuck' at the CII-level leads to the general result that investing in foreign shares through a foreign CII in a third country (the triangular case) is tax disadvantaged on this account (note that this disadvantage may be offset by possible home-country tax deferral opportunities, addressed below.) However, exceptions to this general rule may be observed. The following material reviews factors relevant to the scale and direction of the possible distortions arising on account of withholding tax considerations in the triangular case.

Consider first the situation where a tax treaty applies in the direct investment case, providing for withholding by the source country at its (non-zero) general treaty rate for portfolio dividends (giving full treaty rate reduction from the statutory rate.) This treatment generally would compare more favourably to that possible under the foreign CII option even where a treaty exists between the source and CII countries providing for source country withholding at the same rate as in the direct investment case. The reason for this result rests with the general inability to claim foreign tax credit relief in respect of source country withholding tax in the triangular case.

In the direct investment case, the only potential foreign tax credit constraints are those that may apply at the individual investor level (as for example might occur if the investor's average personal income tax rate is low relative to the withholding rate.) Often such constraints will not be in effect (binding), especially for top-bracket investors, allowing individual investors to claim a foreign tax credit for the full amount of foreign-source country withholding tax, whether imposed at a treaty or non-treaty rate. In contrast, source country withholding tax generally remains unrelieved in the (triangular) intermediated investment case. The implication is that use of the foreign CII will be discouraged relative to the direct investment option on account of this non-creditable tax. The distortion remains unchanged if *CII-level* withholding tax can be credited in full at the individual investor level (as unrelieved withholding at source remains), and is potentially increased if the individual investor is unable to obtain a full credit for the CII-level withholding as a result of foreign tax crediting limitations at the investor level.[13]

Consider now the situation where a treaty is not in effect in the direct portfolio investment case, so that source-country withholding tax is imposed at the statutory rate on portfolio dividends. The general result again will be that the net withholding tax burden is higher under the foreign CII option, even if a tax treaty exists between the source country and the CII-residence country which lowers the applicable source country withholding tax rate below the statutory rate. Once again, the reason for this general result is non-creditable source country withholding tax in the triangular case, as compared to a full offset for (in this case) higher source country withholding tax under the direct investment option.

Several qualifications to the preceding general result should be noted. First, if the withholding tax rate at source is higher in the foreign CII case than in the direct investment case -- as it would be if the source country provides full tax treaty relief in the benchmark case but only partial relief in the CII case (*e.g.*, as under a proportionality approach) or has no tax treaty with the CII country and therefore imposes withholding tax at the statutory rate -- the distortion discouraging the use of the foreign CII, linked to higher net source country withholding tax under the CII option, would be even more pronounced (with increased (net) source country withholding tax being stuck at the CII level).

Second, as noted in the discussion below considering CIIs resident in tax havens, in the event that the net withholding tax burden is higher in the foreign CII case, this tax distortion, operating to discourage the use of the foreign CII, may in certain cases be offset by income tax deferral opportunities when investing through the CII.

Third, a tax distortion favouring the foreign CII option due to withholding tax considerations alone may be observed if the source country withholding tax rate is comparatively high in the benchmark case and if the individual investor is non-taxable, or otherwise subject to restrictions in the claiming of a current direct foreign tax credit in respect of withholding tax on portfolio dividends received.[14] Such a situation could arise where the source and CII countries have concluded a tax treaty, and the CII country and the domestic (home) country have also concluded a tax treaty, but the source country and domestic (home) country have not. The direction and magnitude of the distortion will depend on the foreign tax credit carry-over provisions at the individual investor level, and the degree to which the source country withholding tax rate is lowered below the statutory rate for dividend payments to the foreign CII. Where the net source country withholding tax burden in the direct portfolio investment case exceeds the combined source country and CII country net withholding tax burden under the intermediated investment option, withholding tax considerations alone may encourage investing through a foreign CII.

iii) Possible income conversion possibilities

As in the two-country scenario, dividend income may be converted into capital gains subject to reduced withholding tax by disposing of interests in the foreign CII, with the greatest potential for conversion offered by offshore non-distributor (*i.e.*, 'roll-up') funds. In the *non-treaty* case, source countries may or may not have mechanisms in place to effectively impose withholding tax on such gains.[15] In the *treaty* case, if the CII is regarded as a resident and a company, so that the treaty is deemed to apply directly between the CII and the non-resident individual investor in the CII, then the disposition would be treated in most cases as a tax exempt capital gain.

Thus, depending on whether foreign source dividend income is passed on as dividends or capital gains to the non-resident investor, routing dividend income from a given source country through the foreign CII may result in an increased or decreased withholding tax burden, depending on the particular tax treaty structure.

The tax haven or 'offshore' investment case -- Foreign CIIs subject to low/zero taxation

The three-country portfolio investment case increasingly involves the offshore situation where the CII is resident in a jurisdiction imposing low/no income tax -- a classic 'tax haven' or an otherwise 'high-tax' jurisdiction not attaching a distribution requirement to the non-taxation of a CII.

Under the typical structure, the CII invests in securities generating investment income that is subject to little or no withholding tax at source, little or no income tax or withholding tax is imposed at the CII level, opportunities exist for converting dividend income into capital gains, and there is potential for home country tax deferral. In a typical tax haven situation, a low/zero dividend withholding tax rate would apply to distributions from the CII to non-resident investors, making income conversion unnecessary as regards withholding tax implications (although, as noted above, there may be home country income tax advantages tied to capital gains.)

As regards tax-planning efforts to reduce or eliminate non-resident withholding tax at source, there exist a number of opportunities to earn tax-free returns even for investments in countries which levy substantial rates of withholding tax. While portfolio dividends typically are subject to withholding tax in the source country, there are various tax avoidance strategies available to eliminate the impact of the withholding tax. Methods of avoidance of withholding tax can vary by country, and are not peculiar to the CII sector and so they will be not elaborated here. There are some common features across countries such as the sales of income streams to resident (often tax-exempt) investors to convert dividends into capital gains in the hands of the CII which are not taxed at source, or the use of derivatives, as discussed in the 1994 OECD Report, *Taxation of New Financial Instruments*.[16]

C. Imputation relief considerations

Where, in the two-country situation, integration relief is provided unilaterally by a foreign source (host) country to domestic investors (non-residents from the foreign host country's perspective) through elimination of non-resident withholding tax, generally the same result is achieved in the intermediated investment situation as compared to the direct investment case.[17] Host country tax revenues collected on a dividend distribution would be lower than they would otherwise be, and domestic tax revenues higher through the lowering of foreign tax credit claims, but the existence (or not) of the foreign withholding tax generally would not be a factor influencing investor choice over the direct versus foreign CII option, with foreign tax credit claims available equally in each case.

Similarly, in the three-country case, the absence of withholding tax at source alters host and home country tax revenue sharing. Moreover, unlike the two-country case, source country withholding tax may be non-creditable in the three-country situation, and thus the absence of this tax removes a potential tax impediment to the foreign CII option. Further, if under the intermediated investment option, foreign source dividend income that would be exempt from non-resident withholding tax on a direct payment to a domestic investor is converted into capital gains through a sale/redemption of shares/units in the foreign CII, the neutrality result generally would continue to hold as most countries do not tax capital gains realised by non-resident portfolio investors on the sale/redemption of shares of resident companies.[18]

Where instead a source country offers imputation relief to non-resident investors under tax treaties in the form of an imputation tax credit/refund, such relief generally is made available whether (franked) dividend income is paid directly to a qualifying non-resident investor or is instead routed through a CII in the source (host) country (in the two-country case.) In the intermediated case, imputation relief may be attached to the distribution by the CII of (franked) dividend income either on a pure transparency basis (where the CII is a non-taxpaying entity 'outside' the imputation system, as in the Australian case) or, where the CII is itself involved in the imputation system, with its distributions attracting similar treatment as distributions of the companies in which the underlying investment is made (*e.g.*, where, as in the U.K., distributions by CIIs are subject to ACT on franked dividend payments in excess of franked dividend receipts.) In both cases, the general administrative approach would require the CII to collect withholding tax on, and attach imputation relief to, distributions to non-resident investors of franked investment income. The CII (or its agent) would then apply to the host country for reimbursement of the integration credit/refund (which could be netted against its gross withholding tax payment liability.)

In the three-country situation, inconsistencies are likely to arise. Consider first the case where a foreign source country has a tax treaty with the domestic/home country that provides imputation relief to domestic portfolio individual shareholders. The imputation credit under the direct investment option will differ from the credit attached (if any) to portfolio dividends paid to a CII resident in a third country where the foreign source country and the CII country have not concluded a tax treaty, or have but the treaty does not provide for imputation credits payable to residents of the CII country. Domestic shareholders generally would be discouraged from investing through a foreign CII on account of this tax distortion.

Moreover, if the foreign source country and CII country have concluded a tax treaty extending integration relief to *individuals* resident in the CII country, imputation credits may continue to be denied if the foreign CII is regarded by the host/source country as a company (a separate legal person) as opposed to a transparent entity. If the CII is regarded as purely transparent for this purpose by the host country, it is possible that the domestic investor could apply to the host country for an imputation credit for the portion of his/her return from the CII sourced from that host country, but this information would have to be provided by the CII and may not be forthcoming. In either event, the loss of imputation credits when investing through a foreign CII would tend to discourage its use, relative to the direct investment option.

Alternatively, imputation tax credits may not be provided on a direct portfolio investment, but may be available when investing through a foreign CII resident in a country that has secured such relief for such payments. This suggests treaty shopping opportunities and potential concerns, this time in relation to imputation benefits. Where such benefits are available, the distortion in this case would favour the foreign CII, rather than investing directly.

If portfolio foreign source dividend income that would otherwise attract an imputation tax credit on a direct payment to a domestic investor is converted into capital gains through a sale/redemption of units in the CII, such direct relief would be lost given that it accompanies dividend payments only.[19] (In many cases this loss would be offset by other benefits tied to income conversion -- namely, the elimination of portfolio dividend withholding tax and preferential home country tax treatment of capital gains.)

3.6 Summary

This chapter has examined how the international tax treatment of portfolio foreign investment through domestic CIIs may differ from that when investing directly. Similarly, investing through a foreign CII may result in a different overall tax burden as compared with direct portfolio investment.

Problems may be encountered in the operation of foreign tax credit) mechanisms in the domestic CII case. Tax systems may prevent a mismatch of foreign withholding tax and foreign tax credit; however relief for foreign tax at source in certain cases may not be available. Even where available, compliance and administrative problems in the claiming of the credit may arise.

Another potential source of distortion arises where foreign funds are characterised differently from domestic funds either because a different legal structure is used in a foreign country or because the special rules for transparent tax treatment that apply in the purely domestic case cannot be satisfied by foreign funds (*e.g.*, most simply because only a resident entity can obtain the special tax treatment). This second difference can mean higher tax in the foreign CII case because transparency is lost and the investor is denied credit for tax levied in the foreign country. However, it may also permit lower taxation. Where the foreign CII is not regarded as transparent in the residence country of the investor, it may be possible to roll up income in an 'offshore' CII and defer home country taxation. The offshore case generally provides the most advantage to the investor where there is no tax imposed on the investment income at source or at the CII level. This is the typical scenario with many off-shore funds and some countries have therefore enacted legislation to take away or reduce tax advantages potentially gained by the investor.

This Chapter has also examined how tax treaties may not operate effectively in the case of CIIs. The source country may deny lower withholding tax rates in the CII case and the investor's country of residence may similarly refuse to credit the higher level of tax at source. Or the source country may apply a lower treaty rate of tax on the basis of residence of the CII (in a third country) while the investor resides in a country which would not be entitled to that lower rate, and moreover the investor may not be taxed on a current basis in his/her country of residence.

Lastly, the operation of imputation systems was also shown to potentially different in the CII case. In particular, if a treaty offers imputation benefits to individual investors but does not treat a domestic CII transparently for this purpose, imputation benefits may be denied in the domestic CII case.

NOTES

1. As illustrated in Table 4.2.D, ACT on a distribution of foreign source income by a U.K. AUT generally cannot be set-off in full where such income has attracted foreign withholding tax. This is because ACT is set-off against CII-level income tax reduced first by (measured net of) foreign tax credit claims in respect of foreign withholding tax. Resulting surplus ACT means that the effective tax rate at the CII-level on distributed foreign source dividend income exceeds the ACT rate (which is the rate of creditable tax at the individual shareholder level.) As noted in Table 4.2.D, the U.K. ACT system was removed in 1998.

2. One generally would not observe a situation where a domestic CII is treated as a treaty subject, while a domestic individual is not. Therefore this situation need not be examined.

3. Where a non-resident shareholder is provided with a cash refund in respect of underlying corporate income tax, non-resident withholding tax is typically imposed at the statutory or treaty rate on dividends measured inclusive of this relief. Note that such a system may operate by requiring non-resident shareholders to apply for the refund or more simply, to reduce taxpayer compliance costs, by requiring that the distributing company (or agent) include the refund in the distribution and be reimbursed by the government (with a netting of the withholding tax revenue otherwise payable to the government against its refund.)

4. Treaty access to reduced *withholding tax* rates as a practical matter (see above) generally requires that the CII be regarded as a separate legal person beneficially entitled to the income. If a CII is regarded as a separate legal person and thus eligible for reduced withholding tax, it is relevant to question whether it can be treated on a transparent basis at the same time for the purpose of securing host country imputation tax relief for its resident investors.

5. Similarly, where portfolio foreign source dividend income paid to a domestic CII attracts an imputation credit (as in the direct portfolio investment case), but is converted to capital gains through a sale/redemption of units in the CII, the benefit of the imputation relief would generally be realised by the disposing investor. This follows from the fact that imputation credits in this case generally are 'attached' to the dividend (i.e., the dividend is received gross of the credit amount) and thus should be factored into the sale or redemption price.

6. As explained later in the text, the requirement of no/low tax on the income of an 'offshore' fund includes no/low withholding tax at source on the income of the CII (in the three-country case, where income and the CII are sourced and resident in different countries), and no/low income or withholding tax at the level of the CII.

7. The CII residence country could in principle impose withholding tax on share buybacks (redemptions) by the CII, but may not have legislative (or administrative) rules in place to this end.

8. Under Article 3 of the OECD Model, a company, and any other entity which is taxed as a body corporate (e.g., U.K. AUTs and AITs) is treated for tax treaty purposes as a body corporate.

9. Exemption will arise under tax treaties in the form of Article 13 of the OECD Model Tax Convention in Income and on Capital. Note that a requirement for the waiving of host country withholding tax on capital gains realised by non-resident portfolio investors may be that the shares be listed on a prescribed stock exchange (in the host country.) Certain countries impose tax on capital gains realised on unlisted shares, and on gains on shares (listed or not) realised by foreign direct (as opposed to portfolio) investors, and on gains on other types (e.g., immovable) property.

10. This can be compared with the domestic source income/domestic CII case where the domestic tax regime preserves the character of income. In contrast, with a foreign CII characterised as a company and distributions by it treated as a dividend, any favourable treatment for certain categories of income other than dividends (e.g., for certain capital gains and interest in some of the countries being considered) will be lost to the investor in the foreign CII.

11. As noted earlier, this raises the problem of withholding by the payer/source company. One way in which this problem seems to be solved in some countries (Germany, Japan and Australia have variants of this method) is to shift the withholding obligation to the CII (i.e., the payer of the income is not required to withhold where the recipient is a resident CII, but the CII is.) As the CII should have the necessary information for the application of the treaty, it could then apply the appropriate treaty tax rates when making distributions to investors in the CII. In particular, earnings distributions by the CII would be broken down into constituent parts (e.g., dividend income, interest income and net capital gains), and the appropriate withholding tax rates would be applied (which generally would vary by income type and recipient country.)

12. To achieve full transparency, such a system would require that CIIs keep separate pools/accounts of undistributed domestic and foreign source investment income (dividends, interest and capital gains) and that distributions by CIIs be tagged to show the percentage composition of the underlying income. Information on the residency of CII investors/unitholders (percentage distribution) would be needed by host/source countries to permit application of source country withholding tax rates on a look-through basis. Disaggregation of investment income by income type would be required for foreign unitholders resident in countries requiring that domestic taxpayers calculate separate foreign tax credits for separate categories/types of income. Disaggregation of investment income by source country would be required for foreign investors resident in countries requiring that domestic taxpayers calculate separate foreign tax credits on a country-by-country basis. Moreover, even if such information could be made available to non-resident individual investors, the additional complexity brought to the foreign tax credit calculation at the shareholder level may mean that the credit is not claimed.

The dimensions of the matrix of data could be reduced (full transparency lost, but simplicity gained) if separate foreign tax credit calculations were not required at the investor level for different categories of dividend income received from foreign CIIs (resident in treaty countries, to permit exchange of information.) Under this simplified structure, CIIs would allocate each dollar of investment income (but without a separate pooling of different types or sources of income) across different investors, grouped by residence country, with separate foreign tax credit pools attached to each investor group.

13. In general, the tax distortion against the use of the foreign CII in this case arising on account of withholding tax considerations would be greater where the withholding tax rate on portfolio dividends imposed by the CII-residence country exceeds that imposed by the source country in the direct investment case. A relatively higher withholding tax rate directly imposes a greater tax cost to the investor if he/she is non-taxpaying, and indirectly imposes a greater tax burden where the investor is taxable (but foreign tax credit limitations are binding) by absorbing a larger share of foreign tax credit 'room' (implying reduced foreign tax credit possibilities for other creditable taxes, either on a carry-forward basis, or where different items of foreign source income are pooled for current foreign tax credit purposes.)

14. In general, the net withholding tax burden would tend to be higher in the benchmark case, under the example considered in the text, if $(x>y+z(1-y))$ where x measures the net withholding tax rate on portfolio distributions received directly from the source country in the benchmark case, y measures the (non-creditable) source country withholding tax rate on portfolio dividends paid to the CII, and z measures the net withholding tax rate on portfolio dividends distributed by the CII. Note that x and z are net or effective withholding tax rates, taking into account the present value of current and carryover period foreign tax credit possibilities.

15. The CII residence country could in principle impose withholding tax on share buy-backs (redemptions) by the CII, but may not have legislative (or administrative) rules in place to this end.

16. In the case of interest income earned by a CII, the Euromarkets operate on a tax-free return assumption which has been variously attributed to tax exempt and/or tax evading lenders in those markets. With respect to shares, most countries do not levy capital gains on portfolio investments in companies resident there.

17. If elimination of withholding tax is conditional upon the distributed income having been subject to corporate income tax in the CII country (as under the Australian system which waives non-resident withholding tax on dividends from Australian companies provided that the dividends are 'franked', supported by Australian corporate income tax), it is necessary that franked income at the CII level be pooled separately from other types of income (unfranked dividend income, interest, capital gains) in order to achieve consistent treatment of qualifying distributions.

18. As discussed in section 3.5, 'Withholding Tax Considerations' (the two-country case), withholding tax on capital gains realised by foreign portfolio shareholders is typically exempt under treaty where the CII is regarded by the source country as a company. Where withholding tax is imposed and a foreign tax credit is provided, the neutrality result continues to hold. Where a foreign tax credit is not provided, a tax distortion discouraging the CII option would arise.

19. Note that where imputation relief provided to (resident) shareholders is capitalised into share prices, this consideration would not influence the analysis, as the focus is on the distribution (versus conversion) of a given amount of after-tax earnings at the CII level (as opposed to the company level at which the underlying investment is made.)

Chapter 4

ASSESSING NET SHAREHOLDER TAX RATES UNDER ALTERNATIVE CAPITAL MARKET ARBITRAGE ASSUMPTIONS

4.1 Introduction

This chapter presents net shareholder dividend tax rates for direct and intermediated portfolio investment in domestic and foreign shares of equivalent risk for individual investors resident in Australia, Belgium, Sweden, the U.K. and the U.S. The domestic CII case, the two-country foreign CII case, the three-country foreign CII (triangular) case, and the 'tax haven' CII case, all analysed in Chapter 3, are considered below. While only illustrative, the calculations nonetheless draw out a number of policy relevant considerations.

Two sets of figures are presented. The first set is derived assuming that *pre-personal tax rates of return are equal in all investment cases*. Treating pre-personal tax rates of return as constant across all investment cases implicitly assumes a capital market arbitrage process that tends to equate after-corporate tax rates of return.[1] Where the after-corporate tax return on capital employed in one company exceeds that in another, investment in the former would tend to increase and in the latter to decrease, until the after-corporate tax rates of return were equal (under the assumption that output per unit of capital input falls at the margin as capital increases.) Adjustments tending to equate after-corporate tax rates of return are consistent with an arbitrage process that effectively ignores personal/shareholder-level taxation.

An alternative modelling approach is to assume that *pre-personal tax rates depend on the tax treatment of a 'marginal' shareholder* who buys and sells shares at the margin, influencing share prices and the rates of return that firms must pay. The first set of figures noted above, which treat pre-personal tax rates of return as constant across different investment structures (direct versus intermediated investment) and different source countries, turns out to be consistent with this second modelling approach where the 'marginal' shareholder group consists of tax-exempt investors (*e.g.*, pension funds), which may in fact often be the case.

Section 4.2 presents net shareholder tax rates derived under the assumption of equal pre-personal tax rates of return. Section 4.3 reviews the basic theory behind the view that shareholder level taxation influences pre-tax rates of return on new share issues. Section 4.4 shows the revised set of pre-tax rates of return for the countries considered in the Report, while section 4.5 considers the revised net shareholder tax rates for the direct and intermediated portfolio investment cases, summarised in Table 4.3, and discusses how and why the results differ under the alternative capital market equilibrium condition. Section 4.6 closes by reconciling the two sets of results as reflecting polar cases, and suggests that partial rather than zero or full capitalisation of personal tax considerations may be the most likely outcome. The tax implications (distortions) stemming from this view are considered.

4.2 Net shareholder tax rates assuming equal pre-personal tax returns

Table 4.1 presents net shareholder dividend tax rates for direct and intermediated portfolio investment in domestic and foreign shares for individual investors resident in Australia, Belgium, Sweden, the U.K. and the U.S. The figures consider the domestic CII case, the two-country foreign CII case and the three-country 'offshore' investment case. The figures are derived assuming a fixed pre-tax rate of return at source, held constant over all investment cases.

The detailed tax calculations underlying Table 4.1 are found in Appendix IV, with the domestic CII results in Tables AI.1A-E, the two-country foreign CII case in Tables AI.2A-E, the three-country foreign CII case in Tables AI.3A-E, and the tax haven case in Tables AI.4A-E. Each country table is constructed from the perspective of an individual portfolio investor resident in that (home) country. Columns show possible source countries, including the domestic/home country and the other countries for which the necessary data was available (including the five countries considered throughout the report (Australia, Belgium, Sweden, U.K., U.S.), as well as France, Germany and Italy as other possible source countries.) The sub-headings in Table 4.1 show separately results for the alternative investment structures (*i.e.*, direct, domestic CII, two-country foreign CII, three-country foreign CII, tax haven or 'offshore' CII.)

A. *Direct investment in domestic shares vs. foreign shares*

In those countries with imputation systems (Australia, U.K.), net dividend tax rates are lower for domestic shares held directly as compared with foreign shares held directly, implying a tax distortion in favour of domestic shares over foreign shares paying the same pre-tax (after-corporate tax) rate of return. This result is intuitive. *If all shares pay the same pre-personal tax rate of return*, then domestic shares for which partial or full integration relief is available at the personal level will show a lower net shareholder dividend tax rate. This result occurs even where, as assumed in the examples in Table 4.1, a foreign tax credit can be claimed that offsets in full foreign withholding tax (neutralising a potential tax distortion.) Where this is not the case, the distortion in favour of domestic shares would be even greater.

Where a foreign source (host) country offers integration relief to a domestic investor (a foreign investor from the host country's perspective) who resides in a country also with an imputation or dividend tax credit system, this will tend to lower for that investor the difference between net dividend tax rates on domestic versus foreign shares (and could potentially offset it, or reverse the distortion, depending on the rates of host versus home country tax relief). For the cases examined here involving Australia and the U.K. as host and home countries, host country imputation relief is shown to reduce but not eliminate the tax distortion in favour of domestic shares.

However, for individuals resident in countries with classical tax systems, imputation relief offered by foreign host countries is shown to encourage those investors to choose foreign over domestic shares. For example, the extension of integration relief by the U.K. to direct portfolio investors resident in Sweden and the U.S. is shown to result in a lower net dividend tax rate on U.K. shares compared with domestic shares, encouraging those investors to invest in U.K. shares rather than domestic shares. For portfolio investors resident in Australia, imputation relief on domestic shares provides the highest after-personal tax return, so that while U.K. shares receive preferential tax treatment compared to Belgian, Swedish or U.S. shares, the incentive to invest in domestic shares is the greatest, again under the assumption that all shares pay the same pre-personal tax rate of return.

In the case of Belgian residents, a preference is shown to exist in each case for domestic shares over foreign shares. The result stems from the fact that domestic portfolio dividends are subject to final withholding tax at source at 15 per cent, while foreign portfolio dividend income is taxed in the hands of individuals at a flat rate of 25 per cent without a tax credit for foreign withholding tax. Because the U.K. does not impose withholding tax on portfolio dividends, the net shareholder dividend tax rate is shown to be lower for Belgian shareholders on U.K. shares, as compared to shares issued in Sweden and the U.S. which are subject, in each case, to (non-creditable) withholding tax at source at 15 per cent.

B. Direct investment vs. intermediated investment using domestic CII

Table 4.1 shows identical net shareholder dividend tax rates for direct portfolio investment and investment through a domestic CII in *domestic shares*. These figures reflect the general tax policy adopted in most countries of attempting to achieve tax parity or neutrality for portfolio investment in domestic shares whether made directly or through a domestic CII.[2]

As reviewed in section 4.3, this result stems from the transparent treatment of domestic CIIs in the case of domestic shares, with generally no CII-level tax and, in the case of countries with imputation systems, a flow-through of domestic imputation tax credits to unitholders in the CII. Additionally, the results assume that individual taxpayers are able to comply in each case with imputation tax credit calculations for dividends whether received directly or from a domestic CII.

When considering investments in *foreign shares* held directly versus through a domestic CII, identical net dividend tax rates are calculated in most cases. This result requires that treaty withholding tax rate reductions are passed on in the domestic CII case (*i.e.*, the absence of treaty shopping adjustments to the general tax treaty rate for portfolio dividends),[3] and that foreign tax credits pass through and are claimed at the shareholder level in the domestic CII case. It also requires that host country integration relief, if available to domestic investors (non-residents from the host country's perspective) in the direct portfolio investment case, passes through to unitholders of the domestic CII . In effect, the CIIs in each case are treated as transparent entities, allowing a flow-through of treaty withholding tax relief and source country imputation credits where these would apply in the direct portfolio investor case. While these requirements generally apply in the specific country cases examined, they may not in other situations, as discussed in section 4.3.

A number of exceptions to the general neutrality finding in the domestic CII case (for the countries considered) are identified. First, Australian portfolio investors are discouraged from investing in dividend-paying U.K. shares through an Australian CII, rather than directly. This is because U.K. imputation credits are attached to franked U.K. source income paid directly to an Australian *individual* investor, but are not provided by the U.K. in the case of distributions to an Australian CII (as the U.K. does not treat Australian CIIs as transparent entities.)

Second, under its tax treaty with Sweden, the U.K. attaches imputation credits to franked U.K. source income paid to Swedish portfolio investors *other than* open-ended funds (a closed-end fund would qualify.) Therefore, Swedish portfolio investors would be encouraged to invest in U.K. shares directly rather than through a Swedish CII. This distortion in favour of a direct portfolio investment is similar to that noted under the first exception (*i.e.*, tax distortion due to the denial of host country imputation relief in the domestic CII case.)

Third, in the case of foreign portfolio investment by U.K. individuals through a domestic AUT, the imposition of ACT on distributions by the AUT to U.K. residents of foreign source dividend income can lead to a higher net dividend tax rate on such income as compared with the foreign direct investment case, in the typical situation where tax is withheld at source on the foreign dividend. This result can arise as ACT is set off against mainstream corporate income tax (at the AUT level on foreign dividends) reduced first by foreign tax credit claims in respect of foreign withholding tax, leading to surplus ACT. Thus, for investments by U.K. individuals through a domestic AUT into Belgium, Sweden or the U.S., their net dividend tax rate is shown to be higher when investing through an AUT rather than directly. As in the first two exceptions to the general neutrality result noted above, the interaction of tax systems acts to discourage the use of domestic CIIs, in this instance on account of the interaction of host country withholding tax and the domestic integration system. Neutrality is observed when considering a similar investment through an AUT into Australia, as Australia does not impose withholding tax on franked portfolio dividends paid to U.K. resident shareholders, thus avoiding the surplus ACT problem.

Fourth, in the case of foreign portfolio equity investment by Belgian individuals, a flat 25 per cent Belgian tax rate applies to foreign dividend income net of foreign withholding tax (non-creditable), unless the income is routed through a domestic CII. Where a domestic CII is used, a 15 per cent final withholding tax rate applies on the distribution by the CII of dividend income (net of foreign withholding tax.) Therefore, where foreign dividend income is earned directly (or through a foreign CII), it is subject to a higher net tax rate than if channelled through a domestic CII. Thus, the general finding that foreign dividend income is taxed at the same net tax rate when passed through a domestic CII (or at a higher rate, under the three exceptions noted above), rather than being received directly, is reversed in the Belgian case.

C. *Direct investment vs. intermediated investment using foreign CII*

The two-country case

When considering portfolio investment in *foreign shares* held through a foreign CII resident in the source country (the two-country case) and comparing results with those found in the benchmark case, identical net dividend tax rates are derived in each instance. This neutrality result requires the absence of income tax at the foreign CII level as such tax would be non-creditable. Identical net dividend tax rates when investing through a domestic CII or a foreign CII are also observed in a number of cases. Neutrality here requires no tax at the foreign CII level, and additionally no income tax at the domestic CII level unless this tax can be relieved at the investor level under the domestic integration system (the U.K. system comes close to this.) It also requires that foreign portfolio dividends routed through a foreign CII (and portfolio dividends paid to a domestic CII) be tagged with the same level of integration relief as attached to portfolio dividends received directly from the host country.[4]

A number of exceptions to the general neutrality finding in the foreign CII case (for the countries considered) are identified. In particular, four cases are identified where the net shareholder tax rate is *lower* when investing through a foreign CII rather than a domestic CII. First, as noted in section (3.4), the net tax burden may be higher when investing in foreign shares through a foreign CII rather than a domestic CII. This is observed in Belgium where the net dividend tax burden is higher in the foreign CII case. However, this result is not due to non-creditable host country CII-level tax, or restricted access to treaty-reduced withholding tax rates or host country imputation relief, or neither to foreign tax credit complications. Instead, it rests with the fact that Belgium applies a flat 25 per cent rate at the individual shareholder level to net foreign source dividend income, whether received directly or from a foreign CII, whereas such income is taxed at the individual level at a reduced flat final rate of 15 per cent if passed (tax-free) through a domestic CII. Therefore, in the Belgian case, the domestic tax system is shown to encourage resident individuals to invest in dividend-paying foreign shares through a domestic CII, rather than directly or through a foreign (distributor) CII which show the same net shareholder dividend tax rate.

Second, the net dividend tax rate is shown to be lower for an Australian individual investing into the U.K. through a U.K. AUT. This result shows that foreign CIIs may offer special tax advantages in cases other than 'offshore' situations involving earnings roll-up and tax deferral. In this case, U.K. imputation relief on U.K. source dividends available when investing through a AUT is lost when such income is paid to an Australian CII which is not regarded as a transparent entity. As noted above, the Australian-U.K. tax treaty provides for such relief only for portfolio dividends paid to *individuals.* (Relief could be accessed only if the Australian CII were regarded as transparent, and investors applied to U.K. authorities for such relief.) With host country relief accessed when investing through a U.K. AUT, but not when investing through an Australian CII, an Australian individual wishing to invest in U.K. shares through an intermediary vehicle may, for tax reasons, be encouraged to use a U.K. AUT rather than an Australian CII.

Third, similar to the previous case, dividend payments by a U.K. company to a Swedish (open-ended) CII do not attract imputation relief, while such relief is available to Swedish individuals investing in U.K. shares through a U.K. CII. Again, a tax preference may exist to use a foreign CII resident in the host country.

Fourth, the net dividend tax rate is shown to be lower for U.K. individuals investing in Belgian shares through a Belgian CII, in Swedish shares through a Swedish CII, and in U.S. shares through a U.S. CII, rather than through a U.K. AUT. The reason is essentially the same as that considered above in the direct investment case. In particular, surplus ACT can result on distributions by a U.K. AUT of foreign source dividend income subject to foreign withholding tax. Thus, the net dividend tax rate applicable to U.K. investor returns is shown to be higher when investing in portfolio shares of Belgian, Swedish or U.S. firms through an U.K. AUT, rather than through a foreign CII or directly. As Australia does not impose withholding tax on portfolio dividends paid to U.K. investors, this particular distortion caused by surplus ACT does not arise in the case considered here.

The three-country case

In the three-country case, the foreign CII is assumed to be resident in some (unidentified) third country which waives CII-level income tax, but imposes withholding tax on distributions to non-resident unitholders at 15 per cent. The results in Table 4.1 in general show a higher net shareholder dividend tax rate in the three-country or 'triangular' case, as compared with the other investment structures considered in this Report, for each source country/home country combination.

Tax distortions identified in Table 4.1 discouraging the use of a foreign (distributor) CII in the triangular case are attributable (in some cases fully, in others partly) to the absence of foreign tax credit mechanisms to relieve tax withheld on portfolio dividends at source in each of the countries considered, with the exception of the U.K.[5] Thus, Australian, Belgian, Swedish, U.K. and U.S. investors face lower net dividend tax rates on foreign shares when investing in those shares directly, through a domestic CII, or through a CII resident in the source country, as compared to using a CII resident in a third country (assuming the CII is a distributor fund, and no offsetting income tax deferral advantages are present.)

Two exceptions to this general finding arise in the case of investments in U.K. shares, as the U.K. does not impose withholding tax on portfolio dividends. The immediate implication is that there is no source country taxation in this case that would otherwise remain stuck at the foreign CII level. Thus Australian and Swedish investors are subject to the same net dividend tax rate when investing in U.K. shares through a domestic CII or through a foreign CII resident in a third country (under the assumption of no CII-level income tax) However, investing directly in U.K. shares or through an U.K. AUT yields the highest after-tax result, giving access to host country imputation relief (unavailable on dividend payments to a domestic CII and, by assumption, on dividend payments to the foreign CII.)

Finally, U.K. individuals are subject to the same net dividend tax rate when investing in U.S. shares through a U.K. AUT or through a foreign CII resident in a third country that is assumed to have, like the U.K., a treaty with the U.S. providing for 15 per cent withholding tax. Investing through an AUT creates a surplus ACT problem, while investing through the third-country foreign CII case creates a non-creditable U.S. withholding tax problem, with equivalent effects on the effective dividend tax rate for U.K. investors.

The net dividend tax rates shown in Table 4.1 for the tax haven or 'offshore' CII case are derived assuming that portfolio dividends are 'rolled-up' or retained in an offshore CII for ten years and then distributed to unitholders and reported for tax purposes. No CII-level tax is assumed to apply, and foreign withholding tax imposed at source in each case is assumed to be non-creditable. Certain countries impose portfolio foreign investment fund (PFIF) anti-deferral rules designed to counter and discourage offshore tax-deferral possibilities.

*For those countries (i.e., Australia, U.S.) which have PFIF-type rules in place, these rules have **not** been taken into account in order to illustrate the potential distortive effects posed by 'offshore' jurisdictions.*

For all countries, the net dividend tax rate when investing in foreign shares is the lowest when using an offshore CII, suggesting a potential tax distortion in favour of offshore CIIs over direct investment, or investment through a domestic or foreign CII where a distribution requirement or CII-level tax applies.

Interestingly, in the case of Australia and Belgium, the results show a lower net dividend tax rate on domestic shares held directly or through a domestic CII, rather than through an offshore CII. This result is tied to imputation relief in the domestic investment case, unavailable in the case of distributions to an offshore CII. This situation reverses as the holding/deferral period is extended, and/or the offshore income is not reported.

A Note on the Derivation of Net Dividend Tax Rates in the Offshore CII Case

The net dividend tax rates in the 'offshore' roll-up case are derived as follows. At the beginning of period 1, an individual resident in country (a) is assumed to invest (P) currency units in an offshore CII resident in country (c), which in turn invests this amount in shares of a foreign company resident in source country (b). The source company in turn invests this amount in productive capital which generates a steady-state after-corporate tax rate of return of R, with these returns distributed in full each period. Distributions from country (a) to (c) are subject to withholding tax at rate $w^{a\Diamond c}$. The CII is not subject to income tax, and thus source country withholding tax is the final tax on CII-level income, which can be expressed as $u^{*}=w^{a\Diamond c}$ (alternatively, if the CII is taxable at rate u and source withholding tax is fully creditable, $u^{*}=u$.) The CII is assumed to reinvest its after-tax dividend, either in the same source company or in some alternative asset paying R. At the end of (h) periods, earnings at the CII level are assumed to be distributed to unitholders, subject to tax at the shareholder's marginal personal income tax rate m (under the assumption that withholding tax on distributions from the CII country (if any) is fully creditable at the shareholder level.) This scenario can be compared with one where the individual instead begins the first period by investing P currency units directly in shares of the same foreign company, and reinvests distributed after-tax dividends in the same shares over the same time-frame as the CII. The following table compares the individual's net profit and net shareholder tax rate under alternative holding period assumptions. The example uses the following parameter values: P=1000, R=10%, u^{*}=15% or 0%, m=48.5% (where m is the Australian rate.) The calculations ignore possible capital gains tax on inflationary gains (or alternatively, assume low inflation.)

Illustration of Deferral Advantages with Offshore CII Under Alternative Reinvestment/Roll-up Assumptions

	Direct portfolio investment		*Offshore CII investment*			
			(u^{*}=15%)		(u^{*}=0%)	
reinvestment period (h)	final net return (A)	net dividend tax rate (B)	final net return (A*)	net dividend tax rate (B*)	final net return (A*)	net dividend tax rate (B*)
1	51.5	48.5	43.8	56.2	51.5	48.5
3	162.6	48.5	142.8	52.3	170.5	43.9
5	285.5	48.5	259.4	48.7	314.5	39.7
10	652.5	48.5	649.5	41.2	820.9	30.9
15	1124.2	48.5	1236.1	35.4	1 636.6	24.0
20	1730.7	48.5	2118.1	30.9	2 950.2	18.7

Note: $(A)=P((1+R(1-m))^{h}-1$ $(A^{*})=P((1+R(1-u^{*}))^{h}-1)(1-m)$

$(B)=m$ $(B^{*})=u^{*}+m(1-u^{*})/(1+i(1-m))^{h-1}$

4.3 Pre-personal tax rates of return with tax capitalisation effects

The remaining sections consider the possibility of shareholder-level taxation influencing *pre*-personal tax (after-corporate tax) rates of return on shares. If and how pre-tax returns are influenced by shareholder-level taxation is largely an unresolved theoretical and empirical issue. A number of factors, including the gradual lifting of regulatory controls on capital markets and the resulting globalization of capital flows, arguably have made the task of assessing the linkages more difficult.[6] These developments also make any single characterisation that would apply in all markets and at all times unlikely. One possibility is that capital market arbitrage occurs at the corporate level, tending to equate after-corporate tax rates of return -- implying that personal-level taxes are not directly relevant to the determination of equity prices and pre-personal tax rates of return. This particular assumption was employed in the first part of this chapter.

Under the so-called 'new view' of dividend taxation, shareholder-level taxes are capitalised into share prices and influence pre-personal tax returns.[7] A distinction is drawn between rates of return on investment financed out of retained earnings versus new share issues. Dividend taxes are found to affect equity values, but to have no influence on the firm's after-corporate tax rate of return (the firm's discount rate) in the case of investment financed at the margin by retained earnings.[8] On the other hand, dividend taxes tend to increase the required rate of return on new share issues (as funds not yet committed to the firm can avoid dividend taxation by being invested elsewhere; for example, bonds.) Integration or imputation relief which lowers the effective tax rate on dividends reduces the required rate of return. The following analysis takes *new share issues* as the marginal source of finance, allowing dividend taxes to play a role in determining after-corporate tax returns. The approach of focusing on new share issues as the marginal source of funds is consistent with the focus of the Report on assessing possible tax distortions influencing an individual's choice over investing savings (funds not yet invested in the corporate sector) in domestic shares or foreign shares, directly or through a domestic or foreign CII.

The possibility that certain shareholders exert influence over returns that a competitive firm must offer -- requiring an (expected) after-personal tax rate of return on shares not below that on an alternative investment (*e.g.*, bonds) of equivalent risk -- makes the identification of this shareholder group necessary. This follows from the fact that not all shareholders are taxed at the same rate on their investment returns. This raises the question of the identity of the 'marginal' shareholder group determining equity prices and influencing returns on funds raised to finance corporate investment at the margin. One possibility is that the marginal shareholders are tax-exempt investors, paying no income or withholding tax and receiving no integration relief on their investment returns (*e.g.*, pension funds in some countries.) If this were the case, arbitrage would tend to equate after-corporate tax rates of return (yielding results similar to those observed if instead arbitrage occurred at the corporate level, as noted above.). Alternatively, the marginal shareholders of firms in a given country may be resident individual investors in that country. While other possibilities could be considered, this Report adopts the approach of assuming that the marginal shareholders of firms in a given (source) country are the individual investors resident in that country.

The after-corporate tax rate of return that a company must offer on new share issues is the rate, denoted by R^{NE}, which provides the 'marginal' shareholder with an (expected) after-personal tax rate of return on dividends equal to the after-tax rate on an alternative investment, say bonds, of equivalent risk. This condition may be characterised in either of the following ways:[9]

$$R^{NE}(1\text{-}t^{dm}) = i^{*} \qquad (4.1a)$$

$$R^{NE}(1\text{-}t^{dm}) = i(1\text{-}m^{m}) \qquad (4.1b)$$

where i^{*} is a given (fixed) tax-free interest rate (*e.g.*, on tax-exempt bonds), i is a given (fixed) interest rate on an alternative (taxable) bond, m^{m} is the marginal shareholders personal tax rate on interest income, and t^{dm} is the marginal shareholder's personal tax rate on dividend income. Under (4.1a) and (4.1b), the cost of new share issues to the firm is shown to be higher (lower), the higher (lower) is the marginal shareholder's tax rate on dividend income (t^{dm}) relative to the tax rate on interest income (zero under (4.1a), m^{m} under (4.1b.) It is useful to express the dividend tax term ($1\text{-}t^{dm}$) alternatively as follows:

$$(1\text{-}t^{dm}) = \theta^{m}(1\text{-}m^{m}) \qquad (4.2)$$

where θ^{m} is an *integration parameter* measuring the degree of imputation (or integration) relief provided to the marginal shareholder on the distribution of a dollar (or other currency unit) of earnings (measured after corporate tax.) In classical tax systems, no integration relief is given and the integration parameter θ^{m} is equal to one. In imputation systems, or other systems providing integration relief (*e.g.*, a dividend tax credit) θ^{m} exceeds one. Dividing equation set (4.1) by ($1\text{-}t^{dm}$) and substituting (4.2) gives:

$$R^{NE} = i^{*}/\theta^{m}(1\text{-}m^{m}) \qquad (4.3a)$$

$$R^{NE} = i/\theta^{m}. \qquad (4.3b)$$

Equation (4.3a) shows that the required (after-corporate tax) rate of return on new share issues R^{NE} is lower, the lower is the marginal shareholder's effective tax rate on dividend income. An increase in the integration parameter θ^{m} above one (*e.g.*, accompanying the introduction of imputation relief) lowers the cost of new share issues to the firm, which lowers the discount rate applied to after-corporate tax returns from additional (physical) capital financed at the margin by new shares, thereby encouraging investment. Similarly, a reduction in the marginal shareholders personal income tax rate m^{m} is shown to lower the firm's cost of finance, encouraging investment demand. Changing θ^{m} or m^{m} (or both) alters the *relative* rate of taxation of equity returns and (tax-free) returns on the alternative investment, tax-free bonds.

Equation (4.3b) on the other hand shows R^{NE} to be a function of the integration parameter θ^{m} alone. This follows from the assumption of (4.1b) that the marginal shareholder's alternative investment used to assess the opportunity cost of funds is a taxable bond, interest on which is taxed at the effective rate $\theta^{m}(1\text{-}m^{m})$. Since the term ($1\text{-}m^{m}$) applies to both dividend and interest income, it does not influence the relative rate of taxation of shares and bonds, and so its effect cancels out. This leaves θ^{m} as the sole tax parameter influencing the relative tax rate and therefore R^{NE}, the required rate of return on shares.[10]

An interesting implication of (4.3a) is that tax-exempt investors (*e.g.*, pension funds), as marginal shareholders, would be willing to accept an expected rate of return on new shares equal to the interest rate on tax-exempt bonds. Where tax-exempt investors are granted imputation relief, the required rate of return would be even lower. This would appear unlikely, at least in certain cases. In general, the rate that tax-exempt (and other) investors would demand from firms would depend not only on the rates available on alternative investments of equivalent risk, but also on the rates demanded by other potential investors. These required rates of return on capital supplied would tend to increase with the amount of capital demanded by firms, and rise sharply as available capital supplies become exhausted. In this context, pension funds with relatively large capital pools at their disposal may be able to demand an expected rate of return on a new share issue to finance a large capital project (*i.e.*, where capital demands are large) that exceeds the rate on tax-exempt bonds, and equals the rate paid on conventional (taxable) bonds paying interest rate i, tax-free in the hands of a tax exempt. *This suggests relying on characterisation (4.3b), which is a common approach in the literature.*

To clarify further the implications of equation (4.3b), let the interest rate on taxable bonds be 10 per cent and consider first the case where the marginal investor in a given share issue is a tax-exempt institution (totally outside the tax system.) Since tax-exempt investors are able to earn 10 per cent on bonds, they will require that a company offer an after-corporate tax rate of return on new share issues of at least 10 per cent in order to be willing to purchase those shares. Competitive bidding would lead to an equilibrium price for the shares where the after-corporate tax rate of return just equals 10 per cent, at which point the marginal investors are indifferent between holding shares and bonds.

Alternatively, assume that the marginal investor is a (resident) taxable individual (or a group of taxable individuals) subject to a personal income tax rate at the margin of 40 per cent. Assume for the moment that integration relief is not provided. Since these investors are able to earn an after-tax rate of return of 6 per cent on bonds, the expected after-personal tax rate of return on shares would have to be at least 6 per cent in order for them to be willing to hold those shares. This would require an after-corporate tax (pre-personal tax) rate of return of at least 10 per cent. Competitive bidding between investors would lead to an equilibrium price for the shares such that the after-corporate tax rate of return is 10 per cent. Comparing this case with the preceding one, reveals the result that if interest income and dividend income are taxed in the hands of the marginal investor at the same rate (*e.g.*, 0 per cent in the first case, 40 per cent in the second), the after-corporate tax rate of return, as set by the marginal shareholder, is independent of the value of that shareholder-level income tax rate.[11]

Consider now the situation where the *marginal investor is granted an imputation tax credit* (or a dividend tax credit) as a mitigation of economic double taxation or simply to encourage savings. In this case, the shares of the firm will be valued on the basis of an augmented dividend flow, which includes the imputation credit. An imputation rate of 20 per cent, for example, would mean that the marginal investor receives θ^m=1.25 currency units before personal tax for each currency unit distributed.[12]

As noted above, in the absence of imputation relief, the marginal shareholder would demand a 10 per cent rate of return on shares, measured before personal tax. However, with imputation relief at 20 per cent, the marginal investor would be willing to accept a pre-personal tax rate of return on shares of 8 per cent, given that the imputation tax credit would bump this return up to 10 per cent, which when taxed at 40 per cent would still yield an after-personal tax rate of return of 6 per cent. The introduction of imputation relief would mean that a shareholder eligible for such relief would be willing to pay, for a given stream of distributed after-corporate tax earnings, a share price that is 25 per cent higher, and still be able to earn an after-tax rate of return of 6 per cent.[13]

The introduction of imputation relief would result in a 'windfall' gain to existing shareholders, as the future stream of after-corporate tax earnings generated by invested capital would be subject to a lower effective dividend tax rate. At the same time, the introduction of imputation relief would mean that investors eligible for it would be willing to accept a lower after-corporate tax rate of return on new capital injected into the firm. This lowering of the cost of new share issues to the firm would encourage it to expand its capital stock, which would tend to drive down the after-corporate tax rate of return at the margin on newly installed capital, under the assumption of declining marginal productivity of capital. The final equilibrium would be one which yields an after-corporate tax rate of return of 8 per cent (assuming that the marginal shareholders earn imputation relief at 20 per cent, and a 10 per cent market interest rate applies), which would give an after-personal tax rate of return of 6 per cent, as noted above.

New share issues paying an after-corporate tax rate of return of 8 per cent would not be attractive to investors ineligible for the imputation credit. Tax-exempt investors ineligible for imputation relief could earn 10 per cent on bonds, while individuals denied imputation credits and paying tax at 40 per cent could earn 6 per cent after-tax on interest, as compared to 4.8 per cent on these shares. This observation is important as it illustrates a basic result that integration or dividend tax credit relief, if not available to all shareholders, may encourage or discourage portfolio investors in unintended ways, or give rise to tax arbitrage opportunities. For example, where integration relief is provided and has the intended effect of lowering the required rate of return on new shares (*i.e.*, the cost of funds), it may have the unintended effect of discouraging investors otherwise interested investing in those shares from doing so, as noted in the previous example. Conversely, where integration relief is not provided to the marginal shareholder group -- for example, in the case where tax-exempt marginal shareholders demand a 10 per cent rate of return and are offered this return, due to prospects of after-corporate tax rates of return sufficient to cover that cost -- other shareholder groups entitled to this relief would be able to earn above-normal rates of return by investing in these shares, in this case distorting their investment choice away from alternative portfolio investment choices.

Table 4.2 shows the *pre-tax rate of return* required by domestic shareholders on new shares in Australia, Belgium, Sweden, the U.K. and the U.S., under the assumption that the market interest rate is 10 per cent, and that the marginal investor is a fully taxable resident individual. The pre-tax rate of return is calculated by dividing the market interest rate by the integration parameter for each country, applicable to resident individual taxpayers taken to be the marginal shareholders. In countries which apply the classical system or the zero-rate system (Belgium, Sweden and the U.S.), θ^m equals one and the pre-tax rate of return on portfolio investment equals 10 per cent. In countries where an imputation system applies, θ^m exceeds one and the pre-tax rate of return on shares falls below the market interest rate, depending on the size of the imputation credit (*e.g.* in Australia θ^m=1.563, while in the U.K. θ^m=1.25).

The bottom row of Table 4.2 shows the dividend return (the after-corporate tax, pre-personal tax) received by savers (both marginal and infra-marginal) on a 1 000 currency unit investment in new shares of representative firms in each country. In Australia and the U.K., where the resident marginal shareholder is entitled to a tax credit for underlying corporate tax, the required dividend distribution is lower than in the countries with classical-systems where the pre-tax rate of return on shares equals the interest rate.[14]

Under the assumption that imputation credits offered to the marginal investor cause the pre-tax rate of return on new portfolio shares to fall below the market interest rate, the (effective) net shareholder tax rate on portfolio income may be computed as follows. Consider for example a marginal investor resident in the U.K. subject to a 40 per cent tax rate on investment income. On 1 000 currency units of new equity, the corporation must pay a dividend of 80, as this dividend plus the imputation credit provides the shareholder an after-tax dividend of 60 (=80*1.25*(1-0.4)), the same after-tax amount that would be earned if the same amount had been invested in bonds paying 10 per cent. The net shareholder tax on dividend income of 40 per cent is the same as that on interest. This follows since the UK marginal investor by assumption prices corporate shares such that they provide an after-tax rate of return equal to the after-tax return on the alternative investment in bonds.[15]

Consider next an individual investor resident in Belgium, denied an imputation credit on U.K. shares. On 1 000 currency units invested in U.K. shares, the investor would receive a pre-tax dividend of 80, with the U.K. marginal investor setting the pre-tax rate of return at 8 per cent. Belgian individuals are subject to a flat 25 per cent personal tax rate on investment income (received directly.) His after tax dividend would therefore be 60 (=80*(1-0.25)). The after-tax return of 6 per cent is 4 percentage points below the market interest rate of 10 per cent-- this implies an effective net shareholder dividend tax rate of 40 per cent for the Belgian investor. If the investor chooses bonds, tax of 25 would be due on the pre-tax return of 100, leaving a net return of 75. With the 25 per cent tax rate on interest below the 40 per cent effective tax rate on dividends, the Belgian investor would be discouraged from investing in U.K. shares. The simple economic explanation for this result is that this investor is denied imputation relief, while at the same time the market price of shares (and hence the pre-tax return) has adjusted to the dividend relief available to the U.K. shareholder who is the marginal investor.

4.4 Net shareholder tax rates under the tax capitalisation view

Table 4.3 presents revised net shareholder dividend tax rates based on the tax capitalisation view. In comparing the second set of results in Table 4.3 with the first set shown in Table 4.1, it is first observed that the net shareholder dividend tax rate results for Belgium, Sweden and the U.S. *as source countries* (in the second, third and fifth country-column blocks) are unchanged. This is because pre-personal tax rates of return are unchanged, as each of these countries have classical tax systems. As reviewed above, under the tax capitalisation view represented by equation (4.3b), the pre-personal tax rate of return on new issues set by resident marginal investors *subject to classical tax treatment* will equal the market interest rate. The same pre-personal tax rate of return is observed in Table 4.1 which assumes that market arbitrage occurs at the corporate level with after-corporate tax rates of return equal to the market interest rate in each case.

However, revised net shareholder dividend tax rates are shown for Australia and the U.K. as source countries (the first and fourth country-column blocks.) Imputation relief in these countries lowers the pre-tax rate of return on shares issued by firms resident there, assuming marginal shareholders of these shares are resident individuals. This is shown in Table 4.3 to alter the investment incentive pattern of individual investors resident in Australia, Belgium, Sweden, the U.K. and the U.S. relative to that observed in the first case summarised in Table 4.1.

A. *Direct investment in domestic shares vs. foreign shares*

With pre-tax rates of return on domestic shares lower on account of imputation relief treated as capitalised into share prices, investors resident in Australia and the U.K. are shown to be neutral with respect to the decision to invest directly in domestic versus foreign shares. Imputation credits were found in Table 4.1 to distort resident investor choice in favour of domestic shares, while in Table 4.3 are shown to have a neutral effect as the credits operate to lower the pre-tax return that domestic firms are required to pay. Australian residents are shown to be subject to a net dividend tax rate of 48.5 per cent regardless of whether investing directly in shares issued at home, in Belgium, Sweden, the U.K. or the U.S.

Similarly, U.K. investors in Table 4.3 are shown to face a net dividend tax rate of 40 per cent on domestic shares, and on shares of Belgian, Swedish and U.S. companies, whereas previously net dividend tax rates on U.K. shares were lower. Furthermore, U.K. investors found in Table 4.1 to be indifferent between Australian shares and other foreign shares are shown to be discouraged from investing in shares of Australian companies under the revised figures. Investors in Sweden and the U.S. who previously were indifferent between investing in Australian or domestic shares are also shown to face relatively high net dividend tax rates on Australian shares. Unlike Australian investors for whom the reduction in the pre-tax rate of return on Australian shares is offset by claiming an imputation tax credit, no such offset is available to U.K., Swedish or U.S. investors, as Australia does not extend imputation relief to foreign shareholders.

Swedish and U.S. investors whose portfolio investment decision previously was found to be distorted towards U.K. shares on account of the imputation relief attached to those shares, are shown in Table 4.3 to be neutral, neither encouraged nor discouraged to make this choice. Imputation relief that previously was shown to attract these investors is now shown to be neutralised, offset by the lower pre-personal tax rate of return on U.K. shares.

B. Direct investment vs. intermediated investment using domestic CII

Table 4.3 shows identical net shareholder dividend tax rates for direct portfolio investment and investment through a domestic CII in *domestic shares*, as was the case in Table 4.1. Figures for Belgium, Sweden and the U.S. are unchanged, with Australian and U.K. rates -- while still indicating neutrality over the choice between holding domestic shares directly or using a domestic CII -- now also showing neutrality with respect to the choice between domestic shares and bonds. Considering investments in *foreign shares* held directly or through a domestic CII, identical net dividend tax rates are shown in most cases.

As in the previous set of results in Table 4.1, a number of exceptions to the general neutrality finding in the domestic CII case are identified in Table 4.3. Australian portfolio investors are shown, as in Table 4.1, to face a lower net dividend tax rate when investing in U.K. shares directly, rather than through an Australian CII, as imputation credits are not attached to franked U.K. source income paid to an Australian CII. However, rather than there being a tax incentive to directly hold U.K. shares over other foreign shares, Australian investors are found in Table 4.3 to be neutral with respect to the direct investment option, with imputation relief offsetting the now lower pre-tax rate of return, while facing a tax impediment to investing in U.K. shares through a domestic CII where the net dividend tax rate is 58.8 per cent, the highest value posted for Australian investors in Table 4.3. Similarly, Swedish investors previously shown to be encouraged to invest in U.K. shares directly, now are shown to be neutral on the direct investment option while being discouraged for tax reasons against investing in U.K. shares through a domestic (open-ended) CII and being denied access to the U.K. credit.

Belgian investors are shown to face the highest net dividend tax rate when investing in shares of Australian or U.K. shares, with a flat 25 per cent rate now applied to reduced pre-tax returns on those shares without integration relief. Slightly lower net tax rates are observed when the income is routed through a domestic CII, where a 15 per cent final withholding tax rate applies at the CII level.

C. *Direct investment vs. intermediated investment using foreign CII*

Comparing results for the *two-country case*, involving portfolio investment in foreign shares through a foreign CII resident in the source country, with those in the benchmark case, identical net dividend tax rates are derived in each instance in Table 4.3.

As in Table 4.1, a number of exceptions to the general neutrality finding in the foreign CII case (for the countries considered) are identified. For example, the net dividend tax rate is shown in Table 4.1 to be lower for an Australian individual investing into the U.K. through a U.K. AUT. However, the revised figures shown that the denial of U.K. imputation relief on U.K. source dividends paid to an Australian CII imparts a tax impediment, discouraging this investment option relative to alternatives. Only when investing directly or through a U.K. AUT into U.K. shares are net dividend tax rates sufficiently low to make the U.K. shares as attractive as other portfolio investments. Similarly, dividend payments by a U.K. company to a Swedish (open-ended) CII are no longer found to be competitive, as they do not attract imputation relief, while investing into the U.K. through a U.K. CII, where imputation relief is available, now occupies a neutral position, whereas it was shown to be a preferred option in Table 4.1.

The results reported in Table 4.3 for the *three-country case* generally carryover from Table 4.1, with Australian, Belgian, Swedish, U.K. and U.S. shareholders facing high net dividend tax rates when investing in foreign shares through a CII resident in a third country, due to the absence of foreign tax credit relief to offset source country withholding tax. An exception to this result was identified in Table 4.1 for triangular investments into the U.K., as the U.K. does not impose withholding tax on portfolio dividends -- Australian, Belgian, Swedish and U.S. investors were subject to the lowest net dividend tax rates when investing through the triangular structure into U.K. shares. The same investors are shown in Table 4.3 to face lower net dividend tax rates when investing in Belgian, Swedish or U.S. shares. The attractiveness of U.K. shares linked to the absence of withholding tax at source is offset by the lower pre-tax rate of return U.K. firms can pay, as set by U.K. resident shareholders.

The net dividend tax rates posted for the *tax haven case*, which ignore the possible application of accruals taxation in the home countries, continue to be the most attractive, with net dividend tax rates on investments in Australia and U.K. shares slightly higher, due to the lower pre-personal tax rates of return on these shares at source 4.5 Summary and Reconciliation of Results

The results presented in this chapter underscore many of the considerations raised in Chapters 2 and 3, while adding some additional insights. The simplest results show that if all shares pay the same pre-tax rate of return, then investors in countries with imputation systems would tend to favour investing in domestic shares directly, rather than in foreign shares. At the same time, individuals resident in countries with classical tax systems would be drawn to foreign host countries offering them foreign tax credits.

Table 4.1 **Comparative net shareholder dividend tax rates (%) on Domestic vs Foreign shares under alternative direct vs Intermediated (domestic or foreign CII) investment structures**

	Source country																								
	Australia					**Belgium**					**Sweden**					**U.K.**					**U.S.**				
investor resident in	**dir**	**CII (d)**	**CII (f2)**	**CII (f3)**	**CII (fh)**	**dir**	**CII (d)**	**CII (f2)**	**CII (f3)**	**CII (fh)**	**dir**	**CII (d)**	**CII (f2)**	**CII (f3)**	**CII (fh)**	**dir**	**CII (d)**	**CII (f2)**	**CII (f3)**	**CII (fh)**	**dir**	**CII (d)**	**CII (f2)**	**CII (f3)**	**CII (fh)**
Australia	19.5	19.5	na	na	30.9	48.5	48.5	48.5	56.2	41.2	48.5	48.5	48.5	56.2	41.2	35.6	48.5	35.6	48.5	30.9	48.5	48.5	48.5	56.2	41.2
Belgium	25	15	25	36.3	13.0	15	15	na	na	26.1	36.3	27.8	36.3	45.8	26.1	25	15	25	36.3	13.0	36.3	27.8	36.3	45.8	26.1
Sweden	30	30	30	30	16.3	30	30	30	40.5	28.9	30	30	na	na	28.9	18.8	30	18.8	30.0	16.3	30	30	30	40.5	28.9
U.K.	40	40	40	40	23.7	40	46	40	49	35.1	40	43	40	49	35.1	25	25	na	na	23.7	40	49	40	49	35.1
U.S.	46.6	46.6	46.6	46.6	29.2	46.6	46.6	46.6	54.6	39.8	46.6	46.6	46.6	54.6	39.8	33.3	33.3	33.3	46.6	29.2	46.6	46.6	na	na	39.8

dir=direct (non-intermediated) investment
CII(d)=domestic CII case (*i.e.*, investment through domestic CII into source country)
CII(f2)=foreign CII two-country case (*i.e.*, investment through foreign CII resident in source country)
CII(f3)=foreign CII three-country case (*i.e.*, investment through foreign CII resident in third country, into source country)
CII(fh)=foreign CII tax haven case (*i.e.*, investment through foreign CII resident in tax haven/zero tax country, into source country)
Notes: Individual investor assumed to be taxable and able to fully claim foreign tax credit in respect of foreign withholding tax on dividend income.
CII(fh) figures show shareholder net tax rates in **absence** of anti-deferral portfolio foreign investment fund (PFIF) rules, and assume a ten-year holding period.

Results were also presented which reflect the general tax policy adopted in most countries of attempting to achieve neutrality for portfolio investment in domestic shares whether made directly or via a *domestic CII*. When considering investments in foreign shares through a domestic CII, neutrality with the benchmark case is shown to be dependent on treaty withholding tax rate reductions and foreign tax credits being passed on. Host country integration relief, if available to domestic investors in the direct portfolio investment case, would also have to pass through to unitholders of a domestic CII. In effect, the domestic CII must be treated as a transparent entity.

In the *foreign CII* case, neutrality was shown to require that income tax not apply at the foreign CII level, and foreign portfolio dividends routed through a foreign CII be tagged with the same level of integration relief as attached to portfolio dividends received directly from the host country. In the three-country foreign CII case, the main distortion identified was shown to be the absence of foreign tax credit mechanisms to relieve tax withheld on portfolio dividends at source, which gets stuck at the CII level. However, it was also shown that these potential disadvantages associated with the use of a foreign CII could be offset if the CII was resident in a jurisdiction that did not tax CIIs or impose a distribution requirement, allowing for home country tax deferral.

The second set of results also reflected the importance of the preceding considerations, but added a different perspective by admitting the possibility that integration relief could encourage corporate-level investment, and not just savings, by getting shifted back and allowing a reduction in the cost of capital. The first set of results showed integration credits as having the effect of attracting investors able to access those credits, while leaving other investors generally indifferent. The second set of results instead showed integration credits as having the effect of leaving investors able to access those credits generally indifferent between choosing those shares or an alternative investment, while leaving other investors discouraged from purchasing those shares.

It may be that where imputation relief is provided, its actual effects lie somewhere between the two sets of results, with that relief only partially capitalised into share prices. This however implies distortions on both sides of the coin -- with investors able to claim imputation relief in respect of given shares encouraged to purchase them (although less so than indicated by the results in Table 4.1), while those without access to the credit generally discouraged from purchasing those shares (again, less so than indicated by the second set of results in Table 4.3.)[16.]

Table 4.2 Imputation parameter (θ^m) and Required pre-tax returns

(marginal investor resident in source country, market interest rate = 10 per cent)

Country	AU	B	S	U.K.	US
θ^m	1.563	1	1	1.25	1
required pre-tax rate of return on new shares (%)	6.4	10	10	8	10
dividend paid by corporation (on 1 000 unites invested)	64	100	100	80	100

AU=Australia, B=Belgium, S=Sweden, U.K.=United Kingdom, U.S.=United States.

Table 4.3 **Comparative net shareholder dividend tax rates (%) on Domestic vs Foreign shares under alternative direct vs intermediated (Domestic or foreign CII) investment structures and under assumption that the 'marginal' investor is a resident individual portfolio investor**

	Source country																								
	Australia					Belgium					Sweden					U.K.					U.S.				
investor resident in	dir	CII (d)	CII (f2)	CII (f3)	CII (fh)	dir	CII (d)	CII (f2)	CII (f3)	CII (fh)	dir	CII (d)	CII (f2)	CII (f3)	CII (fh)	dir	CII (d)	CII (f2)	CII (f3)	CII (fh)	dir	CII (d)	CII (f2)	CII (f3)	CII (fh)
Australia	48.5	48.5	na	na	55.8	48.5	48.5	48.5	56.2	41.2	48.5	48.5	48.5	56.2	41.2	48.5	58.8	48.5	58.8	44.7	48.5	48.5	48.5	56.2	41.2
Belgium	52	45.6	52	59.2	44.4	15	15	na	na	26.1	36.3	27.8	36.3	45.8	26.1	40	32	40	49	30.4	36.3	27.8	36.3	45.8	26.1
Sweden	55.2	55.2	55.2	55.2	46.4	30	30	30	40.5	28.9	30	30	na	na	28.9	30	44	30	44	33.1	30	30	30	40.5	28.9
U.K.	61.6	61.6	61.6	61.6	51.2	40	46	40	49	35.1	40	43	40	49	35.1	40	40	na	na	38.9	40	49	40	49	35.1
U.S.	65.8	65.8	65.8	65.8	54.7	46.6	46.6	46.6	54.6	39.8	46.6	46.6	46.6	54.6	39.8	46.6	46.6	46.6	57.3	43.3	46.6	46.6	na	na	39.8

dir=direct (non-intermediated) investment
CII(d)=domestic CII case (*i.e.*, investment through domestic CII into source country)
CII(f2)=foreign CII two-country case (*i.e.*, investment through foreign CII resident in source country)
CII(f3)=foreign CII three-country case (*i.e.*, investment through foreign CII resident in third country, into source country)
CII(fh)=foreign CII tax haven case (*i.e.*, investment through foreign CII resident in tax haven/zero tax country, into source country)
Notes: Individual investor assumed to be taxable and able to fully claim foreign tax credit in respect of foreign withholding tax on dividend income. CII(fh) figures show shareholder net tax rates in **absence** of anti-deferral portfolio foreign investment fund (PFIF) rules, and assume a ten-year holding period.

NOTES

1. The calculations consider domestic shares and foreign shares of equivalent risk. Exchange controls or other regulatory impediments (generally not an issue in OECD countries) are also assumed away in such an analysis focusing on tax considerations.

2. Given this neutrality result, it follows that the tax distortions influencing investor choice between direct portfolio investment in domestic shares versus foreign shares, discussed in the preceding section, carry over equally and apply to the choice between domestic intermediated investment in domestic shares versus direct portfolio investment in foreign shares.

3. Alternatively, the (higher) foreign withholding tax would have to be fully creditable at the shareholder level.

4. In addition, host country integration relief attached to distributions to a domestic CII must pass through to individual unitholders of a domestic CII for the neutrality result to hold. Also note that the examples assume that the individual taxpayer is taxable and thus able to claim withholding tax credits in full. As discussed in the main text, where foreign tax credit constraints apply, neutrality will generally require that source country withholding tax be imposed at the same (treaty) rate in each case.

5. Similar results would have been found under the assumption that the foreign CII was subject to income tax, and source country withholding tax could be credited against this tax (given that CII-level income tax would be non-creditable at the investor level in each of the countries considered.)

6. The globalization of capital markets has at the same time simplified certain aspects of the analysis of taxation and its possible effects on equilibrium equity returns and prices. For example, the gradual de-segmentation of capital markets has made the concept of a 'world' interest rate for a debt instrument of a given risk no longer an abstract construct. However, the opening of domestic equity markets to foreign investors has also opened up the range of possible shareholder-level taxes, making the identification of the 'marginal' investor group more difficult.

7. See Sinn, H.W. (1990.)

8. The basic reason for this result is that earnings in the firm are 'trapped' and cannot avoid dividend taxation, being subject to dividend taxation if currently distributed rather than retained, or in the future if retained and eventually distributed. Note that, in practice, dividend taxation may be avoided in certain cases through share repurchases (or perhaps other means) -- models assume either that share repurchases are not possible (as is the case in certain instances), or that capital gains realised on share repurchases are characterised as dividends for tax purposes.

9. In this simplified illustration, inflation is assumed to be negligible so that there is no need to distinguish between nominal and real returns. The characterisation of the taxation of dividend and/or interest income in equation (4.1) is not representative of all countries. However, the equation can be modified as necessary, and the required after-corporate tax rate of return derived under the same

assumption that the marginal (domestic individual) investor equates the after-tax rate of return on equity with the after-tax rate of return on bonds.

10. Note that personal taxation of interest income (though not necessarily at the marginal shareholder's tax rate mm) would indirectly enter equations (4.1b) and (4.3b). Arbitrage in bond markets would tend to force up the interest rate on taxable bonds to match that on tax-exempt bonds, such that i(1-m)=i*, or i=i*/(1-m). Only where m equals mm would (4.3a) and (4.3b) give the same value for RNE.

11. Consider a share paying a perpetual stream of dividends (after-corporate tax earnings) of 100 currency units per period, or 60 after personal tax assuming a 40 per cent shareholder tax rate. Assume that this stream is discounted using a interest rate on bonds of equivalent risk of 10 per cent, implying an after-tax discount rate of 6 per cent.
This yields a share value (v) of 1000 units, where v=(1- mm)d/i(1- mm)=d/RNE.

12. A 20 per cent imputation rate means that relief is provided for underlying corporate income tax at 20 per cent. Providing relief for corporate income tax at the rate of 0.20 for each currency unit of pre-tax corporate profit requires an imputation credit of 0.25 currency units for each currency unit of after-tax distributed corporate profit. Note that θm=1+u/(1-u)=1.25 where u is the imputation rate (0.2).

13. In the absence of imputation relief, a share paying a perpetual stream of dividends of 100 currency units per period would be valued by a 40 per cent taxpayer at 1000=100(1-.4)/0.10(1-.04). If imputation relief is available at 20 per cent, paying 0.25 per currency unit of distributed income, the share paying 100 currency units per period would be valued at 1250=100(1.25)(1-.4)/0.10(1-.04).

14. The after-corporate, pre-personal tax rates of return on portfolio investment, shown in Table 4.2, may be interpreted as discount rates for firms in each country (for investment financed at the margin by new share issues, and assuming accrual-equivalent capital gains taxes (if any) are negligible.) The wedge between the market interest rate and the company's discount rate is zero in a classical system of corporate taxation (e.g., Belgium, Luxembourg, Sweden, the U.S.) and negative for tax systems that provide mitigation of double taxation at the shareholder level (e.g., Australia, France, Germany, Italy, the U.K.) The wedge itself conveys limited information on overall investment incentives at the company level, and to compare the numbers across countries is difficult. A company's pre-tax cost of capital depends on the combined impact of dividend relief and the corporate tax wedge (which in turn depends on both the corporate tax rate and the base of the tax, e.g. the tax rules governing depreciation).

15. For an explanation of the link between this analysis and formal 'marginal effective tax rate' (METR) analysis, see Appendix IV.

16. These tentative conclusions have a bearing on the interpretation of other types of taxes and/or tax subsidies that might apply to direct or intermediated portfolio investment. First, the theory considered in this chapter would suggest that tax burdens and/or tax reliefs should be capitalised into share prices and influence rates of return (if at all) only where they apply to affect the net rate of return on the asset in question relative to that on alternative investment determining the opportunity cost of funds. This explains why dividend taxes may influence share prices and returns in the case of investment financed at the margin by new share issues, as opposed to retained earnings, and why the integration parameter (and not the marginal investor's income tax rate) matter where the opportunity cost of funds is taken to be the after-tax rate of return on bonds (taxed also at the same income tax rate.) Second -- given that if a tax applies, incentives exist to plan around it, while if a tax subsidy applies, incentives exist to plan for it -- it may be that there is a greater likelihood that subsidies to portfolio investment are more important than taxes themselves in influencing portfolio investment behavior.

Chapter 5

POLICY CONSIDERATIONS IN THE TAXATION OF CROSS-BORDER INVESTMENT THROUGH COLLECTIVE INVESTMENT INSTITUTIONS

5.1 Introduction

Most countries have a fiscal regime specially designed for domestic CIIs that aims at ensuring that the tax burden of participants in a CII which invests in domestic shares on their behalf does not exceed the tax burden which would have resulted with a direct portfolio investment. This aim is achieved sometimes by making the CII 'transparent', meaning that the CII is considered not to exist separately for tax purposes. Other times this aim is achieved by exempting the CII from tax entirely. Such provisions are typically developed with the primary objective of ensuring a flow-through of *domestic* source income and equivalent tax treatment. Certain problems, reviewed in Chapters 3 and 4, may arise in the context of earning *foreign* investment income through domestic CIIs. Similarly, the interaction of foreign and home country tax systems may imply that earning foreign source income through a foreign CII may not yield an equivalent result to that observed in the foreign direct portfolio investment case.

A number of the potential problems related to the taxation of investments through CIIs are considered below, along with possible design considerations and policy options that may be relevant to countries when considering introducing or modifying their tax rules as they apply to investment income earned through CIIs.

5.2 Foreign portfolio investment via CIIs -- Policy considerations and options

Four potential areas of policy concern are addressed in this section. Sub-section (A) reviews income tax deferral possibilities when using offshore CIIs, and how these might be dealt with. Sub-section (B) considers withholding tax rate differentials that might arise when using foreign or domestic CIIs, rather than investing in foreign portfolio shares directly, and reviews some past and recent analysis of how this area might be addressed. Sub-section (C) deals with imputation tax relief and draws on the findings of Chapter 4 in addressing possible policy considerations that under certain assumptions may argue in favour of (and under alternative assumptions, caution against) the provision of imputation relief to non-resident shareholders investing through a foreign or domestic CII. Finally, sub-section (D) considers possible foreign tax credit complications and suggests that these be dealt with bearing in mind both transparency and compliance considerations.

A. *Addressing income tax deferral possibilities*

Using a foreign CII to make foreign portfolio investment raises the possibility of an additional layer of non-creditable tax at the CII level. However, as noted in Chapter 3, countries that tax the income of resident CIIs typically impose a zero/low effective tax rate, while others exempt CIIs from income taxation altogether. Thus, in most cases, income tax at the CII level, which for a non-resident portfolio investor in the CII would be a non-creditable tax, constitutes no great problem. In fact, as the present Report notes, the residence country of the CII may not attach a distribution requirement to CII income tax relief, implying income tax savings through deferral opportunities for investors in the CII -- savings that are not available when investing directly in the underlying shares (or through a domestic CII in the country of residence of the investor.)

A potential deferral advantage arises because countries typically do not impose domestic tax on the investment income or capital gains of foreign entities. Moreover, such income is typically not subject to income tax in the CII's country of residence. Income tax or more specifically domestic income tax on earnings at the CII level therefore may be deferred until the investor receives distributions from the CII or disposes of his/her interest in the CII, absent special rules to tax investors in the CII on their pro-rata share of that income as its accrues (*i.e.*, on an accrual basis.)

Tables 4.1 and 4.3 illustrate the effect of income tax deferral possibilities, which lower the net dividend tax rate on foreign (and domestic) shares held through an offshore 'roll-up' CII that reinvests earnings at the CII level. The potential tax savings can operate to encourage individuals to invest in portfolio equities through offshore CIIs, rather than through domestic CIIs or directly where investment returns are taxed on a current basis. This distortion may be viewed by tax policy makers as inappropriate, posing revenue loss, efficiency and equity concerns.[1]

Such concerns have led a number of OECD countries, including Australia, Canada, New Zealand and the United States, to adopt anti-deferral rules in the portfolio investment area, sometimes referred to as passive foreign investment fund (PFIF) rules. Although the specific PFIF rules differ from one country to the next, they share a common goal of eliminating domestic income tax deferral benefits otherwise available when investing in offshore CIIs. In addition, PFIF rules can address domestic tax avoidance tied to the conversion of dividends into capital gains subject in some countries to a preferential tax rate.

An alternative approach for eliminating income tax deferral advantages and attendant distortions tied to the use of offshore CIIs would be for all countries to impose income tax at some minimum significant rate (*e.g.*, 25 per cent) on resident CIIs, which could be creditable against withholding tax on CII distributions. However, such an approach might be viewed as difficult and too radical a departure from existing tax treatment designed to ensure transparency in the resident CII resident investor situation. Moreover, given the virtual certainty that not all countries could be convinced of such a structure, tax deferral opportunities would continue through the use of CIIs resident in those countries. This would appear to leave the PFIF-approach as the more appropriate policy direction.

Policy Option 1: *Countries that do not have anti-deferral passive foreign investment fund (PFIF) rules may consider adopting such rules as a means to curtail domestic tax base erosion, and to address efficiency and equity concerns linked to the avoidance of domestic tax on passive investment income earned via offshore CIIs.*

B. Addressing withholding tax differential possibilities

The possibility of different source country withholding tax levied on direct versus intermediated investment may arise where a domestic investor uses a *domestic CII* to earn foreign source income. In this situation, the withholding tax rate applied to foreign portfolio dividends paid to a domestic CII might be higher than that applied if the dividends were received directly, tending to discourage the domestic CII option.

Similarly, the use of a *foreign CII* raises the possibility of withholding at source on portfolio dividends at a rate different from that applied if dividends were received directly (or through a domestic CII.) This generally does *not* occur where the distributing (source) company is resident in the same country as the foreign CII, as most countries apply the same non-resident withholding tax rate to portfolio dividends whether paid abroad directly by a resident (source) company or through a resident CII (with the withholding occurring either at source or at the CII level.)

However, the withholding tax rate at source on a distribution to a CII in a third country may be higher than that applied to a dividend paid directly to a domestic investor, tending to discourage portfolio investment through the foreign CII. This situation could arise where the source and CII countries have concluded a tax treaty that provides for a reduced withholding tax rate for portfolio dividends paid (directly) to *individuals* resident in the CII country, but not for portfolio dividends paid to CIIs. Moreover, investing through a foreign CII generally will be tax discouraged on account of withholding tax considerations alone even where the withholding tax rate at source is the same in the foreign CII and direct investment cases, owing to foreign tax credit limitations under the foreign CII option.

Alternatively, the withholding tax rate at source on a distribution to a foreign CII might be lower than that applied to a dividend paid directly to a domestic investor and, despite such tax being non-creditable, may result in an overall tax saving when choosing the foreign CII, tending to encourage this option.[2] Indeed, individual investors may 'treaty shop' for a CII resident in a foreign country that has a broad treaty network providing resident CIIs with reduced source country withholding tax.

In general, from a source (host) country's perspective, two competing interests would influence the decision of whether or not to attach treaty benefits to portfolio dividends paid to a CII resident in a treaty country. On the one hand, recognising that a CII may be a preferred vehicle to investors for sound non-tax reasons (*e.g.*, portfolio management/diversification benefits), a host country may be encouraged to extend to individuals resident in the treaty country, investing through a resident CII, treaty benefits that would be available on a direct portfolio investment, as the same policy reasons that would argue in favour of extending such relief in the direct investment case generally would carry over. However, a CII resident in a treaty country may also be a preferred investment vehicle for portfolio investors not resident in the CII country, for purely tax reasons -- in particular, if investing in the CII provides treaty benefits unavailable on a direct portfolio investment. For this reason, a given source country may be unwilling to apply a treaty rate to dividend payments to a non-resident CII if it perceives that interests in the CII by investors resident in other (non-treaty) countries are significant.

Under some of Germany's treaties, the practice is to follow the proportionality approach, which limits withholding tax relief based on the treaty between the source country (Germany) and the CII residence country to the proportion of (individual) investors in the CII that are resident in the country of residence of the CII. The relief (in the form of a greater cash receipt) goes to the CII which then allocates it among its investors as it sees fit. This approach seems to be premised on the view that the treaty operates at the level of the investor, but that for practical reasons treaty relief can only operate at the level of the CII.

The 1977 OECD Study and the 1997 IFA report propose that treaties be operated at the level of the CII, regardless of whether or not the CII strictly satisfies the treaty requirements as to being a person which is a treaty resident and beneficial owner of the income, in order to avoid complications involved with the alternative of operating treaties at the individual investor level, and suggest a limitation of benefits approach in situations where treaty abuse may be expected.[3]

The 1977 OECD Study

The 1977 OECD Study proposes a combined domestic and treaty regime operating treaty benefits at the level of the CII and separately at the level of the investor, through a withholding tax on distributions by the CII against which withholding at source against the CII could be offset. The 1977 Study proposes that, in respect of triangular situations (source country, CII country and investor country all different):

a) Conventions should be expanded to include a rule that a CII which satisfies the conditions described below should always be regarded as a treaty subject entitled to a reduction of withholding taxes, irrespective of the legal form of the CII.

b) Measures should be incorporated in national legislation whereby the CII as an independent unit is not subjected to actual taxation.

c) When income is distributed by a CII to a foreign investor, a withholding tax should always be levied irrespective of the legal form of the CII (*e.g.*, at a rate of 25 per cent.) The chosen withholding tax rate should be sufficiently high to permit crediting of the foreign withholding tax levied at source (on the foreign income of the CII) against CII-level withholding tax. Withholding tax at the CII level, which in spite of the crediting procedure remains formally at 25 per cent, should be creditable against the income tax liability of a CII participant/investor resident in the CII state. In the case of a non-resident participant, the 25 per cent rate may be reduced under a tax treaty between the CII state and the non-resident participant state. The participant state (*i.e.*, residence country of the foreign investor in the CII) should provide the participant with a foreign tax credit for the CII-level withholding tax (imposed at 25 per cent in the non-treaty case, or some lower amount (*e.g.*, 15 per cent) in the treaty case.)

An example of this structure is set out below, where a CII receives a dividend of 100 from a foreign source state. Under a convention between the source state and the CII-residence state, tax is withheld at source at 15 per cent, reduced from 25 per cent. The CII thus receives 85. Under the proposal, the CII would have to withhold tax at 25 per cent, or 25, on distributions to non-treaty participants. However, the CII is allowed to offset the withholding tax paid to the source state (15), so a balance of 10 would be paid to the CII state. The CII would then distribute 75 to its non-resident participants. Alternatively, under any convention between his/her state and the CII state, the participant would apply for a 15 per cent withholding tax rate (*i.e.*, a 10 per cent withholding tax rate reduction, of 10.) The participant would thus receive in total a net sum of 85 and would be allowed to offset the remaining withholding tax of 15 against his/her income tax payable in respect of the distribution.

The net effect in the treaty situation is that the CII dividend is subject to only one withholding tax (at source) at the convention rate for portfolio investment income, which can be offset by the participant investor against his/her income tax. This yields the same result as would occur had the participant invested directly in the source state. In particular, if the participant had invested directly, he/she would have received a dividend of 100, less withholding tax of 15 (reduced from 25 under terms of the tax convention between the source state and participant state), arriving at a net receipt of 85. For non-treaty participants, 15 is withheld at source and an additional 10 in the CII state for a total of 25 as would have occurred had the participant invested directly in the source state. The CII is in effect transparent but the withholding tax mechanism prevents tax avoidance.

Example of CII Withholding tax structure proposed in 1977 OECD study

Row		**Direct portfolio investment:** ***Treaty benchmark***	**Intermediated portfolio Investment --** ***treaty situation***	**Direct portfolio investment:** ***Non-treaty benchmark***	**Intermediated portfolio Investment --** ***Non-treaty situation***
1	Dividend paid by company(1)	100	100	100	100
2	Foreign withholding tax	15	15	25	15
3	Cash receipt (CII)	na	85	na	85
4	Dividend plus gross-up	na	100	na	100
5	Gross withholding tax (CII)	na	15	na	25
6	Foreign tax credit	na	15	na	15
7	Net withholding tax (CII)	na	0	na	10
8	Cash receipt (individual)(2)	85	85	75	75
9	Dividend plus gross-up	100	100	100	100
10	Personal income tax @40%	40	40	40	40
11	Foreign tax credit	15	15	25	25
12	Net personal tax	25	25	15	15
13	Net return (individual)	60	60	60	60

(1) Distributing company and CII are resident in different countries.
(2) Final return if investment income is not reported for home country tax purposes.

The aim of the 1977 OECD Study was to achieve a situation where the tax to which the CII participant is subject, is as similar as possible to that levied on a direct portfolio investor. In the case of capital gains, it is suggested that this aim could be achieved by the CII distributing capital gains on a separate coupon, since this would enable capital gains tax to be refunded under a convention procedure. The separate coupon would also enable the participant state to accord the appropriate treatment to the capital gain. States would then be left free to choose the regime they wish to apply to capital gains.

In the numerical example set out above, it is possible that the participant may not ask the CII state for a reduction of the withholding tax because he/she wishes to remain anonymous (*i.e.*, wishes not to report such income for domestic income tax purposes.) In this case, the CII state will retain the 10 per cent withheld by the CII. It seems in this case as if only the CII state has benefited -- this may be referred to as a shifting of revenue and considered a problem with the scheme. However, it should be noted that such shifting already occurs in many cases where a corporate form CII obtains a reduction in withholding tax from the source state under a convention. In such cases, if the CII state imposes a withholding tax on distributions by the CII and the investors, wishing to remain anonymous, do not submit returns and thereby claim a credit, there has in effect been a shifting of revenue to the CII state. Intensive efforts to remedy this problem have not been successful.

Lastly, it should be noted that the scheme implicitly assumes a treaty network covering the relevant countries in uniform terms.[4] The 1977 Study assumed in the tax treaty area that the OECD Model was used by all countries. Also, it was originally contemplated laying down the proposed arrangements in a multi-lateral convention to which all countries could accede. However, it was considered that this would lead to difficulties. It should be emphasised that the 1977 Study is in favour of a national CII regime under which the CII itself is in principle not subject to taxation.

This solution is directed at the true triangular case (where the source country, country of residence of the CII, and country of residence of the investor are different (and not insignificant withholding tax applies at source)) -- which in terms of overall international tax treaty problems with CIIs is unlikely to be a dominant case. Moreover, it requires significant changes to the domestic law of many countries and even then it is premised on treaties in uniform terms between the countries concerned (the proposal could work in other cases but only at the cost of misallocation of tax revenue between the countries concerned.)

The 1997 IFA Report

The 1997 IFA report takes a similar approach to that of the 1977 OECD Study. In dealing with the international tax treatment of CIIs, it proposes, like the 1977 OECD Study, that CIIs should be entitled to treaty benefits, subject to certain conditions. The Report argues that whatever the legal form of CIIs, they should be treated as treaty persons, since they are treated as being separate entities for regulatory purposes. Similarly, they should be treated as treaty residents in the country where they are subject to tax on a residence-type basis (even if no tax is levied) or subject to a withholding tax on distributions if themselves not subject to tax.

Although the IFA report vacillates on the question of ownership of CIIs' investments, it considers that for treaty purposes CIIs should be treated as beneficial owners, whether as a matter of general operation of that treaty concept, or where necessary by special deeming. The overall result is that CIIs are entitled to treaty benefits in their country of residence.

The IFA report recognises that entitling CIIs to treaty benefits may open the way to treaty shopping, and therefore deals with limitation of benefits in some detail. As a general matter, it does not regard limitation of benefits based on transparency, base erosion or treaty exclusion as appropriate in view of the special nature of CIIs (*i.e.*, transparency is often achieved by deduction of distributions or by tax exemption.) Specifically, it proposes that *limitation of benefits would <u>not</u> be necessary if*:

1. The CII is itself subject to tax at a reasonable rate, or
2. Withholding tax is levied at a reasonable rate on distributions or redemptions by the CII, or
3. There is some safeguard that the investor is subject to tax on distributions and gains (*e.g.*, limitation of benefits by reference to regionality of investors, having in mind particularly the developing treaty approach between the US and EU countries, or disclosure requirements.)

The specific treatment of dividends flowing through a CII in a triangular structure where the above tests (1-3) are not satisfied would be left to treaty negotiators. The report gives a simple example of how to effect limitation of benefits in such situations which is virtually identical to the solution considered in the 1977 OECD Study, illustrated above. Aside from some of the variations contemplated under the proposal, especially in relation to treaty shopping, the solution is essentially the same as the one adopted in the 1977 OECD Study.

Proportionality (providing for partial access to treaty benefits) is reluctantly accepted even where the above tests (1-3) are not satisfied -- that is, even where the CII is not taxed at a reasonable rate in its country of residence, and retentions and distributions are not subject to withholding (or home country income tax) at reasonable rates. Where the CII does not meet a proportionality test (*i.e.*, it is essentially an offshore fund) no treaty benefits would be available. While this approach precludes the investor from accessing treaty benefits stipulated in the treaty between the investor's country and the country of source of the income, this lack may not regarded as problematic as the offshore industry could reconstruct itself as necessary into funds with and funds without access to treaty benefits to suit investor profiles (*i.e.*, the lack of access may be seen as solvable by appropriate structuring.)

Measured against the array of international tax impediments associated with the use of CIIs in certain cases, the triangular case (where the source country, country of residence of the CII, and country of residence of the investor are different) may not be particularly problematic, at least currently. However, given the likelihood of increased internationalisation and growth in the CII area, work should continue to resolve this issue. Given that similar problems arise in the context of other forms of institutional investment, this work should run parallel with those efforts.

Policy Option 2: *Countries follow projects underway by Working Party No 1 on Double Taxation of the Committee on Fiscal Affairs concerning the treatment of transparent entities and pension funds under tax treaties, and consider the findings and conclusions of reports on those projects before considering possible treaty approaches to address differential withholding tax treatment in the CII case. This would permit consideration of a similar or tailored approach to a similar problem which arises in the context of other transparent entities and pension funds*.

C. Addressing differential imputation relief possibilities

The following two policy options concern distortions and possibly undesired revenue losses linked to the extension or not of imputation relief by a source country to non-resident shareholders. These are addressed in two contexts. The first involves non-resident portfolio investment in shares through a *CII resident in the host (source) country*. The discussion focuses on the (outbound) foreign source income /foreign CII/domestic investor case (Case 6 in Chapter 3, section 3.2.) However, the points raised also concern the (inbound) domestic source income/domestic CII/ foreign investor case (Case 2 in section 3.2.) The second context involves portfolio investment in foreign shares through a *CII resident in the home country*. The discussion focuses on the (outbound) foreign source income/domestic CII/domestic investor case (Case 5), with the considerations applying also to the (inbound) domestic source income/foreign CII/foreign investor case (Case 4.) The results depend on the assumptions of the model and are therefore tentative. As more evidence becomes available on the impact of imputation relief on capital markets, countries may wish to revisit this area, with a view to further examining the advantages of an imputation system versus a dual income tax system, or a classical system with a final flat dividend tax rate.

i) Foreign portfolio investment through a foreign CII

As discussed in Chapter 2, a country may provide its resident shareholders with integration relief in respect of corporate income tax imposed on resident firms, with the objective of lowering the cost of capital and thereby encouraging real investment and economic growth, and/or with the objective of encouraging domestic savings incentives. As considered in Chapter 4, where the intention is to lower the cost of capital for resident companies, the same (source) country may grant integration relief to non-resident direct portfolio shareholders as well, while recognising that part of the relief may be taxed away by the investor's home country tax system, resulting in a partial transfer of revenues from the source country to the home country of foreign investors.

Taking the taxation of direct foreign portfolio investment case as a policy benchmark, integration relief attached to dividends paid directly to non-resident portfolio investors in treaty countries should also be granted -- on pure neutrality grounds and if possible -- where the dividends are routed instead through a CII resident in the source country (the two-country case.) Attaching relief to tax-paid dividends flowing through a resident CII adds complexity, requiring a separate pooling of qualifying income, but this would occur at the CII level where investor residence information should be available. The policy of granting imputation relief to non-resident portfolio shareholders when investing through a resident CII holds out the advantage that these investors would not be discouraged from providing capital to firms in the source country through this channel. Moreover, it may be that for certain investors, direct investment in foreign portfolio shares would not be considered despite the availability of source country integration relief, due to relatively high transactions and monitoring costs in foreign as compared to domestic equity markets. Placing the direct investment option and the intermediated (source country) CII option on an equal footing, as regards integration provisions, may be required in order to draw in portfolio capital.

However, before taking a policy position, it is important to consider the incidence of imputation relief and the economic effects of extending such relief (or not) to inbound *direct* portfolio investors, taken as the policy benchmark, and by extension through a resident CII. As illustrated in Chapter 3, where integration relief is provided and gets 'shifted-back', resulting in a lowering of the cost of capital -- *i.e.*, a lowering of the after-corporate tax (pre-shareholder tax) rate of return that a firm must pay -- the extension of integration relief to non-resident portfolio shareholders on inbound direct and intermediated portfolio investments may be necessary if the host country desires that this investor group not be discouraged from investing in portfolio shares issued by firms in the host country, favouring domestic (home country) or other foreign shares instead. Concerns could arise, for example, where foreign capital is needed to finance domestic investment projects.

Alternatively, integration relief may not get shifted back and reduce the cost of funds of resident firms. In particular, the practice of denying integration relief to certain investors -- who may be the 'marginal' investors in newly-issued shares, setting required rates of return and equity prices -- while providing it to others (*e.g.*, taxable resident investors and possibly certain non-resident investors) may mean that such relief generates only windfall gains to those eligible for it, with no real investment effects. Where this is the case, host country imputation relief may operate to distort portfolio savings decisions and cross-border portfolio flows by encouraging non-resident individuals to invest in host country shares, purely for tax reasons, directly or via a host country CII where integration relief passes through. This outcome may be viewed as unsatisfactory by both host and home countries. For the host country, if imputation relief does not result in a lowering of the cost of capital (*i.e.*, a lowering of shareholder required rates of return) for companies resident there, implying little or no boost to real investment activity, the revenue loss from granting windfall integration relief to non-resident shareholders might be viewed as unwarranted.[5] Furthermore, the residence (home) country of portfolio individuals investing in foreign shares offering imputation credits may be concerned that the attraction of domestic taxpayers to foreign shares paying excess rates of return, supported by integration relief, might make the collection of domestic tax revenues more difficult, given the increased problems in obtaining information on foreign investment income. Where imputation relief is found to have mostly windfall effects, attracting savings from abroad, while having a negligible impact on the cost of capital to firms, it may be appropriate for host countries to deny such relief to non-resident shareholders in direct and intermediated investment cases. While recognising the general policy goal of most tax systems of not providing windfall gains, and the fact that possible windfall gains in relation to integration relief are not limited to intermediated investment cases, the following policy option (as well as option 4) may be considered.

Policy Option 3: *Countries that maintain an imputation system and extend imputation relief to non-resident individuals on direct portfolio investments may consider providing the same relief when those individuals invest through a CII resident in the host country, and where such relief is believed not to provide purely windfall effects. Where imputation relief is believed to provide purely windfall effects, consideration might be given to not granting such relief to non-resident investors unilaterally, and to refrain from granting such relief when negotiating/renegotiating tax treaties.*

ii) Foreign portfolio investment through a domestic CII

Once again taking the *direct* portfolio investment case as a policy benchmark, integration relief attached to dividends paid directly to non-resident portfolio investors arguably should be made available to those investors on pure neutrality grounds, if possible, and perhaps with limitations (noted below), where the dividend is routed through a domestic CII (*i.e.*, a CII resident in the investor's home country.) This policy, which the U.K., France, Germany and Italy adhere to in certain treaty situations (see section 3.4), removes a possible impediment to inbound portfolio investment through non-resident CIIs.[6]

As considered above, extending imputation relief to non-resident individuals investing directly or through a CII may generate purely windfall gains and corresponding tax distortions, depending on the operation of capital markets, and in particular on the effects (if any) of imputation relief on pre-personal tax rates of return. Where windfall effects occur (*i.e.*, imputation relief causes pre-personal tax rates of return to exceed the market interest rate on bonds of equivalent risk), imputation relief, whether provided directly to non-resident portfolio shareholders or indirectly through a domestic (or foreign) CII, may cause unintended and undesired shifts in savings towards securities issued in the host country. On the other hand, where such relief is passed back and lowers pre-tax rates of return, the extension of such relief to non-resident individuals investing directly or indirectly through a CII may be necessary in order that these investors -- as a result of this tax factor -- not be discouraged from investing in host country shares.

Where a foreign host country wishes to attach imputation relief to distributions to a non-resident CII, to be passed on to individual shareholders resident in the CII country, the potential for unintended spillover or leakage of imputation benefits to other investors in the CII should be recognised. In particular, a domestic CII in receipt of dividends with imputation credits attached may attract investors resident in other countries that have not concluded a tax treaty with the host country providing for integration relief on portfolio dividends paid directly to individual investors resident in those (third) countries.

One approach to address this potential concern would be to adopt the German *proportionality approach* applied to determine treaty withholding rate reductions, but in this case applied to determine imputation relief benefits. Where a host country's intention is to target imputation relief to resident individuals in a given treaty country, the imputation credit attached to a portfolio dividend paid to a CII in the treaty country could be limited to the proportion of investors in the CII that are individuals resident in the same country.

Policy Option 4: *Countries that maintain an imputation system and extend on a bilateral treaty basis imputation relief to non-resident individuals on direct portfolio investments, may consider providing the same relief when those individuals invest through a domestic CII (resident in the investor country) where such relief is believed not to provide purely windfall effects. Further, countries that extend imputation relief to non-resident CIIs may consider restricting this relief to account for possible treaty shopping abuses. One approach might be to apply the proportionality approach, and limit imputation relief to the proportion of individual investors in the CII that are resident in the CII country.*

D. Addressing possible foreign tax credit concerns

A further issue in relation to the use by domestic investors of domestic CIIs through which to earn foreign dividend income concerns the possibility that a foreign tax credit in respect of withholding tax at source may be in question. It was noted in Chapter 3 that this concern may arise even in exemption countries, as exemption provisions generally are not operative for foreign portfolio income (especially if a reduction of tax at source has occurred under a tax treaty.)

From a compliance perspective, it might be argued that foreign tax credit claims in respect of foreign withholding tax on investment income paid to domestic CIIs should be taken at the CII level. However, for this approach to be viable, there must be tax at the CII level, whether in the form of income tax on the CII, or withholding tax on distributions to its investors. Moreover, to prevent flow-on (*i.e.*, double taxation) effects at the individual investor level, it would be necessary that tax at the CII level be final, whether in the form of income tax or withholding tax (as in the case of Japan), or for CII distributions to be dealt with under an integration system which effectively ignores the foreign source of the income generating the distribution (the U.K. system comes fairly close to this paradigm.)

Treating tax at the CII level as final may be objected to where progressive taxation of such income is sought. The alternative of providing individual investors with a tax credit in respect of income tax paid by domestic CIIs on foreign source income, net of foreign tax credits, may also be seen as unacceptable to countries that have not adopted a domestic integration system. Moreover, in countries where CIIs are not subject to tax, as a means of achieving transparency, introducing tax at the CII level may prove difficult.

From the neutrality perspective of seeking to achieve the same outcome for intermediated investment via CIIs as for direct portfolio investments in foreign securities, the appropriate solution would seem to be the provision of foreign tax credits at the investor level. This approach permits progressive taxation, and by not requiring the imposition of tax at the CII level for foreign tax credit claiming purposes, by-passes the potential problem of introducing an additional (non-creditable) tax wedge at the CII level that would not arise on a direct portfolio investment. However, this approach may raise administrative and compliance concerns.

Providing foreign tax credits at the shareholder level raises difficulties for foreign unitholders of domestic CIIs who generally will not be able to access a foreign tax credit in respect of withholding tax imposed by the source country. Considering the possibility of both foreign and domestic unitholders of domestic CIIs, and the desire to extend foreign tax credit relief to all unitholders, a variant on the Japanese system might be recommended, as it was in the 1977 OECD Study and the 1997 IFA Report. Such a solution was, however, apparently not acceptable to a majority of countries in 1977, and may not be any more acceptable today as it requires most countries to give up their current domestic tax methods for dealing with CIIs.

Policy Option 5*: Until it is demonstrated that the triangular case is very common, a simpler solution to a potential foreign tax credit problem may be that countries seek within the context of their domestic regimes for CIIs to produce an outcome consistent with transparency, but with the compliance burden falling mainly at the CII level.. If foreign tax credit claims are to occur at the individual investor level, consideration may be given to changes to simplify the operation of the system, as in the U.S. and U.K. systems.*

NOTES

1 The 1997 IFA Report takes the view that a requirement for the distribution by a CII of its income is unnecessary, with the taxation of undistributed income being a matter for the country of residence of the investor. The report however proceeds on the assumption of disclosure by the investor (i.e., the reporting of foreign investment income and gains) as required in the investor's country of residence and generally by-passes the problem of such home country taxation. Arguably, the report is too focused on achieving transparency in the home country of the CII and not focused enough on appropriate ultimate taxation of the income derived through the CII (i.e., on the need for PFIF-type accrual taxation rules and exchange of information provisions.)

2 Withholding tax at source (if any) in the intermediated investment case together with net withholding tax (if any) on distributions from the CII to the individual investor, or on share buy-backs (redemptions), may compare favourably to net withholding tax on distributions received directly. Where it does, a tax treaty will typically exist between the foreign source and CII countries, where the source country regards the CII as a resident person, beneficially entitled to the income, permitting a lowering of the source withholding tax rate. Similarly, the treaty may provide for reduced withholding tax on interest income and capital gains. It is also likely in this case that the home country of the investor has not concluded a treaty with the source country. In such cases, investments in foreign CIIs may be encouraged on account of withholding tax considerations alone.

3 Under a *proportionality approach*, treaty benefits are reduced (in proportion to the number of investors in a CII that are resident in a country other than the residence country of the CII) but not necessarily eliminated. In contrast, under a *limitation of benefits approach*, treaty benefits are eliminated.

4 Even assuming a treaty network covering the relevant countries concerned in uniform terms, the solution would require the tracing of distributions by a CII to the underlying income and its source(s).

5 It has been argued in the present report that possible tax policy reasons behind the provision of imputation/integration relief are (a) a desire to encourage investment by lowering the cost of equity capital, and (b) to encourage savings by resident individuals. In the situation where integration relief has no effect on the cost of funds to domestic firms, one could argue that the provision of imputation relief to non-resident shareholders, and the foregone domestic revenue that it entails, would not be in the host country's interest (other than bringing additional tax treaty negotiating power.) This assumes that the savings rates of non-resident shareholders are of no policy relevance to the host country (which is presumably the case where such savings rates have no bearing on the availability/cost of equity funds to host country firms.)

6 Where a domestic CII does not get imputation benefits available on a direct foreign portfolio investment (or more generally, does not get imputation benefits provided to investors resident in the foreign source country, on the same underlying investment), a number of mechanisms are available to gain access to such relief. One such method is a security lending agreement, in which the dividend stream is sold to investors able to use the imputation credits, in exchange for payments (to the CII) which do not attract withholding tax in the source country and reflect in part the value of the transferred tax credit. Despite this, certain countries may desire to extend imputation relief to non-resident CIIs, and further to limit imputation relief in such cases to limit treaty shopping opportunities.

REFERENCES

BOADWAY, R. and N. BRUCE (1992), 'Problems with Integrating Corporate and Personal Income Taxes in an Open Economy', Journal of Public Economics, 48, North Holland.

HURLEY et al. (1995) 'The Coming Evolution of the Investment Management Industry: Opportunities and Strategies', Goldman Sachs.

International Fiscal Association (1997), 'The Taxation of Investment Funds', Studies on International Fiscal Law, Vol. LXXXIIb, 51st Congress of the International Fiscal Association, 1997 New Kelhi Congress.

JORGENSON, D. (1992), 'Tax Reform and the Cost of Capital: An International Comparison', Harvard University, HIER Discussion Paper No. 1621.

KING, M. A. and D. FULLERTON (1984), 'The Taxation of Income from Capital', Chicago: University of Chicago Press.

OECD (1972) 'Standard Rules for the Operations of Institutions for Collective Investment', Paris: OECD.

OECD (1977) 'The Taxation of Collective Investment Institutions', Paris: OECD.

OECD (1991) 'Taxing Profits in a Global Economy: Domestic and International Issues', Paris: OECD.

OECD (1994) 'Taxation and Household Saving', Paris: OECD.

OECD (1994) 'Taxation of New Financial Instruments', Paris: OECD.

SINN, H.W. (1990) 'Taxation and the Cost of Capital: the 'Old' View, the 'New' View and Another View', Working Paper N. 3501, NBER Cambridge Mass.

Appendix I

NET SHAREHOLDER TAX RATE TABLES

Table AI.1.A **Taxation of Domestic and Foreign source dividends via Domestic CII**
Portfolio investment by Australia resident individual through Australian CII into

Row		AU	B	S	U.K.	US	F	G	It	L
1	Dividend payment (at source)	**100**	100	100	100	100	100	100	100	100
2	Tax credit (at source)	**56.25**	n.a.	n.a.	0[1]	n.a.	0	0	0	n.a.
3	Dividend plus gross-up (if any)	**156.25**	100	100	100	100	100	100	100	100
4	Foreign withholding tax	**n.a.**	15	15	0	15	15	15	15	30
	Domestic CII level									
5	Cash receipt	**100**	85	85	100	85	85	85	85	70
6	Tax paid by CII	**0**	0	0	0	0	0	0	0	0
7	Dividend distributed by CII	**100**	85	85	100	85	85	85	85	70
	Shareholder level (PIT@48.49%)									
8	Cash receipt	**100**	85	85	100	85	85	85	85	70
9	Grossed-up dividend	**156.25**	100	100	100	100	100	100	100	100
107	IT liability	**75.78**	48.5	48.5	48.5	48.5	48.5	48.5	48.5	48.5
118	less withholding tax credit	**n.a.**	15	15	0	15	15	15	15	30
129	less imputation credit	**56.25**	0	0	0	0	0	0	0	0
13	Tax due	**19.53**	33.5	33.5	48.5	33.5	33.5	33.5	33.5	18.5
14	**Net return**	**80.47**	**51.5**	**51.5**	**51.5**	**51.5**	**51.5**	**51.5**	**51.5**	**51.5**
15	**Net shareholder tax rate (%)**	**19.53**	**48.5**	**48.5**	**48.5**	**48.5**	**48.5**	**48.5**	**48.5**	**48.5**

AU = Australia, B = Belgium, S = Sweden, U.K. = United Kingdom, US = United States; F = France, G = Germany, It = Italy, L = Luxembourg.

(1) The U.K. provides imputation credits only on distributions paid directly to Australian resident *individuals* and does not withhold against portfolio dividends that do not attract an imputation credit.

Table AI.1.B **Taxation of Domestic and Foreign source dividends via Domestic CII**

Portfolio investment by Belgium resident individual through Belgian CII into

Row		AU	B	S	U.K.	US	F	G	It	L
1	Dividend payment (at source)	100	**100**	100	100	100	100	100	100	100
2	Tax credit (at source)	0	**n.a.**	n.a.	0	n.a.	0	0	0	n.a.
3	Dividend plus gross-up (if any)	100	**100**	100	100	100	100	100	100	100
4	Domestic/foreign withholding tax	0	**15**[(1)]	15	0	15	15	15	15	15
	Domestic CII level									
5	Cash receipt	100	**85**	85	100	85	85	85	85	85
6	Net CT paid by CII	0	**0**[(1)]	0	0	0	0	0	0	0
7	Domestic withholding tax on dividends from CII (15%)	15	**15**	12.75	15	12.75	12.75	12.75	12.75	12.75
8	Dividend distributed by CII	85	**85**	72.25	85	72.25	72.25	72.25	72.25	72.25
	Shareholder level (final WT@15%)									
9	Cash receipt	85	**85**	72.25	85	72.25	72.25	72.25	72.25	72.25
10	Grossed-up dividend	0	**n.a.**	n.a.	0	n.a.	0	0	0	n.a.
11	IT liability	0	**0**	0	0	0		0	0	0
12	less withholding tax credit	n.a.	**n.a.**	n.a.	n.a.	n.a.	n.a.	n.a.	n.a.	n.a.
13	Tax due	0	**0**	0	0	0		0	0	0
14	**Net return**	85	**85**	72.25	85	72.25	72.25	72.25	72.25	72.25
15	**Net shareholder tax rate (%)**	**15**	**15**	**27.75**	**15**	**27.75**	**27.75**	**27.75**	**27.75**	**27.75**

AU = Australia, B = Belgium, S = Sweden, U.K. = United Kingdom, US = United States; F = France, G = Germany, It = Italy, L = Luxembourg.

(1) The mutual fund is fully credited for the payment of withholding tax on dividends distributed by a domestic company.

Table AI.1.C **Taxation of Domestic and Foreign source dividends via Domestic CII**
Portfolio investment by Sweden resident individual through Swedish CII into

Row		AUS	B	S	U.K.	US	F	G	It	L
1	Dividend payment (at source)	100	100	**100**	100	100	100	100	100	100
2	Tax credit (at source)	0	n.a.	**n.a.**	0[(1)]	n.a.	50	0	0	n.a.
3	Dividend plus gross-up (if any)	100	100	**100**	100	100	150	100	100	100
4	Foreign withholding tax (15%)	0	15	**n.a.**	n.a.	15	22.5	15	15	15
	Domestic CII level									
5	Cash receipt	100	85	**100**	100	85	127.5	85	85	85
6	Net CT paid by CII	0	0	**0**	0	0	0	0	0	0
7	Dividend distributed by CII	100	85	**100**	100	85	127.5	85	85	85
	Shareholder level (PIT@30%)									
8	Cash receipt	100	85	**100**	100	85	127.5	85	85	85
9	Grossed-up dividend	100	100	**100**	100	100	150	100	100	100
10	IT liability	30	30	**30**	30	30	45	30	30	30
11	less withholding tax credit	0	15	**n.a.**	0	15	22.5	15	15	15
12	Tax due	30	15	**30**	30	15	22.5	15	15	15
13	**Net return**	**70**	**70**	70	**70**	**70**	**105**	**70**	**70**	**70**
14	**Net shareholder tax rate (%)**	**30**	**30**	**30**	**30**	**30**	**-5**	**30**	**30**	**30**

AU = Australia, B = Belgium, S = Sweden, U.K. = United Kingdom, US = United States; F = France, G = Germany, It = Italy, L = Luxembourg.

(1) The U.K. does not withhold against payments of portfolio dividends that do not attract an imputation credit (note that the U.K. denies imputation credits to (Swedish) open-ended funds (but provides them in certain cases to closed-end funds (e.g., U.S. case.)))

Table AI.1.D **Taxation of Domestic and Foreign source Dividends via domestic CII (AUT)**
Portfolio investment by U.K. resident individual through U.K. CII (AUT) into

Row	Country	AU	B	S	U.K.	US	F	G	It	L
1	Dividend payment (at source)	100	100	100	**100**	100	100	100	100	100
2	Tax credit (at source)	0	n.a.	n.a.	**25**[1]	n.a.	50	0	56.25	n.a.
3	Dividend plus gross-up (if any)	100	100	100	**125**	100	150	100	156.25	100
4	Foreign withholding tax	0	10 (10%)	5 (5%)	**n.a.**	15	22.5 (15%)	15	23.44 (15%)	15
	Domestic CII level									
5	Cash receipt	100	90	95	**100**	85	127.5	85	132.81	85
6	Grossed-up dividend	100	100	100	**125**	100	150	100	156.25	100
7	Corporate tax (20%)	20	20	20	**0**	20	30	20	31.25	20
8	less foreign tax credit	0	10	5	**n.a.**	15	22.5	15	23.44	15
9	Net CT paid by CII	20	10	15	**0**	5	7.5	5	7.81	5
10	Dividends distributed by CII	80	72	76	**100**	68	102	68	106.25	68
11	ACT (1/4 of distribution)	20	18	19	**25**[2]	17	25.5	17	26.56	17
12	ACT setoff/repayment	-20	-10	-15	**-25**[2]	-5	-7.5	-5	-7.81	-5
13	Surplus ACT	0	8	4	**0**	12	18	12	18.75	12
	Shareholder level (PIT@40%)									
14	Cash receipt	80	72	76	**100**	68	102	68	106.25	68
15	Tax credit(1/4 x cash receipt)	20	18	19	**25**	17	25.5	17	26.56	17
16	Grossed-up dividend	100	90	95	**125**	85	127.5	85	132.81	85
17	IT liability	40	36	38	**50**	34	51	34	53.13	34
18	less tax credit	20	18	19	**25**	17	25.5	17	26.56	17
19	Tax due	20	18	19	**25**	17	25.5	17	26.56	17
20	**Net return**	**60**	**54**	**57**	**75**	**51**	**76.5**	**51**	**79.7**	**51**
21	**Net shareholder tax rate (%)**	**40**	**46**	**43**	**25**	**49**	**23.5**	**49**	**20.3**	**49**

AU = Australia, B = Belgium, S = Sweden, U.K. = United Kingdom, US = United States; F = France, G = Germany, It = Italy, L = Luxembourg.

[1] FII = Franked investment income. [2] Where AUT receives dividends (franked investment income) from a U.K. company (see previous table) it is entitled to a tax credit equal to the rate of ACT paid by the U.K. company on the dividend in question. The credit for ACT can be set off against AUT tax liabilities or against the ACT levied on dividends of the unitholders.

Table AI.1.E **Taxation of Domestic and Foreign source Dividends via domestic CII (AIT)**

Portfolio investment by U.K. resident individual through U.K. CII (AIT) into

Row	Country	AU	B	S	**U.K.**	US	F	G	It	L
1	Dividend payment (at source)	100	100	100	**100**	100	100	100	100	100
2	Tax credit (at source)	0	n.a.	n.a.	**25**[1]	n.a.	50	0	56.25	n.a.
3	Dividend plus gross-up (if any)	100	100	100	**n.a.**	100	150	100	156.25	100
4	Foreign withholding tax	0	10 (10%)	5 (5%)	**n.a.**	15	22.5 (15%)	15	23.44 (15%)	15
	Domestic CII level									
5	Cash receipt	100	90	95	**100**	85	127.5	85	132.81	85
6	Grossed-up dividend	100	100	100	**125**	100	150	100	156.25	100
7	Corporate tax (33%)	33	33	33	**0**	33	49.5	33	51.56	33
8	less foreign tax credit	0	10	5	**n.a.**	15	22.5	15	23.44	15
9	Net CT paid by CII	33	23	28	**0**	18	27	18	28.13	18
10	Dividends distributed by CII	67	67	67	**100**	67	100.5	67	104.69	67
11	ACT (1/4*dividends distributed)	16.75	16.75	16.75	**25**[2]	16.75	25.13	16.75	26.17	16.75
12	ACT setoff/repayment	-16.76	-16.76	-16.76	**-25**[2]	-16.76	-25.13	-16.76	-26.17	-16.76
13	Surplus ACT	0	0	0	**0**	0	0	0	0	0
	Shareholder level (PIT@40%)									
14	Cash receipt	67	67	67	**100**	67	100.5	67	104.69	67
15	Tax credit(1/4*cash receipt)	16.75	16.75	16.76	**25**	16.75	25.13	16.75	26.17	16.75
16	Grossed-up dividend	83.75	83.75	83.75	**125**	83.75	125.63	83.75	130.86	83.75
17	IT liability	33.5	33.5	33.5	**50**	33.5	50.25	33.5	52.34	33.5
18	less tax credit	16.75	16.75	16.75	**25**	16.75	25.13	16.75	26.17	16.75
19	Tax due	16.75	16.75	16.75	**25**	16.75	25.13	16.75	26.17	16.75
20	**Net return**	**50.25**	**50.25**	**50.25**	**75**	**50.25**	**75.38**	**50.25**	**78.52**	**50.25**
21	**Net shareholder tax rate (%)**	**49.75**	**49.75**	**49.75**	**25**	**49.75**	**24.62**	**49.75**	**21.48**	**49.75**

AU = Australia, B = Belgium, S = Sweden, U.K. = United Kingdom, US = United States; F = France, G = Germany, It = Italy, L = Luxembourg.

[1] FII = Franked investment income. [2] Where AIT receives dividends (franked investment income) from a U.K. company (see previous table) it is entitled to a tax credit equal to the rate of ACT paid by the U.K. company on the dividend in question. The credit for ACT can be set off against AIT tax liabilities or against the ACT levied on dividends of the unitholders.

Table AI.1.F **Taxation of Domestic and Foreign source dividends via Domestic CII**

Portfolio investment by U.S. resident individual through U.S. CII into

Row		AU	B	S	U.K.	US	F	G	It	L
1	Dividend payment (at source)	100	100	100	100	**100**	100	100	100	100
2	Tax credit (at source)	0	n.a.	n.a.	25	**n.a.**	50	5.88	0	n.a.
3	Dividend plus gross-up (if any)	100	n.a.	100	125	**n.a.**	150	105.88	100	100
4	Foreign withholding tax	0	15	15	18.75	**n.a.**	22.5	15.88	15	15
					(15%)		(15%)	(15%)		
	Domestic CII-level tax									
5	Cash receipt	100	85	85	106.25	**100**	127.5	90	85	85
6	Net CT paid by CII	0	0	0	0	**0**	0	0	0	0
7	Dividend distributed by CII	100	85	85	106.25	**100**	127.5	90	85	85
	Shareholder- level tax (46.6% rate)									
8	Cash receipt	100	85	85	106.25	**100**	127.5	90	85	85
9	Grossed-up dividend	100	100	100	125	**n.a.**	150	105.88	100	100
10	IT liability	46.6	46.6	46.6	58.25	**46.6**	69.9	49.34	46.6	46.6
11	less withholding tax credit	0	15	15	18.75	**n.a.**	22.5	15.88	15	15
12	Tax due	46.6	31.6	31.6	39.5	**46.6**	47.4	33.46	31.6	31.6
13	**Net return**	**53.4**	**53.4**	**53.4**	**66.75**	**53.4**	**80.1**	**56.54**	**53.4**	**53.4**
14	**Net shareholder tax rate (%)**	**46.6**	**46.6**	**46.6**	**33.25**	**46.6**	**19.9**	**43.46**	**46.6**	**46.6**

AU = Australia, B = Belgium, S = Sweden, U.K. = United Kingdom, US = United States; F = France, G = Germany, It = Italy, L = Luxembourg.

Table AI.2.A **Taxation of Foreign source dividends via Foreign CII (two-country case)**

Portfolio investment by Australian resident individual through foreign CII in shares of foreign company both resident in:

Row		AU	B	S	U.K.	US	F	G	It	L
1	Dividend payment (at source)	n.a.	100	100	100	100	100	100	100	100
	Foreign CII level									
2	Cash receipt	n.a.	100	100	100	100	100	100	100	100
3	Tax paid by CII	n.a.	0	0	0	0	0	0	0	0
4	Dividend payment by CII	n.a.	100	100	100	100	100	100	100	100
5	Tax credit (at source)	n.a.	n.a.	n.a.	25	n.a.	0	0	0	n.a.
6	Dividend plus gross-up (if any)	n.a.	100	100	125	100	100	100	100	100
7	Foreign withholding tax	n.a.	15	15	18.75[(1)]	15	15	15	15	30
	Shareholder level (PIT@48.49%)									
8	Cash receipt	n.a.	85	85	106.25	85	85	85	85	70
9	Grossed-up dividend	n.a.	100	100	125	100	100	100	100	100
10	IT liability	n.a.	48.49	48.49	60.61	48.49	48.49	48.49	48.49	48.49
11	less withholding tax credit	n.a.	15	15	18.750	15	15	15	15	30
12	Tax due	n.a.	33.49	33.49	41.86	33.49	33.49	33.49	33.49	18.49
13	**Net return**	n.a.	**51.51**	**51.51**	**64.39**	**51.51**	**51.51**	**51.51**	**51.51**	**51.51**
14	**Net shareholder tax rate (%)**	n.a.	**48.49**	**48.49**	**35.61**	**48.49**	**48.49**	**48.49**	**48.49**	**48.49**

AU = Australia, B = Belgium, S = Sweden, U.K. = United Kingdom, US = United States; F = France, G = Germany, It = Italy, L = Luxembourg.

(1) The U.K. provides imputation credits on distributions paid directly to Australian resident *individuals* and withhold against such payments at 15%.

Table AI.2.B **Taxation of Foreign source dividends via Foreign CII (two-country case)**

Portfolio investment by Belgian resident individual through foreign CII in shares of foreign company both resident in:

Row		AU	B	S	U.K.	US	F	G	It	L
1	Dividend payment (at source)	100	n.a.	100	100	100	100	100	100	100
	Foreign CII level									
2	Cash receipt	100	n.a.	100	100	100	100	100	100	100
3	Tax paid by CII	0	n.a.	0	0	0	0	0	0	0
4	Dividend payment by CII	100	n.a.	100	100	100	100	100	100	100
5	Tax credit (at source)	n.a.	n.a.	n.a.	0	n.a.	0	0	0	0
6	Dividend plus gross-up (if any)	100	n.a.	100	100	100	100	100	100	100
7	Foreign withholding tax	0	n.a.	15	0	15	15	15	15	15
	Shareholder level (PIT@25%)[1]									
8	Cash receipt	100	n.a.	85	100	85	85	85	85	85
9	Grossed-up dividend	n.a.	n.a.	n.a.	n.a.	n.a.	n.a.	n.a.	n.a.	n.a.
10	IT liability	25	n.a.	21.25	25	21.25	21.25	21.25	21.25	21.25
11	less withholding tax credit	0	n.a.	0	0	0	0	0	0	0
12	Tax due	25	n.a.	21.25	25	21.25	21.25	21.25	21.25	21.25
13	**Net return**	**75**	n.a.	**63.75**	**75**	**63.75**	**63.75**	**63.75**	**63.75**	**63.75**
14	**Net shareholder tax rate (%)**	**25**	n.a.	**36.25**	**25**	**36.25**	**36.25**	**36.25**	**36.25**	**36.25**

AU = Australia, B = Belgium, S = Sweden, U.K. = United Kingdom, US = United States; F = France, G = Germany, It = Italy, L = Luxembourg.

(1) Belgium applies a flat 25% rate to foreign source dividend income, with no foreign tax credit.

Table AI.2.C **Taxation of Foreign source dividends via Foreign CII (two-country case)**

Portfolio investment by Swedish resident individual through foreign CII in shares of foreign company both resident in:

Row		AU	B	S	U.K.	US	F	G	It	L
1	Dividend payment (at source)	100	100	n.a.	100	100	100	100	100	100
	Foreign CII level									
2	Cash receipt	100	100	n.a.	100	100	100	100	100	100
3	Tax paid by CII	0	0	n.a.	0	0	0	0	0	0
4	Dividend payment by CII	100	100	n.a.	100	100	100	100	100	100
5	Tax credit (at source)	n.a.	n.a.	n.a.	25	n.a.	50	0	0	0
6	Dividend plus gross-up (if any)	100	100	n.a.	125	100	150	100	100	100
7	Foreign withholding tax	0	15	n.a.	18.75[(1)]	15	22.5	15	15	15
	Shareholder level (PIT@30%)									
8	Cash receipt	100	85	n.a.	106.25	85	127.5	85	85	85
9	Grossed-up dividend	100	100	n.a.	125	100	150	100	100	100
10	IT liability	30	30	n.a.	37.5	30	45	30	30	30
11	less withholding tax credit	0	15	n.a.	18.75	15	22.5	15	15	15
12	Tax due	30	15	n.a.	18.75	15	22.5	15	15	15
13	**Net return**	**70**	**70**	n.a.	**87.5**	**70**	**105**	**70**	**70**	**70**
14	**Net shareholder tax rate (%)**	**30**	**30**	n.a.	**18.75**	**30**	**-5**	**30**	**30**	**30**

AU = Australia, B = Belgium, S = Sweden, U.K. = United Kingdom, US = United States; F = France, G = Germany, It = Italy, L = Luxembourg.

(1) The U.K. provides imputation credits on distributions paid directly to Swedish resident individuals and withhold against such payments at 15%.

Table AI.2.D **Taxation of Foreign source dividends via Foreign CII (two-country case)**

Portfolio investment by U.K. resident individual through foreign CII in shares of foreign company both resident in:

Row		AU	B	S	U.K.	US	F	G	It	L
1	Dividend payment (at source)	100	100	100	n.a.	100	100	100	100	100
	Foreign CII level									
2	Cash receipt	100	100	100	n.a.	100	100	100	100	100
3	Tax paid by CII	0	0	0	n.a.	0	0	0	0	0
4	Dividend payment by CII	100	100	100	n.a.	100	100	100	100	100
5	Tax credit (at source)	n.a.	n.a.	n.a.	n.a.	n.a.	50	0	56.25	0
6	Dividend plus gross-up (if any)	100	100	100	n.a.	100	150	100	156.25	100
7	Foreign withholding tax	0	15	5	n.a.	15	22.5	15	23.44	15
	Shareholder level (PIT@40%)									
8	Cash receipt	100	85	95	n.a.	85	127.5	85	132.81	85
9	Grossed-up dividend	100	100	100	n.a.	100	150	100	156.25	100
10	IT liability	40	40	40	n.a.	40	60	40	62.5	40
11	less withholding tax credit	0	15	5	n.a.	15	22.5	15	23.44	15
12	Tax due	40	25	35	n.a.	25	37.5	25	39.06	25
13	**Net return**	**60**	**60**	**60**	n.a.	**60**	**90**	**60**	**93.75**	**60**
14	**Net shareholder tax rate (%)**	**40**	**40**	**40**	n.a.	**40**	**10**	**40**	**6.25**	**40**

AU = Australia, B = Belgium, S = Sweden, U.K. = United Kingdom, US = United States; F = France, G = Germany, It = Italy, L = Luxembourg.

Table AI.2.E **Taxation of Foreign source dividends via Foreign CII (two-country case)**

Portfolio investment by U.S. resident individual through foreign CII in shares of foreign company both resident in:

Row		AU	B	S	U.K.	US	F	G	It	L
1	Dividend payment (at source)	100	100	100	100	n.a.	100	100	100	100
	Foreign CII level									
2	Cash receipt	100	100	100	100	n.a.	100	100	100	100
3	Tax paid by CII	0	0	0	0	n.a.	0	0	0	0
4	Dividend payment by CII	100	100	100	100	n.a.	100	100	100	100
5	Tax credit (at source)	n.a.	n.a.	n.a.	25	n.a.	50	5.88	0	0
6	Dividend plus gross-up (if any)	100	100	100	125	n.a.	150	105.88	100	100
7	Foreign withholding tax	0	15	15	18.75(1)	n.a.	22.5	15.88	15	15
	Shareholder level (PIT@46.6%)									
8	Cash receipt	100	85	85	106.25	n.a.	127.5	90	85	85
9	Grossed-up dividend	100	100	100	125	n.a.	150	105.88	100	100
10	IT liability	46.6	46.6	46.6	58.25	n.a.	69.9	49.34	46.6	46.6
11	less withholding tax credit	0	15	15	18.75	n.a.	22.5	15.88	15	15
12	Tax due	46.6	31.6	31.6	39.5	n.a.	47.4	33.46	31.6	31.6
13	**Net return**	**53.4**	**53.4**	**53.4**	**66.75**	n.a.	**80.1**	**56.54**	**53.4**	**53.4**
14	**Net shareholder tax rate (%)**	**46.6**	**46.6**	**46.6**	**33.25**	n.a.	**19.9**	**43.46**	**46.6**	**46.6**

AU = Australia, B = Belgium, S = Sweden, U.K. = United Kingdom, US = United States; F = France, G = Germany, It = Italy, L = Luxembourg.

(1) The U.K. provides imputation credits on distributions paid directly to U.S. resident individuals and withhold against such payments at 15%.

Table AI.3.A **Taxation of Foreign source dividends via Foreign CII (three-country case)**

Portfolio investment by Australian resident individual through CII resident in third country in shares of foreign company resident in:

Row		AU	B	S	U.K.	US	F	G	It	L
1	Dividend payment (at source)	n.a.	100	100	100	100	100	100	100	100
2	Foreign withholding tax	n.a.	15	15	0	15	15	15	15	30
	Foreign CII level									
3	Cash receipt	n.a.	85	85	100	85	85	85	85	70
4	Tax paid by CII	n.a.	0	0	0	0	0	0	0	0
5	Dividend payment by CII	n.a.	85	85	100	85	85	85	85	70
6	Foreign withholding tax (@15%)	n.a.	12.75	12.75	15	12.75	12.75	12.75	12.75	10.5
	Shareholder level (PIT@48.49%)									
7	Cash receipt	n.a.	72.25	72.25	85	72.25	72.25	72.25	72.25	59.5
8	Grossed-up dividend	n.a.	85	85	100	85	85	85	85	70
9	IT liability	n.a.	41.22	41.22	48.5	41.22	41.22	41.22	41.22	33.94
10	less withholding tax credit	n.a.	12.75	12.75	15	12.75	12.75	12.75	12.75	10.5
11	Tax due	n.a.	28.47	28.47	33.5	28.47	28.47	28.47	28.47	23.44
12	**Net return**	n.a.	**43.78**	**43.78**	**51.5**	**43.78**	**43.78**	**43.78**	**43.78**	**36.06**
13	**Net shareholder tax rate (%)**	n.a.	**56.22**	**56.22**	**48.5**	**56.22**	**56.22**	**56.22**	**56.22**	**63.94**

AU = Australia, B = Belgium, S = Sweden, U.K. = United Kingdom, US = United States; F = France, G = Germany, It = Italy, L = Luxembourg.

Table AI.3.B **Taxation of Foreign source dividends via Foreign CII (three-country case)**

Portfolio investment by Belgian resident individual through CII resident in third country in shares of foreign company resident in:

Row		AU	B	S	U.K.	US	F	G	It	L
1	Dividend payment (at source)	100	n.a.	100	100	100	100	100	100	100
2	Foreign withholding tax	0	n.a.	15	0	15	15	15	15	30
	Foreign CII level									
3	Cash receipt	100	n.a.	85	100	85	85	85	85	70
4	Tax paid by CII	0	n.a.	0	0	0	0	0	0	0
5	Dividend payment by CII	100	n.a.	85	100	85	85	85	85	70
6	Foreign withholding tax (@15%)	15	n.a.	12.75	15	12.75	12.75	12.75	12.75	10.5
	Shareholder level (PIT@25%)[1]									
7	Cash receipt	100	n.a.	72.25	85	72.25	72.25	72.25	72.25	59.5
8	Grossed-up dividend	n.a.	n.a.	n.a.	n.a.	n.a.	n.a.	n.a.	n.a.	n.a.
9	IT liability	21.25	n.a.	18.06	21.25	18.06	18.06	18.06	18.06	14.88
10	less withholding tax credit	0	n.a.	0	0	0	0	0	0	0
11	Tax due	21.25	n.a.	18.06	21.25	18.06	18.06	18.06	18.06	14.88
12	**Net return**	**63.75**	n.a.	**54.19**	**63.75**	**54.19**	**54.19**	**54.19**	**54.19**	**44.62**
13	**Net shareholder tax rate (%)**	**36.75**	n.a.	**45.81**	**36.25**	**45.81**	**45.81**	**45.81**	**45.81**	**55.38**

AU = Australia, B = Belgium, S = Sweden, U.K. = United Kingdom, US = United States; F = France, G = Germany, It = Italy, L = Luxembourg.

(1) Belgium applies a flat 25% rate to foreign source dividend income, with no foreign tax credit.

Table AI.3.C **Taxation of Foreign source dividends via Foreign CII (three-country case)**

Portfolio investment by Swedish resident individual through CII resident in third country in shares of foreign company resident in:

Row		AU	B	S	U.K.	US	F	G	It	L
1	Dividend payment (at source)	100	100	n.a.	100	100	100	100	100	100
2	Foreign withholding tax	0	15	n.a.	0	15	15	15	15	30
	Foreign CII level									
3	Cash receipt	100	85	n.a.	100	85	85	85	85	70
4	Tax paid by CII	0	0	n.a.	0	0	0	0	0	0
5	Dividend payment by CII	100	85	n.a.	100	85	85	85	85	70
6	Foreign withholding tax (@15%)	15	12.75	n.a.	15	12.75	12.75	12.75	12.75	10.5
	Shareholder level (PIT@30%)									
7	Cash receipt	85	72.25	n.a.	85	72.25	72.25	72.25	72.25	59.5
8	Grossed-up dividend	100	85	n.a.	100	85	85	85	85	70
9	IT liability	30	25.5	n.a.	30	25.5	25.5	25.5	25.5	21
10	less withholding tax credit	15	12.75	n.a.	15	12.75	12.75	12.75	12.75	10.5
11	Tax due	15	12.75		15	12.75	12.75	12.75	12.75	10.5
12	**Net return**	**70**	**59.5**	n.a.	**70**	**59.5**	**59.5**	**59.5**	**59.5**	**49**
13	**Net shareholder tax rate (%)**	**30**	**40.5**	n.a.	**30**	**40.5**	**40.5**	**40.5**	**40.5**	**51**

AU = Australia, B = Belgium, S = Sweden, U.K. = United Kingdom, US = United States; F = France, G = Germany, It = Italy, L = Luxembourg.

Table AI.3.D **Taxation of Foreign source dividends via Foreign CII (three-country case)**

Portfolio investment by U.K. resident individual through CII resident in third country in shares of foreign company resident in:

Row		AU	B	S	U.K.	US	F	G	It	L
1	Dividend payment (at source)	100	100	100	n.a.	100	100	100	100	100
2	Foreign withholding tax	0	15	15	n.a.	15	15	15	15	30
	Foreign CII level									
3	Cash receipt	100	85	85	n.a.	85	85	85	85	70
4	Tax paid by CII	0	0	0	n.a.	0	0	0	0	0
5	Dividend payment by CII	100	85	85	n.a.	85	85	85	85	70
6	Foreign withholding tax (@15%)	15	12.75	12.75	n.a.	12.75	12.75	12.75	12.75	10.5
	Shareholder level (PIT@40%)									
7	Cash receipt	85	72.25	72.25	n.a.	72.25	72.25	72.25	72.25	59.5
8	Grossed-up dividend	100	85	85	n.a.	85	85	85	85	70
9	IT liability	40	34	34	n.a.	34	34	34	34	28
10	less withholding tax credit	15	12.75	12.75	n.a.	12.75	12.75	12.75	12.75	10.5
11	Tax due	25	21.25	21.25	n.a.	21.25	21.25	21.25	21.25	17.5
12	**Net return**	**60**	**51**	**51**	n.a.	**51**	**51**	**51**	**51**	**42**
13	**Net shareholder tax rate (%)**	**40**	**49**	**49**	n.a.	**49**	**49**	**49**	**49**	**58**

AU = Australia, B = Belgium, S = Sweden, U.K. = United Kingdom, US = United States; F = France, G = Germany, It = Italy, L = Luxembourg.

Table AI.3.E **Taxation of Foreign source dividends via Foreign CII (three-country case)**

Portfolio investment by U.S. resident individual through CII resident in third country in shares of foreign company resident in:

Row		AU	B	S	U.K.	US	F	G	It	L
1	Dividend payment (at source)	100	100	100	100	n.a.	100	100	100	100
2	Foreign withholding tax	0	15	15	0	n.a.	15	15	15	30
	Foreign CII level									
3	Cash receipt	100	85	85	100	n.a.	85	85	85	70
4	Tax paid by CII	0	0	0	0	n.a.	0	0	0	0
5	Dividend payment by CII	100	85	85	100	n.a.	85	85	85	70
6	Foreign withholding tax (@15%)	15	12.75	12.75	15	n.a.	12.75	12.75	12.75	10.5
	Shareholder level (PIT@46.6%)									
7	Cash receipt	85	72.25	72.25	85	n.a.	72.25	72.25	72.25	59.5
8	Grossed-up dividend	100	85	85	100	n.a.	85	85	85	70
9	IT liability	46.6	39.6	39.6	46.6	n.a.	39.6	39.6	39.6	32.6
10	less withholding tax credit	15	12.75	12.75	15	n.a.	12.75	12.75	12.75	10.5
11	Tax due	31.6	26.86	26.86	31.6	n.a.	26.86	26.86	26.86	22.1
12	**Net return**	**53.4**	**45.4**	**45.4**	**53.4**	n.a.	**45.4**	**45.4**	**45.4**	**37.4**
13	**Net shareholder tax rate (%)**	**46.6**	**54.6**	**54.6**	**46.6**	n.a.	**54.6**	**54.6**	**54.6**	**62.6**

AU = Australia, B = Belgium, S = Sweden, U.K. = United Kingdom, US = United States; F = France, G = Germany, It = Italy, L = Luxembourg.

Table AI.4.A **Taxation of Foreign source dividends via 'Offshore' CII (three-country case) in absence of PFIF (anti-deferral) rules**

Portfolio investment by Australian resident individual through 'off-shore' CII in shares of foreign company resident in:

Row	*Ten Year Holding Period*	AU	B	S	U.K.	US	F	G	It	L
	Year 1									
1	Dividend payment (at source)	100	100	100	100	100	100	100	100	100
2	Tax credit (at source)	n.a.	n.a.	n.a.	0	n.a.	0	0	0	n.a.
3	Dividend plus gross-up (if any)	100	100	100	100	100	100	100	100	100
4	Foreign withholding tax	0	15	15	0	15	15	15	15	30
	Foreign CII level									
5	Cash receipt	100	85	85	100	85	85	85	85	70
6	Tax paid by CII	0	0	0	0	0	0	0	0	0
	Year 10									
7	Dividend distributed by CII	100	85	85	100	85	85	85	85	70
8	Foreign withholding tax	0	0	0	0	0	0	0	0	0
	Shareholder level (PIT@48.49%)									
9	Cash receipt	100	85	85	100	85	85	85	85	70
10	Grossed-up dividend	100	85	85	100	85	85	85	85	70
11	IT liability	48.49	41.22	41.22	48.49	41.22	41.22	41.22	41.22	33.94
12	less withholding tax credit	0	0	0	0	0	0	0	0	0
13	Tax due (year 10)	48.49	41.22	41.22	48.49	41.22	41.22	41.22	41.22	33.94
14	**Present value of PIT due (year 10)**	**30.86**	**26.23**	**26.23**	**30.86**	**26.23**	**26.23**	**26.23**	**26.23**	**21.60**
15	**Net shareholder tax rate (%) (P.V.)**	**30.86**	**41.23**	**41.23**	**30.86**	**41.23**	**41.23**	**41.23**	**41.23**	**51.60**

AU = Australia, B = Belgium, S = Sweden, U.K. = United Kingdom, US = United States; F = France, G = Germany, It = Italy, L = Luxembourg.

Table AI.4.B **Taxation of Foreign source dividends via 'Offshore' CII (three-country case) in absence of PFIF (anti-deferral) rules**

Portfolio investment by Belgian resident individual through 'off-shore' CII in shares of foreign company resident in:

Row	*Ten Year Holding Period*	AU	B	S	U.K.	US	F	G	It	L
	Year 1									
1	Dividend payment (at source)	100	100	100	100	100	100	100	100	100
2	Tax credit (at source)	n.a.	n.a.	n.a.	0	n.a.	0	0	0	n.a.
3	Dividend plus gross-up (if any)	100	100	100	100	100	100	100	100	100
4	Foreign withholding tax	0	15	15	0	15	15	15	15	30
	Foreign CII level									
5	Cash receipt	100	85	85	100	85	85	85	85	70
6	Tax paid by CII	0	0	0	0	0	0	0	0	0
	Year 10									
7	Dividend distributed by CII	100	85	85	100	85	85	85	85	70
8	Foreign withholding tax	0	0	0	0	0	0	0	0	0
	Shareholder level (PIT@25%)									
9	Cash receipt	100	85	85	100	85	85	85	85	70
10	Grossed-up dividend	100	85	85	100	85	85	85	85	70
11	IT liability	25	21.25	21.25	25	21.25	21.25	21.25	21.25	17.5
12	less withholding tax credit	0	0	0	0	0	0	0	0	0
13	Tax due (year 10)	25	21.25	21.25	25	21.25	21.25	21.25	21.25	17.5
14	**Present value of PIT due (year 10)**	**13.04**	**11.08**	**11.08**	**13.04**	**11.08**	**11.08**	**11.08**	**11.08**	**9.13**
15	**Net shareholder tax rate (%) (P.V.)**	**13.04**	**26.08**	**26.08**	**13.04**	**26.08**	**26.08**	**26.08**	**26.08**	**39.13**

AU = Australia, B = Belgium, S = Sweden, U.K. = United Kingdom, US = United States; F = France, G = Germany, It = Italy, L = Luxembourg.

Table AI.4.C **Taxation of Foreign source dividends via 'Offshore' CII (three-country case) in absence of PFIF (anti-deferral) rules**

Portfolio investment by Swedish resident individual through 'off-shore' CII in shares of foreign company resident in:

Row	*Ten Year Holding Period*	AU	B	S	U.K.	US	F	G	It	L
	Year 1									
1	Dividend payment (at source)	100	100	100	100	100	100	100	100	100
2	Tax credit (at source)	n.a.	n.a.	n.a.	0	n.a.	0	0	0	n.a.
3	Dividend plus gross-up (if any)	100	100	100	100	100	100	100	100	100
4	Foreign withholding tax	0	15	15	0	15	15	15	15	30
	Foreign CII level									
5	Cash receipt	100	85	85	100	85	85	85	85	70
6	Tax paid by CII	0	0	0	0	0	0	0	0	0
	Year 10									
7	Dividend distributed by CII	100	85	85	100	85	85	85	85	70
8	Foreign withholding tax	0	0	0	0	0	0	0	0	0
	Shareholder level (PIT@30%)									
9	Cash receipt	100	85	85	100	85	85	85	85	70
10	Grossed-up dividend	100	85	85	100	85	85	85	85	70
11	IT liability	30	25.5	25.5	30	25.5	25.5	25.5	25.5	21
12	less withholding tax credit	0	0	0	0	0	0	0	0	0
13	Tax due (year 10)	30	25.5	25.5	30	25.5	25.5	25.5	25.5	21
14	**Present value of PIT due (year 10)**	**16.32**	**13.87**	**13.87**	**16.32**	**13.87**	**13.87**	**13.87**	**13.87**	**11.42**
15	**Net shareholder tax rate (%) (P.V.)**	**16.32**	**28.87**	**28.87**	**16.32**	**28.87**	**28.87**	**28.87**	**28.87**	**41.42**

AU = Australia, B = Belgium, S = Sweden, U.K. = United Kingdom, US = United States; F = France, G = Germany, It = Italy, L = Luxembourg.

Table AI.4.D **Taxation of Foreign source dividends via 'Offshore' CII (three-country case) in absence of PFIF (anti-deferral) rules**

Portfolio investment by U.K. resident individual through 'off-shore' CII in shares of foreign company resident in:

Row	*Ten Year Holding Period*	AU	B	S	U.K.	US	F	G	It	L
	Year 1									
1	Dividend payment (at source)	100	100	100	100	100	100	100	100	100
2	Tax credit (at source)	n.a.	n.a.	n.a.	0	n.a.	0	0	0	n.a.
3	Dividend plus gross-up (if any)	100	100	100	100	100	100	100	100	100
4	Foreign withholding tax	0	15	15	0	15	15	15	15	30
	Foreign CII level									
5	Cash receipt	100	85	85	100	85	85	85	85	70
6	Tax paid by CII	0	0	0	0	0	0	0	0	0
	Year 10									
7	Dividend distributed by CII	100	85	85	100	85	85	85	85	70
8	Foreign withholding tax	0	0	0	0	0	0	0	0	0
	Shareholder level (PIT@40%)									
9	Cash receipt	100	85	85	100	85	85	85	85	70
10	Grossed-up dividend	100	85	85	100	85	85	85	85	70
11	IT liability	40	34	34	40	34	34	34	34	28
12	less withholding tax credit	0	0	0	0	0	0	0	0	0
13	Tax due (year 10)	40	34	34	40	34	34	34	34	28
14	**Present value of PIT due (year 10)**	**23.68**	**20.12**	**20.12**	**23.68**	**20.12**	**20.12**	**20.12**	**20.12**	**16.57**
15	**Net shareholder tax rate (%) (P.V.)**	**23.68**	**35.12**	**35.12**	**23.68**	**35.12**	**35.12**	**35.12**	**35.12**	**46.57**

AU = Australia, B = Belgium, S = Sweden, U.K. = United Kingdom, US = United States; F = France, G = Germany, It = Italy, L = Luxembourg.

Table AI.4.E **Taxation of Foreign source dividends via 'Offshore' CII (three-country case) in absence of PFIF (anti-deferral) rules**

Portfolio investment by U.S. resident individual through 'off-shore' CII in shares of foreign company resident in:

Row	*Ten Year Holding Period*	AU	B	S	U.K.	US	F	G	It	L
	Year 1									
1	Dividend payment (at source)	100	100	100	100	100	100	100	100	100
2	Tax credit (at source)	n.a.	n.a.	n.a.	0	n.a.	0	0	0	n.a.
3	Dividend plus gross-up (if any)	100	100	100	100	100	100	100	100	100
4	Foreign withholding tax	0	15	15	0	15	15	15	15	30
	Foreign CII level									
5	Cash receipt	100	85	85	100	85	85	85	85	70
6	Tax paid by CII	0	0	0	0	0	0	0	0	0
	Year 10									
7	Dividend distributed by CII	100	85	85	100	85	85	85	85	70
8	Foreign withholding tax	0	0	0	0	0	0	0	0	0
	Shareholder level (PIT@46.6%)									
9	Cash receipt	100	85	85	100	85	85	85	85	70
10	Grossed-up dividend	100	85	85	100	85	85	85	85	70
11	IT liability	46.6	39.61	39.61	46.6	39.61	39.61	39.61	39.61	32.62
12	less withholding tax credit	0	0	0	0	0	0	0	0	0
13	Tax due (year 10)	46.6	39.61	39.61	46.6	39.61	39.61	39.61	39.61	32.62
14	**Present value of PIT due (year 10)**	**29.18**	**24.8**	**24.8**	**29.18**	**24.8**	**24.8**	**24.8**	**24.8**	**20.42**
15	**Net shareholder tax rate (%) (P.V.)**	**29.18**	**39.8**	**39.8**	**29.18**	**39.8**	**39.8**	**39.8**	**39.8**	**50.42**

AU = Australia, B = Belgium, S = Sweden, U.K. = United Kingdom, US = United States; F = France, G = Germany, It = Italy, L = Luxembourg.

Appendix II

COUNTRY RULES APPLICABLE TO TAXATION OF DOMESTIC SOURCE INCOME

Table AII.1 **Legal form and domestic regulation of CIIs**

Country	Type(s) of investment fund(2)	Description	Form of investment	Regulatory framework	Removal from fund	Brief overview of general principles of tax treatment of fund and participant (greater detail in following tables)	Relative importance of financial assets	Type of investor and relative importance
Australia	Unit Trust	A trust where the interests of beneficiaries are divided into equal sub-interests (called units) in the income and assets of the trust.	Unit; i.e. the investor's proportional interest in the income and assets of the trust.	Australian company legislation has since the 1930s contained provisions strictly controlling investment companies which is viewed by most investment managers as too rigid for the effective operation of collective investments. This regime was not applied to unit trusts although public marketing of unit trusts does attract considerable regulation designed to protect investors.	Sale of the unit on the market to another investor, or redemption by the trustee of the trust.	The trust is not a tax entity but the net taxable income is calculated at trust level. Each unitholder is subject to tax on his/her share of the income and net capital gains of the trust at the year end, regardless of whether a distribution has been made. As a result, a unit trust is treated as a conduit for tax purposes.	Total financial assets at end '95 as a per cent of GDP: 75.9%.	Total financial assets by type of investor at end '95: Invest. fund: 12%; Pens. Fund 18%; Life insurance: 32.2%; others: 37.8%
Belgium	The most common type of fund is SICAV (open-ended investment company)	Incorporated entity with a variable paid-in capital whose legal purpose is to invest and manage a portfolio of investment securities, and where the purchase of units results in a contribution to the capital of the company.	Units of two types: Capitalisation units: the investor obtains income by selling the units; Dividend paying units: the share of profits due to the dividend-earning units must be distributed: the investor then obtains a dividend.	Subject to all the relevant provisions of the co-ordinated laws on commercial companies. Must register with Banking and Financial Commission. This registration in fact means that the management or investment undertaking has been authorised and that its management rules or instruments of incorporation have been accepted. Second, the Commission has general supervisory powers over investment undertakings	Sale of the units.	SICAV are corporate entities and are therefore liable to corporation tax. The tax base is, however, limited: reserved and distributed profits are not liable to corporation tax and the tax base therefore includes only rejected costs (non-approved expenditure) and abnormal benefits.	Total financial assets at end '96 as a per cent of GDP: 11.4%.	Total financial assets by type of investor: Invest. fund: 40%; Pens. Fund: 5%; Life insurance: 25%; others: 30%

Table AII.1 (cont'd) **Legal form and domestic regulation of CIIs**

Country	Type(s) of investment fund(2)	Description	Form of investment	Regulatory framework	Removal from fund	Brief overview of general principles of tax treatment of fund and participant (greater detail in following tables)	Relative importance of financial assets	Type of investor and relative importance
Germany	Investment fund (Sondervermogen)	The investment fund can be either general (retail) or special (i.e. a fund in which unit certificates are held by no more than 10 unit holders who are not natural persons). The investment fund is managed by an investment company (Kapitalanlage-gesellschaft) with minimum paid up capital of DM 3m and with registered office and head office situated in Germany.	Participation in the fund takes the form of a unit certificate.	Act on Investment Companies Act on the marketing of foreign investment units and concerning the taxation of income from foreign investment units. In the case of the management company: Regulations for credit institutions (Sec 1(1) No. 6 Banking Act).	Redemption by fund.	The fund is regarded in principle as transparent. The fund is a tax subject for corporate tax purposes. Its income is exempt, except that it pays corporate tax on dividends from German companies and gets a credit for the corporation tax paid by the dividend distributing company. There is a withholding tax of 25% on dividends which is refunded to the fund on application. Other income of the fund is taxed as if received without interposing the fund except that with accumulated income there may be a difference in the time of taxation of the unitholder. In general there is no difference in treatment between distributed and undistributed income of the fund.	Total financial assets at end '95 as a per cent of GDP: 46%.	Total financial assets by type of investor at end '95: Invest. fund: 33%; Pens. Fund: 6%; Life insurance: 42%; others: 15%
Japan	Security Investment Trust	Trust-type open-ended structure. There are different types; e.g. bond trusts and stock trusts.	Investors acquire trust beneficiary certificates which are redeemable.	Securities Investment Trust Law. Investment Trust Management Companies must be licensed by the Minister of Finance.	Investors may exit from the investment by disposal or redemption.	The trust is not an independent taxable entity and tax is not imposed at trust level. Investors are taxed when they receive a distribution from the trust. Characterisation of income depends on trust type; e.g. distributions from bond trusts are income; distributions from stock trusts are dividends. Such distributions, because they are either income or dividend income, are subject to a flat 20% withholding tax at source.	Total financial assets at end '95 as a percent of GDP: 77.4%.	Total financial assets by type of investor at end '95: Invest. fund: 13%; Pens. Fund: 0%; Life insurance: 46%; others 41%:

Table AII.1 (cont'd) **Legal form and domestic regulation of CIIs**

Country	Type(s) of investment fund	Description	Form of investment	Regulatory framework	Removal from fund	Brief overview of general principles of tax treatment of fund and participant (greater detail in following tables)	Relative importance of financial assets	Type of investor and relative importance
Sweden	Mutual Fund (open ended)	The open mutual fund is not a legal entity. It is constructed in three part contractual form: a managing company that manages the portfolio, a financial institution such as a bank to act as repository for the portfolio and thirdly, the individual shareholder. Although the fund is not a legal entity, the capital in the fund is independent of the management company and belongs to the shareholders.	Shares.	Mutual Funds Act. Supervision by the Financial Supervisory Authority.	Redemption of shares by fund.	Mutual funds normally do not pay Swedish tax. Income and tax liability is transferred to shareholders. Such transfer is only possible with income from equities and derivatives thereof. The same principle applies to investment companies. There is no obligation to distribute or roll-up income.	Total financial assets at end '95 as a percent of GDP: 114.8%. Life Insurance: 666bn; Pension funds: 37bn; Invest fund:177bn.	Total financial assets by type of investor at end '95: Invest. fund: 19%; Pens. Fund: 2%; Life insurance: 35%; others: 44%
U.K.	Authorised Unit Trust (AUT)	Trust formed, trustee holds assets; investors are the trust beneficiaries	The unit; i.e. the investor's proportional interest in the trust assets.	Trust law Financial Services Act 1986	Sale of unit or redemption by AUT	AUT deemed to be an investment company for tax purposes and taxable profits are calculated on corporate tax principles; however, AUT is exempt from tax on chargeable gains. AUT is regarded as distributing all its income to unitholders even where income is re-invested or accumulated. Where income is retained, cost of units is adjusted for capital gains purposes	Total financial assets at end '95 as a per cent of GDP: 162.3%	Total financial assets by type of investor at end '95: Invest. fund: 13%; Pens. Fund: 42%; Life insurance: 39.6%; others: 5.4% AUT as a per cent of invest. fund: 70%
	Approved investment trust company (AIT)	Company listed on London SE. Invests in shares and securities for benefit of shareholders.	Shares	Corporations law, Stock Exchange law.	Sale of shares	Basis of taxation is the same as for a private investment company; however, investment trusts can obtain Inland Revenue approval under the Income and Corporation Taxes Act 1988 to secure exemption for chargeable gains		AIT as a per cent of invest. fund: 30%
	Open-ended investment company (OEIC)	Several features of the AUT but in a corporate rather than a trust form	Shares	EC Directive, Undertakings for Collective Investment in Transferable Securities	Sale of shares or redemption by OEIC.	Regulations taking effect in January 1997 will modify tax legislation to assimilate the taxation of OEIC's to the taxation of unit trusts	Introduced in 1997. Over time may replace AUT	No data

Table AII.1 (cont'd) **Legal form and domestic regulation of CIIs**

Country	Type(s) of investment fund(2)	Description	Form of investment	Regulatory framework	Removal from fund	Brief overview of general principles of tax treatment of fund and participant (greater detail in following tables)	Relative importance of financial assets	Type of investor and relative importance
USA	Mutual Fund (open-ended)	The most common mutual fund. Open-ended fund requiring active investment management.	Shares	Investment Company Act of 1940	Shares redeemable at option of investor at price based on net asset value of fund.	A mutual fund which qualifies as a regulated investment company (RIC) is treated as a conduit for tax purposes. This tax regime is contingent on the fund distributing substantially all of its income. Where requirements are met, the fund is not taxed on distributed tax and net capital gains and shareholders are taxed directly on these amounts. Fund is taxed at corporate rates on retained income. Net capital gains and, in some cases, tax exempt interest, retain their character as they pass through the mutual fund.	Total assets at end '96 as a per cent of GDP: 171%.	Total financial assets by type of investor at end '95: Invest. fund: 23%; Pens. Fund: 35%; Life insurance: 18%; others: 24% Mutual fund as a per cent of invest. fund: 97%
	Unit investment trust (close-ended)	Less common mutual fund structure. Has a fixed size and portfolio and requires little or no investment management.	Shares. Usually listed.	Investment Company Act of 1940	Sold on market.	As above.		Unit investment trust as a per cent of invest. fund: 3%

Table AII.2 **Taxation of the underlying investment, 1st January 1997**

Country	Rate of tax levied on profits of domestic companies in which investment funds typically invest	Tax levied at source on domestic dividend, interest and similar income paid to ...	
		resident investment fund	*other investor; e.g. individual/company*
Australia	The standard corporate tax rate is 36%.	There is no tax levied at source on domestic dividends, interest, rents or other types of income. In the case of companies, a full imputation system operates in Australia in respect of tax paid on income distributed by the company . However, tax credits arising under such system relate to tax paid by the company on its pre-distribution income, rather than to tax paid by the company on dividends which it pays (as in the case of ACT in the U.K.).	As for investment fund.
Belgium	The standard corporate tax rate is 39%. (40.17% when the 'crisis' levy of 3% is incorporated). A lower rate applies to companies owned more than 50% by individuals.	There is a withholding tax of 15% on dividends. The withholding tax rate is 25% for dividends from shares issued before 1.1.1994. However, CII are fully credited for the payment of domestic withholding tax, effectively eliminating the dividend tax of the CII. There is a withholding tax of 15% on interest payments to the SICAV. The withholding tax rate is 25% for interest on loan agreements concluded prior to 1.3.1990. Both the withholding tax on interest and the withholding tax on dividends are fully creditable against corporate income tax.	Interest payments and dividends are subject to a withholding tax if they constitute income from Belgian sources or income from foreign sources collected through an intermediary established in Belgium. In principle the rate for dividends is 25%. However the rate is reduced to 15% for: - dividends issued as of 1.1.1994 if the shares are either issued to the public or the shares are registered shares or held by a financial institution registered by the Belgian Banking Commission; - dividends from Belgian investment companies. Interest is subject to a withholding tax of 15% and to a tax of 25% for loan agreements concluded prior to 1 March 1990. The withholding tax is final for proviate savers. However the taxpayer has the option to declare the income in order for it to be chargeable to tax at normal personal income tax rate. For corporations, the withholding tax is not final, but creditable against corporate income tax
Germany	On distributed profits of companies: 30% (48% when local taxes are included); on undistributed profits: 45% (59.2% when local taxes are included).	There is a 25% withholding tax on dividends, which tax is refundable upon application by the investment fund. In the case of interest there is no withholding tax.	There is a 25% withholding tax on dividends which is not refundable and there is also a withholding tax on interest. This tax is not levied if dividends are distributed through a fund.
Japan	The standard corporate tax rate is 37.5% (49.98% when local taxes are included).	Interest and dividends paid to investment trusts are exempt from withholding tax, provided it has registered its exemption status.	The treatment of other domestic investors is different from that of investment trusts. [No further information given]
Sweden	Corporate profits are taxed at 28% before distribution.	There is no tax levied at source on domestic dividends, interest, rents or other types of income.	Dividends are taxed in the hands of the individual recipient at the rate of 30%. If the recipient is a corporation holding the share as part of an investment portfolio, the dividend will be taxed at the rate of 28%. If the corporation holds more than 25% of the shares in the dividend distributing company, the dividends are not taxed in the recipient's hands. Interest income and realised capital gains of an individual tax payer are subject to the capital income tax of 30%. Interest income and realised capital gains of a company are subject to regular business taxation.

Table AII.2 (cont'd) **Taxation of the underlying investment, 1st January 1997**

Country	Rate of tax levied on profits of domestic companies in which investment funds typically invest	Tax levied at source on domestic dividend, interest and similar income paid to ...	
U.K.	The main corporate tax rate is 33% and applies to companies with profits above the upper profit limit of GBP 1.5 M. The small company rate applies to companies with profits below the lower limit of GBP 0.3 M. With profits between the two limits the rate varies smoothly between the small company and main rates.	U.K. company pays Advance Corporation Tax (ACT) on dividends paid by it. Current rate is 25% of dividends. ACT is offset against company's mainstream corporate tax (MCT). Dividends paid by one U.K. company to another are known as franked investment income (FII). FII paid to recipient company carries a tax credit equal to the ACT paid on the dividend. Recipient company can pass the dividend on without paying further ACT or it may claim the credit, in which case subsequent dividends paid by the recipient company are subject to ACT. To qualify for the credit, shareholder must be resident in U.K. or entitled to it under a double taxation treaty. These rules apply to AUT (which is deemed to be an investment company for tax purposes) and to the investment trust company. Interest income paid to AUTs may be subject to a withholding tax at a rate of 20% (an AUT can receive gross interest.) The withholding tax can be offset against the withholding tax levied on distribution to unitholders.	An ACT credit also attaches to dividends paid to an individual; i.e. shareholder treats dividend plus ACT credit as dividend income. Dividends paid to corporations: see previous column. Companies and individuals are subject to a withholding tax on interest payments. The withholding tax rate is equivalent to the lower personal income tax rate of 20%.
USA	The top corporate income tax rate is 35% (39.5% when local taxes are included).	There are no taxes levied at source on domestic dividends, interest and similar income. There is no corporate imputation system and dividend income is taxable in full. Dividend income is assessable when received. Interest income is also generally assessable on a cash basis.	No domestic withholding tax.

Table AII.3 **Taxation of the CII**

Country	Tax on domestic gains and income derived by the resident fund	Exemption or transparent treatment	Residence of fund established by	Capital tax payable by resident fund on domestic assets [rate]	Tax credits allowed to resident fund for tax paid by resident body in which fund invests when income from the underlying investment is derived by the fund	Withholding tax at source on domestic gains/income of the fund distributed to resident investors [rate]	Tax credits/set-off available to resident fund for use against liability of fund to withhold tax at source on distribution
Australia	If unitholders are entitled to the entire income of the trust, the trust itself will not be subject to tax on any of its assessable income, including capital gains. If there is any income to which unitholders are not presently entitled, the trustee would be assessed on that income at the 48.5% rate.	See previous table and column.	No data.	No data..	There is an imputation system in terms of which there is attached to dividends a tax credit in respect of tax paid by the company on its income. A dividend carrying such a credit is a "franked dividend". In the unlikely event in which the dividend does not carry an imputation credit at the full company tax rate, it is partly franked and partly unfranked.	None.	Not applicable.
Belgium	It is subject to corporation tax but only on exceptional income items and non-deductible costs. It cannot benefit from the (95%) dividend received deduction or from the deemed foreign tax credit. It is also subject to domestic withholding tax on dividend income (see column 2 in Table A1.1). There is no withholding tax on foreign source dividends, even if received through a Belgian Bank, if the resident recipient has applied for exemption available under Belgian law.	Transparency applies.	No data available	A SICAV is liable to an annual tax of 0.06 per cent on its net assets as of 1 July 1997.	None.	Income from dividend-paying units is liable to a withholding tax of 15 per cent in lieu of final tax. The sale and purchase of capitalisation units as well as movements from a dividend to a capitalisation unit or vice versa is subject to tax at 0.5%.	The mutual fund is fully credited for the payment of withholding tax on dividends distributed by a domestic company.

Table AII.3 (cont'd) **Taxation of the CII**

Country	Tax on domestic gains and income derived by the resident fund	Exemption or transparent treatment	Residence of fund established by	Capital tax payable by resident fund on domestic assets [rate]	Tax credits allowed to resident fund for tax paid by resident body in which fund invests when income from the underlying investment is derived by the fund	Withholding tax at source on domestic gains/ income of the fund distributed to resident investors [rate]	Tax credits/set-off available to resident fund for use against liability of fund to withhold tax at source on distribution
U.K.							
1. Authorised Unit Trust (AUT)	AUT is regarded as distributing all its income to unitholders even where income is reinvested in new units or accumulated. Dividend income paid by U.K. resident company to AUT is franked investment income (see previous table) and does not form part of taxable profits of AUT. AUT pays corporation tax on balance of unfranked income less expenses at current rate of 20%, subject to double taxation treaty relief. Management expenses are deductible; costs of buying and selling investments are not. Capital gains realised by an AUT are exempt at the institution level.	AUT exempt from tax in respect of income derived from futures or options contracts. AUT does not pay corporations tax on dividend income, which is subject instead to the franked investment income regime described in the previous table.	A foreign investment fund will become a U.K. resident if it becomes centrally managed and controlled in the U.K.. This involves control of the fund's overall investment policy: mere day-to-day management of the fund's investments will not result in residence being established.	None.	Where AUT receives dividends (franked investment income) from a U.K. company (see previous table) it is entitled to a tax credit equal to the rate of ACT paid by the U.K. company on the dividend in question. The credit for ACT can be set off against AUT tax liabilities or against the ACT levied on dividends of the unitholders.	Where there is a distribution by AUT characterised as yearly interest, unitholder is treated as receiving interest net of lower rate of tax (see table A1.1, last column).	Not applicable.
2. Approved Investment Trust Company	As for AUT, as described in first paragraph above. However, the corporation tax rate paid by AITs is the same as for regular companies reported in table AII.1.1, column 1.	The AIT is allowed to retian up to 15% of its income. However, this is still taxable at the normal rate of corporate tax if it is interest income received by the fund. Exemption for chargeable gains realised on investments. Falls outside rules which tax foreign currency gains/losses (incl. those on currency instruments) as income.	To secure Inland Revenue approval, an investment trust must be resident in the United Kingdom.	None.	Tax credit for ACT, in terms of the franked investment income regime.	None.	Not applicable.

Table AII.3 (cont'd) **Taxation of the CII**

Country	Tax on domestic gains and income derived by the resident fund	Exemption or transparent treatment	Residence of fund established by	Capital tax payable by resident fund on domestic assets [rate]	Tax credits allowed to resident fund for tax paid by resident body in which fund invests when income from the underlying investment is derived by the fund	Withholding tax at source on domestic gains/ income of the fund distributed to resident investors [rate]	Tax credits/set-off available to resident fund for use against liability of fund to withhold tax at source on distribution
USA	Provided a mutual fund qualifies as a regulated investment company (RIC), it will not be subject to its earnings to the extent that such earnings are distributed to shareholders. To qualify as an RIC, the mutual fund must be a domestic operation registered under the Investment Company Act as a management company or unit investment company. Among other conditions, 90% of the fund's taxable income must be distributed to shareholders. Tax is imposed on the RIC, in respect of undistributed income, on the same basis as for a resident corporation, subject to some differences in respect of exclusions and deductions from income. The fund is taxed on retained capital gains, being net capital gains not distributed to shareholders by way of a capital gains dividend. The fund may designate that shareholders be treated as if retained capital gains have been distributed but the fund still pays the tax on the gains.	Provided the mutual fund qualifies as a regulated investment company, transparent treatment applies - see previous column. Tax-exempt interest dividends - see following table on taxation of the investor.	No data.	0 if distribution requirements are satisfied.	None.	None.	Not applicable.

Table AII.4 **Taxation of the investor**

Country	Tax paid by investor on domestic gains/incomes	Character of income earned by fund maintained when passed to investor	Amount distributed to investor differs from proportionate share of fund's income for tax purposes	Tax on capital gains realised on disposal by investor of investment in fund	Capital tax payable by investor on investment in fund	Capital tax payable by investor on underlying assets of the investment fund	Access by investor to overall loss incurred by investment fund	Tax credits available to investor
Australia	Each unitholder is subject to tax on his/her share of the income and capital gains of the trust at the year end, regardless of whether a distribution has been made. First, the "income of the trust" is determined in accordance with the trust deed, then the "net income of the trust" is determined, being the total assessable income of the trust less allowable deductions under the Tax Act. The assessable income of the unitholder includes that share of the net income of the trust attributable to the time he is resident and, when not resident, the income which is Australian sourced. The unitholder's share normally depends on the proportion of the total units held by him. Where the net income is less than the income under the deed, which is the usual case, it is clear that a unitholder need only include in his assessable income the proportionate share of the net income. Any excess distribution is not assessable income but may have consequences for the cost base in the units.	Distributions by fund to individual investors are treated as dividends and do not retain the character of the fund's underlying income. When trust receives franked dividends, the unitholder is treated as having received them directly (see column on tax credits).	Usually, "net income of the trust" is less than "income of the trust". Unitholder includes in his income only his share of trust's net income. If any excess of income over net income is distributed, this is not assessable income but has capital gains implications. (See next column).	Capital gains tax is payable on gains realised on disposal of units. Where excess of trust's income over net income is distributed (see previous column) the indexed cost base of the units is reduced by the amount of the non-assessable distribution. If the distribution exceeds the indexed cost base of the units, a capital gain equal to the excess is realised.	None.	None.	Unitholder has no access to tax losses incurred by the trust. Trust may carry losses forward to absorb future income. If the trust is in a loss position, imputation credits (see next column) may not flow through to the unitholders.	In determining net income of the trust, franked dividend income is grossed up for the attached imputation credits and the additional amounts are included in the assessable income of the unitholder. The unitholder is allowed a tax credit for the portion of the gross-up which has been included in his/her assessable income. A corporate unitholder is allowed a tax credit for the gross-up and a rebate for the underlying dividend. It is also allowed a credit to its franking account to reflect the franked amount of the dividend which has flowed through.

Table AII.4 (cont'd) **Taxation of the investor**

Country	Tax paid by investor on domestic gains/incomes	Character of income earned by fund maintained when passed to investor	Amount distributed to investor differs from proportionate share of fund's income for tax purposes	Tax on capital gains realised on disposal by investor of investment in fund	Capital tax payable by investor on investment in fund	Capital tax payable by investor on underlying assets of the investment fund	Access by investor to overall loss incurred by investment fund	Tax credits available to investor
Belgium	Capitalisation units are in the form of capital gains and are tax exempt. Income from paying units is liable to a final withholding tax of 15%.	No data.		Tax exempt.	None.	None.	No data.	None.
Germany	Resident investors pay tax on the accumulated or distributed profits of the fund. If accumulated income is distributed, the distributed income is reduced by the proportion of that part of the income that has already been taxed when accumulated.	Character of the income is maintained when distributed.	The income of the fund serves as the basis of taxation of the investor's entitlement or distribution from an investment fund. differentiation between the income of the fund and the that of the investor is therefore not possible.	Capital gains tax is only payable if the units are sold less than 6 months after acquisition or if the investor carries on an enterprise of investment. The accumulated income component of capital gains realised by the fund is taxed as if it had been distributed and is therefore not subject to capital gains tax.	Resident investors must pay capital tax on their investment in the investment fund.	None.	Investors have no access to any overall loss incurred by the fund.	An imputation credit is granted against the income tax of the investor. Withholding tax paid by the fund on accumulated interest income of the fund (see previous table) can be credited against the income of the investor.
Japan	Investors are taxed on amounts received, not on income accrued by the investment trust. Individual investors incur a flat 20% tax at source, made up of a 15% National Income Tax and a 5% Local Inhabitants Tax. The tax is final and is calculated on a gross basis without deduction of expenses. Corporate investors incur a 20% withholding tax on distributions from trusts, being 15% national tax and 5% local tax. Corporations can claim a credit against corporate tax for the amount withheld.	Income from bond investment trusts is deemed to be interest and income from stock investment trusts is deemed to be dividend income.	As there is no tax at trust level, the amount of the resident investor's entitlement cannot differ from his proportionate share of the trust income as calculated for tax purposes. However, new investors in an investment trust pay a premium where there is accretion in trust property value, to account for the shares of existing investors. The premium may be distributed to existing investors. This "special distribution" is exempt from tax in the hands of individuals but is included in the taxable income of corporate investors.	Individuals: Gains arising from the transfer of trust certificates are not subject to income tax. On redemption, payments to investors are divided into distributions and capital gains. The distribution portions are taxed under the 20% withholding tax regime. The capital gain portion is exempt from tax. Corporate investors: Gains on disposal by a corporate investor are subject to normal corporate tax rules. Amounts received on redemption are part capital and part distribution. There is no capital gains tax on the capital portion. The distribution portion is subject to a withholding tax of 20%. The corporate investor can claim a tax credit for this.	None.	None.	There is no access by individuals to losses of the fund. With corporate investors, if the certificate is sold or redeemed at a loss, the amount of the loss can be used to offset other income of the company	If the investment trust were to suffer a withholding tax on any amount paid to the trust, the investor would be able to claim a tax credit in respect of such withholding tax. Corporate investors can also claim a tax credit against the withholding tax.

Table AII.4 (cont'd) **Taxation of the investor**

Country	Tax paid by investor on domestic gains/incomes	Character of income earned by fund maintained when passed to investor	Amount distributed to investor differs from proportionate share of fund's income for tax purposes	Tax on capital gains realised on disposal by investor of investment in fund	Capital tax payable by investor on investment in fund	Capital tax payable by investor on underlying assets of the investment fund	Access by investor to overall loss incurred by investment fund	Tax credits available to investor
Sweden	Income from investment funds is made available to investors either as dividends or as capital gains. Investors are liable for tax on dividends and capital gains. Individuals pay tax at a rate of 30% and corporate investors at a rate of 28%. Investors are not taxed on income retained in the fund (no attribution).	No.	No.	Capital gains tax is payable - see first column.	The value of the individual investor's investment is subject to wealth tax if the individual's total overall capital exceeds SEK 900,000.	None.	Investment funds are valued at market prices for wealth tax purposes. The value of the underlying asset in the fund and any overall loss incurred by the fund is implicitly taxed through wealth taxation (see column 5).	There are no tax credits available to the investor in respect of any tax paid by the fund.
U.K.								
1. Authorised Unit Trust	Depends on identity of unitholder and characterisation of distribution by AUT. Where AUT presents distributable income as conventional dividend: (a) individual unitholders treated as receiving conventional dividend with associated tax credit in respect of ACT, and is taxed on the dividend (unless exempt; e.g. as with personal equity plans or where income does not exceed personal allowance). Pension funds are exempt from tax on dividends. Exempted taxpayers may claim the ACT credit; (b) for U.K. resident corporate unitholder, the portions of the dividend attributable to the AUT's franked and unfranked income are treated as franked and unfranked income respectively in the hands of the corporate unitholder. Where AUT presents distributable income as yearly interest (having met certain criteria): (a)unitholders treated as receiving interest net of the lower rate of personal income tax; (b) company holding units in an AUT which is entitled to pay interest distributions must value units on a mark-to-market basis in each accounting period and take gain/loss into account for tax purposes.	Subject to the restriction on yearly interest, an AUT has in theory complete freedom to decide how to show its income available for distribution. In practice, however, the most tax efficient presentation will be to match the form of its accounts presentation to the underlying income of the trust. Thus the characterisation of dividend income as franked or unfranked investment income in AUT's hands is maintained when distribution made to corporate unitholder (see previous column).	No it is the same	Unitholders are liable to capital gains tax in respect of any disposal of their units, subject to the usual annual and other exemptions and indexation. Where a person acquires units during an income period, the price paid will include an amount in respect of accrued income. The accrued income is effectively paid to the unitholder at the next distribution date in the form of an equalisation payment. An equalisation payment is not treated as income but reduces the allowable cost of the units in a future capital gains tax computation.	None.	None.	No data.	Where AUT characteris es distribution as a dividend, tax credits in respect of ACT are available to the unitholders (see first column).

Table AII.4 (cont'd) **Taxation of the investor**

Country	Tax paid by investor on domestic gains/incomes	Character of income earned by fund maintained when passed to investor	Amount distributed to investor differs from proportionate share of fund's income for tax purposes	Tax on capital gains realised on disposal by investor of investment in fund	Capital tax payable by investor on investment in fund	Capital tax payable by investor on underlying assets of the investment fund	Access by investor to overall loss incurred by investment fund	Tax credits available to investor
U.K.								
2. ***Approveded Investment Trust Company***	Dividends paid to corporate and individual shareholders are subject to the same rules as those set out above in respect of AUT's.	AITs must derive their income wholly/ mainly from shares or securities or certain property rents and can only distribute income in the form of dividends. Dividends and gains realised on AIT shares are taxed at the shareholder level in sme way as ordinary dividends.	No it is the same. An AIT can retain not more than 15% of its income.	Shareholders are subject to capital gains tax on gains realised on disposal of shares in the company.	None.	None.	No data.	Shareholders entitled to tax credits in respect of ACT paid by company on dividends paid (as for AUT - see first column above).
USA	Provided a mutual fund qualifies as an RIC (see previous table), the fund is not taxed on its income to the extent that the income is distributed to its shareholders, and income is taxed in the hands of investors. If at the end of a quarter, the fund's investments in tax exempt securities make up at least 50% of its total assets, the fund can pay interest dividends which are exempt from tax in the hands of the investor.	Distributions by fund to individual investors are treated as dividends and do not retain the character of the fund's underlying income, subject to the following. Distributions to corporate investors are dividends to the extent that they are referable to underlying dividend income of the fund. Exempt interest dividends retain their character as exempt interest. In some cases, foreign income of fund retains its character in the hands of the investor - see next table.	Not applicable.	Capital gains dividends (see previous table) are taxable as long term capital gains in the investor's hands. Where the fund designates that investors be treated as if retained capital gains have been distributed (see previous table), investors are credited with the tax paid on those retained capital gains by the fund.	None.	None.	No data.	Tax credit available in respect of capital gains tax paid by fund on undistributed capital gains where fund has designated that shareholders be treated as if retained capital gains have been distributed.

Appendix III

COUNTRY RULES APPLICABLE TO TAXATION OF FOREIGN SOURCE INCOME

Table AIII.1 **Domestic investor, domestic CII, foreign source income**

Country	Domestic tax levied on foreign investment income received by fund	Application of anti-avoidance / deferral regime to fund's investment in foreign securities	Domestic capital tax payable by fund on foreign assets	Tax credits available to fund in r/o foreign tax paid by foreign body in which fund invests	Tax credits available to fund in r/o foreign tax paid by fund	Tax treatment of investor where foreign source income is distributed by the fund	Brief note on tax treaty policy on collective investment institutions / foreign funds
Australia	Foreign sourced dividend and interest income is generally subject to tax in the hands of a resident taxpayer on a receipts basis. Gains on disposal of foreign investment assets are subject to capital gains tax. Foreign tax credits apply - see column 6. The foreign investments of a resident unit trust are likely to include investments in foreign companies and trusts. Such entities are FIFs and an interest in a FIF includes a share in a foreign company and an interest in the income and/or corpus of a foreign trust. Most resident unit trusts would seek to take advantage of the various exemptions from the FIF provisions, particularly the balanced portfolio exemption. If one of the various exemptions is not available, the net income of the trust will include accrued FIF income. Therefore, unitholders will usually also be required to include their share of this income in assessable income.	The FIF provisions described in the previous column operate to prevent deferral of tax by subjecting accrued income to tax.	None.	The tax credit is generally not provided by the home country for foreign underling taxes. The Unite Kingdom provide the tax credit for the domestic underling corporate tax to Australian portfolio investors if the latter pay taxes in the home country (e.g. the U.K..). Funds which take advantage of the FIF exemption provision would not be entitle to the U.K. tax credit.	A foreign tax credit is available to the fund in respect of foreign taxes incurred, subject to a world-wide limit applied separately to various categories of income (including passive income).	Foreign source income of the fund which is included in the net income of the trust will form part of the unitholder's assessable income. The beneficiary of a trust which has paid foreign tax is deemed to have paid those taxes him/herself. His/her assessable income is grossed up and a tax credit is available for all or some of the foreign tax. However, with some unit trusts, practical difficulties mean that some trusts no longer make available to unitholders the information needed to calculate this credit. Where accrued income is included in the trust's income in terms of the FIF provisions, unitholders must include their share of such income in their assessable income. But if the trust is a "resident public unit trust"(3) a small investor exemption may apply: if the interest of the unitholder in FIFs, resident public unit trusts and foreign life policies does not exceed $50 000, the unitholder's share of the net income of the trust will not include the trust's FIF income.	No data.
Belgium	Domestic tax levied on foreign investment income received by the fund at 25% (fully creditable) on dividends from foreign shares. For interest, see Table AII.2.	No FIF rules.	Same as in column 4 of Table A1.3.	None	None	Same as for domestic source income distributed by the fund.	No data.

Table AIII.1 (cont'd) **Domestic investor, domestic CII, foreign source income**

Country	Domestic tax levied on foreign investment income received by fund	Application of anti-avoidance / deferral regime to fund's investment in foreign securities	Domestic capital tax payable by fund on foreign assets	Tax credits available to fund in r/o foreign tax paid by foreign body in which fund invests	Tax credits available to fund in r/o foreign tax paid by fund	Tax treatment of investor where foreign source income is distributed by the fund	Brief note on tax treaty policy on collective investment institutions / foreign funds
Germany	No tax on foreign investment income is levied upon its receipt by a resident investment fund.	No special anti-avoidance/deferral regime applies. However, income of the fund not used to cover costs or to make distributions is considered to have accrued by the end of the financial year in which it is received.	None.	As the fund is exempt from tax, no foreign tax paid by foreign entities is allowed as a credit to the fund.	As the fund pays no tax, no credit for any foreign tax paid by the fund is allowed to the fund.	A foreign tax credit for foreign withholding taxes is granted to the investor on his/her corresponding income. In the case of investment in share capital of French companies, imputation of the French corporation tax is allowed on the income of the investor.	In German tax treaties, distributions by resident investment funds are generally expressly mentioned as being dividends in the sense of the dividend article. There are no further provisions as to residence of the fund. Specific residence provisions apply in the German DTAs with Switzerland, France, Britain and the Netherlands. If the fund is not regarded as a resident person under the DTA, it operates only on the level of the investors. As it is difficult for individuals to claim treaty relief, the DTA with Switzerland and France allows for the fund to apply for a refund of source taxes. The refund is limited pro-rata to German investors in the fund.. As unit certificates are bearer documents, identifying the residence of unitholders is impossible and a mechanism is therefore used whereby the coupons presented by German banks to the management company are deemed to belong to German residents and those presented by foreign banks are deemed to belong to foreign investors.

Table AIII.1 (cont'd) **Domestic investor, domestic CII, foreign source income**

Country	Domestic tax levied on foreign investment income received by fund	Application of anti-avoidance / deferral regime to fund's investment in foreign securities	Domestic capital tax payable by fund on foreign assets	Tax credits available to fund in r/o foreign tax paid by foreign body in which fund invests	Tax credits available to fund in r/o foreign tax paid by fund	Tax treatment of investor where foreign source income is distributed by the fund	Brief note on tax treaty policy on collective investment institutions/ foreign funds
Japan	No tax is levied on foreign investment income received by an investment trust.	Not applicable.	None.	As the investment trust is not a taxable entity this is not applicable.	Foreign withholding tax on interest and dividends paid to a Japanese investment rust is creditable against the 20% withholding tax payable upon distributions from such trusts.	No data.	since a Japanese investment trust is not a taxable entity, it is not clear whether such trust is eligible for treaty benefits. Answer to the issue depends on the interpretation of each treaty.
Sweden	Mutual fund's profits from foreign sources are subject to corporate taxation. Dividends from the fund are deductible if transferred to the investor. The tax is not levied on receipt: the foreign source income is treated as part of gross income and the tax is levied in principle at the end of the fiscal year. [confirm] Foreign share portfolios are ascribed an imputed income to be taxed at 30% (28% for investment companies). [confirm]	No data.	None.	A mutual fund is not credited with any foreign taxes paid by any foreign body in which the fund invests, subject to any relief given in double taxation treaties.	Mutual funds do not benefit from credit of tax when tax has been withheld on dividends and interest in other countries. The internal rules only allow such tax to be deducted as a cost against the fund's taxable income.	The tax treatment is the same as for domestic source income.	The treaties between Sweden and certain OECD countries (e.g. Australia, France, Germany, Japan, U.K., USA) provide that investment funds will fall within the ambit of the treaty if they qualify as a body corporate or if they are treated as a body corporate for tax purposes.
U.K. ***(AUT and AITC)***	Foreign source dividends earned by an AUT are taxable at the 20% rate, as is foreign source interest. Foreign source dividends and interest earned by an AIT are taxable at the normal marginal rate of corporation tax. Foreign source interest income and capital gains realised on the sale of foreign shares are tax exempt.	AUTs are regarded as distributing all income to unit holders even where income is accumulated. AITs are regarded as distributing income, while allowed to retain up to 15% of income.	None.	It depends on the treaty against double taxation. For example France grants to the British fund a tax credit of 50% for the underlying French corporate tax	The U.K. operates a credit system (rather than an exemption system) for foreign withholding taxes. Accordingly foreign source income received by an investment company that has born a foreign withholding tax must be grossed-up for the foreign tax. The foreign tax may than be credited against the U.K. CT charged on the particular institution. However, if the withholding tax exceeds the residence tax liability, the institution will only be able to claim the credit up to, but not exceeding, the U.K. CT	Where U.K. company (including AUT or AITC) derives foreign source income in respect of which a foreign tax credit is allowed, the company may distribute the income as a foreign income dividend (FID). No ACT is payable in respect of a FID and no tax credit attaches to a FID; a FID is not franked investment income in the hands of another company. *Corporate investor* is exempt from tax on a FID but cannot claim any credit. *Individual investor* is regarded as receiving dividend income equal to the FID grossed up at the lower rate of income tax (currently 20%). Where individual liable to pay tax on savings income at only 20%, no further tax is due on the FID. Those paying higher rate on savings pay tax at the difference between the lower and higher rates of tax.	No data

Table AIII.1 (cont'd) **Domestic investor, domestic CII, foreign source income**

Country	Domestic tax levied on foreign investment income received by fund	Application of anti-avoidance / deferral regime to fund's investment in foreign securities	Domestic capital tax payable by fund on foreign assets	Tax credits available to fund in r/o foreign tax paid by foreign body in which fund invests	Tax credits available to fund in r/o foreign tax paid by fund	Tax treatment of investor where foreign source income is distributed by the fund	Brief note on tax treaty policy on collective investment institutions / foreign funds
USA	As with other corporations, mutual funds must include income and gains from all sources in its taxable income.	No data.	None.	It depends on the treaty against double taxation. For example France grants to the US fund a tax credit of 50% for the underlying French corporate tax. data.	Fund may have access to foreign tax credits for withholding taxes imposed, in the source country, on distribution to the US fund. As an RIC (see previous table) is not subject to tax on most of its income, it will generally not be able to use such tax credits. The tax credit passes on to investor - see next column	If the mutual fund has more than 50% of its assets invested in stock or securities of foreign corporations, it may pass foreign tax credits on to the investor. Investor must include the foreign taxes in his/her income in order to claim the credit. Investor treats the grossed up (of credit for underlying foreign corporate tax and of credit for withholding tax) distribution as foreign sourced income.	No data.

Notes

(1) Taxpayer may also be subject to tax on an accrual basis if the tax regimes known as the controlled foreign company (CFC) provisions the transfer trust provisions apply. The CFC rules apply when a resident taxpayer has a direct as opposed to a portfolio interest in the CFC and the CFC is a resident in a low tax country but excludes from the regime income earned from active business operations. The transfer trust provisions subject a resident to tax on the income earned by a trust which is a resident in a low tax country where the resident has transferred property or services to the trust. These regimes are not applicable for the purposes of this study.

(2) The market value method (stock exchange results or redemption values may be used), the deemed rate of return method (based on the interest rate payable on 13 week Australian Treasure notes plus 4%) or the calculation method (the notional profit of the FIF must be determined as well as the investor's entitlement thereto).

(3) A "resident public unit trust" is a widely held or publicly listed unit trust where either the central management and control of the trust is in Australia or more than 50% of the beneficial interests in the trust is held by residents.

Table AIII.2 **Domestic investor, foreign CII, foreign source income**

Country	Foreign funds recognised as transparent for tax purposes	Domestic tax levied on income from foreign fund received by investor	Tax paid by resident investor on gains/income of foreign fund	Anti-avoidance or de-ferral regimes applicable	Tax paid by investor on capital gains realised on disposal of investment in foreign fund	Domestic capital tax paid by investor on investment in foreign fund	Domestic capital tax payable by investor on underlying assets of foreign fund	Tax credits available to investor	Tax treaty policy on collective investment insituations / foreign funds
Australia	Foreign funds are classified as FIFs (see previous table). No income of fund is included in assessable income of unitholder under normal trust look-through rules. If FIF provisions do not apply to the foreign fund normal look-through rules will apply.	Generally there is no domestic tax on income from foreign fund. However, if FIF provisions do not apply, and the unitholder is presently entitled to a share of the income of a non-resident trust, the unitholder could be assessed under the ordinary look-through provisions. Due to difficulties of calculation, most small investors would be likely simply to include trust income on receipt of a distribution.	Generally no tax paid by resident investor on gains of foreign fund. However, FIF accrued income might be included in unitholder's assessable income if the small investor exemption is not available (see previous table)	FIF accrued income provisions, referred to in previous column, would operate to prevent deferral.	On disposal of unit, investor will be required to calculate any capital gain or loss. The consideration received is translated into Australian dollars at the rate at the time of the disposal. If the FIF regime applies, the consideration received on disposal will be reduced by any amount previously taxed to the investor.	None.	None.	Where FIF provisions do not apply and domestic tax is levied on income from a foreign fund, the investor would be entitled to a foreign tax credit in respect of foreign taxes, including withholding taxes, borne by the unit trust, but in practice he/she would probably not have the information needed to claim the credit. Where FIF provisions apply, foreign tax credits are only available to the unitholder when the calculation method has been elected (see notes to previous table). A foreign tax credit is available for any foreign tax levied on a gain on disposal of the unit, and relief for any income previously attributed.	No data.

Table AIII.2 (cont'd) **Domestic investor, foreign CII, foreign source income**

Country	Foreign funds recognised as transparent for tax purposes	Domestic tax levied on income from foreign fund received by investor	Tax paid by resident investor on gains/income of foreign fund	Anti-avoidance or deferral regimes applicable	Tax paid by investor on capital gains realised on disposal of investment in foreign fund	Domestic capital tax paid by investor on in-vestment in foreign fund	Domestic capital tax payable by investor on underlying assets of foreign fund	Tax credits available to investor	Tax treaty policy on collective investment institutions / foreign funds
Belgium	Foreign fund must accordingly register with the Banking and Financial Commission. In the case of investment undertakings which are subject to the European Directive and have been authorised to carry out their activity by the competent authority in their country of origin, the Banking and Financial Commission will simply check whether the necessary information has been provided; it will also examine the methods of marketing shares. The requirements which must be met by foreign CIUs which are not subject to the European Directive are stipulated by Royal Decree. Such undertakings have to appoint a depositary and are subject to the same supervisory and information requirements as Belgian CIUs.	A domestic final withholding tax of 25% is levied on foreign source dividend income. On interest payments there is a 15% final withholding tax.	Capital gains from sale of units in a foreign fund are tax exempt.	No FIF or anti-deferral rules.	None.	None.	None.	A credit for foreign withholding taxes on distribution by foreign fund.	No data.

Table AIII.2 (cont'd) **Domestic investor, foreign CII, foreign source income**

Country	Foreign funds recognised as transparent for tax purposes	Domestic tax levied on income from foreign fund received by investor	Tax paid by resident investor on gains/income of foreign fund	Anti-avoidance or deferral regimes applicable	Tax paid by investor on capital gains realised on disposal of investment in foreign fund	Domestic capital tax paid by investor on investment in foreign fund	Domestic capital tax payable by investor on underlying assets of foreign fund	Tax credits available to investor	Tax treaty policy on collective investment institutions / foreign funds
Germany	Foreign fund is regarded as transparent if a) unit certificates are offered to the public or traded on a German stock exchange, and the fund has a representative in Germany; and b) the fund certifies the types of income and the taxes that can be credited against the income tax of the investor.	A domestic withholding tax of 30% is levied on receipt of income from the foreign fund if paid out by a German bank. If income is less than DM6000 or DM12000 for a married couple, application can be made for exemption. Resident investors in foreign fund must pay income tax on the distributed profits of the fund and, in the case of accumulated income, the deemed distributed profits of the fund. The tax treatment varies according to the legal framework of the foreign fund.	No data.	No data.	Capital gains tax is not payable unless the investor buys and sells the unit within 6 months, or if the investor carries on an investment business.	Domestic capital tax on the investment is payable if certain amounts of assets are exceeded.	None.	Tax paid by the underlying foreign entities cannot be credited against German income tax. A tax levied by withholding at source paid by a foreign investment fund on income received by it can be credited against German tax as far as the underlying tax has led to a reduction of the tax withheld on the distribution of the fund.	German tax treaties contain no special provisions regarding residency of investment funds, except in the DTA with France. Distributions on certificates of funds are explicitly included in the dividend article. Foreign investment funds are generally not regarded as treaty residents and in the case of non-transparent funds the treaties only operate at the level of the investor. The treaty can only be applied properly if the fund has the right to claim benefits on behalf of the investors. A method of determining percentages of investors resident in the state of the foreign fund must therefore by agreed between the contracting states. In the case of non-transparency, the fund may claim treaty benefits itself, as with the U.K..

Table AIII.2 (cont'd) **Domestic investor, foreign CII, foreign source income**

Country	Foreign funds recognised as transparent for tax purposes	Domestic tax levied on income from foreign fund received by investor	Tax paid by resident investor on gains/income of foreign fund	Anti-avoidance or deferral regimes applicable	Tax paid by investor on capital gains realised on disposal of investment in foreign fund	Domestic capital tax paid by investor on investment in foreign fund	Domestic capital tax payable by investor on underlying assets of foreign fund	Tax credits available to investor	Tax treaty policy on collective investment institutions / foreign funds
Japan	The concept "transparent" does not apply if taken to mean a complete pass-through of fund income. With foreign investment trusts there is no tax at trust level. Foreign Corporate type funds are not subject to Japanese tax on foreign source income.	When distributions by foreign investment trusts are received through paying agents in Japan the distributions are taxed in the same way as distributions by Japanese investment trusts, and the 20% withholding tax is payable. Foreign withholding taxes are creditable against the local withholding tax. When distributions are made through paying agents outside Japan and the non-resident trusts are publicly placed, the 20% withholding tax does not apply. Distributions by corporate funds are taxed as dividends (20% withholding tax). If distribution was subject to foreign withholding taxes, the 20% tax is imposed on the after-tax amount.	No data.	Investments in corporate type funds may be subject to anti-Tax Haven legislation, in terms of which accumulated profits of controlled foreign corporations are taxed in the hands of investors who own directly or indirectly more than 5% of the shares in such controlled foreign corporation. A controlled foreign corporation is one where 50% or more of the shares are owned by a resident, directly or indirectly.	When certificates of publicly placed foreign trusts are sold through security companies in Japan the proceeds are taxed in the same manner as described for domestic taxation in Table A1.2. Where there is a disposal of shares in a foreign corporate fund, the investor must report gains that are taxed at 20% tax rates plus 6% Local Inhabitants Tax. Investors may choose to have 1% of the gross receipt withheld on the condition that the shares in the fund are traded on a foreign stock exchange.	None.	None.	Foreign taxes on amounts distributed by foreign trusts through paying agents in Japan are creditable against the 20% withholding tax on the distribution. When distributions are made through paying agents not in Japan and when the non-resident trusts are publicly placed, the income is aggregated with other income of the investor and the investor can claim a credit in respect of foreign taxes paid. Distributions from corporate type funds are taxed as dividends (20% withholding tax). The withholding tax can be claimed as a credit. Where foreign taxes were paid, the withholding tax is calculated on an after-tax amount.	The same issues apply as those referred to in the previous table.

Table AIII.2 (cont'd) **Domestic investor, foreign CII, foreign source income**

Country	Foreign funds recognised as transparent for tax purposes	Domestic tax levied on income from foreign fund received by investor	Tax paid by resident investor on gains/income of foreign fund	Anti-avoidance or deferral regimes applicable	Tax paid by investor on capital gains realised on disposal of investment in foreign fund	Domestic capital tax paid by investor on investment in foreign fund	Domestic capital tax payable by investor on underlying assets of foreign fund	Tax credits available to investor (2)	Tax treaty policy on collective investment institutions / foreign funds
Sweden	Tax treatment unclear. Shares in foreign funds are treated as shares in Swedish funds. Shares in company-type mutual funds are treated as ordinary shares. With non-corporate foreign fund, tax treaties indicate that they should be transparent but this is not applied in practice.	Residents are taxed at 30% on dividends and capital gains from abroad (distributions by foreign funds being treated as dividends). Resident investors are liable to pay wealth tax pertaining to the market value of their shares in the foreign investment fund.	Activities of foreign investment funds are not subject to taxation in Sweden.	No data. It is possible that anti-deferral regimes do not apply since the treatment of Swedish resident's shares in foreign mutual funds are commonly treated as Swedish's residents' shares in Swedish mutual fund.	Capital gains on shares in foreign funds are taxed at 30%.	Investor is liable to pay wealth tax on the value of shares in foreign funds.	No data.	No data.	No data.
U.K.	Offshore funds are divided into two categories in terms of U.K. legislation: distributor funds, which distribute at least 85% of the fund's U.K. equivalent profits, and non-distributor funds. Off-shore funds are not subject to taxation in the U.K..	Distributions by offshore funds rank as income in the hands of U.K. resident recipients and are liable to U.K. tax subject to a credit for any foreign withholding tax suffered.	No.	See next column: rules regarding capital gains used as an anti-avoidance measure in respect of offshore funds which do not make distributions.	Capital gains tax is payable by the investor in respect of gains made upon the disposal of interests in a distributor fund. With non-distributor funds, tax is only levied on actual distribution thereby allowing income in the fund to accumulate tax-free. Gains on the disposition of interests in non-distributor funds (offshore income gains) are taxed as ordinary income and will not benefit from capital gains tax relief and indexation.	None.	None.	Foreign taxes paid in respect of distributions by offshore funds are allowed as a credit in respect of U.K. income tax payable by investor.	No data.

Table AIII.2 (cont'd) **Domestic investor, foreign CII, foreign source income**

Country	Foreign funds recognised as transparent for tax purposes	Domestic tax levied on income from foreign fund received by investor	Tax paid by resident investor on gains/income of foreign fund	Anti-avoidance or deferral regimes applicable	Tax paid by investor on capital gains realised on disposal of investment in foreign fund	Domestic capital tax paid by investor on investment in foreign fund	Domestic capital tax payable by investor on underlying assets of foreign fund	Tax credits available to investor (2)	Tax treaty policy on collective investment insituations / foreign funds
USA	There are specific provisions aimed at investments of US persons in foreign mutual funds, the passive foreign investment company ("PFIC") rules. In relation to a US citizen or resident investor, a PFIC is a foreign corporation where, for the income year, either 75 per cent or more of gross income is passive income or the average percentage of assets which produce passive income is at least 50 per cent. Passive income is defined as dividends, interest, royalties, rents, annuities, net gains on the disposal of assets which give rise to this type of income, net gains from commodity trading, net foreign currency gains and income equivalent to interest. There is also a look-through provision where one foreign corporation owns at least 25 per cent of another corporation when applying these threshold tests. Once a foreign corporation is a PFIC in relation to a shareholder, it remains a PFIC in relation to that investor even if the income and assets tests are not met in a subsequent year.	Foreign sourced income is generally taxable on receipt by the taxpayer unless the PFIC provisions apply (see next column 4).	None	To avoid deferral of tax, if there is an excessive distribution by a PFIC, the excess is taxed at the highest marginal rate applicable over the last three years, and interest is charged on such tax. Alternatively, a shareholder can elect to have the PFIC treated as a "qualified electing fund". The shareholder must include in income his/her share of the PFIC's income and capital gains currently, that is, whether distributed or not. If an amount is later distributed which is attributable to an amount previously included in the shareholder's income, that distribution is tax free and the basis in the shares in reduced by the amount excluded from income. As deferral is no longer utilised, the interest charge and highest marginal rates are not applicable when amounts are actually distributed.	The same interest charge principles described in the previous column also apply to gains realised on the sale of shares in a PFIC.	None.	None.	No data.	No data.

Appendix IV

A FORMAL MODEL FOR MEASURING TAX INCENTIVES

AIV.1 Introduction

The overall objective of this annex is to explain in greater detail the methodology applied in the main text. This methodology, while unable to cover all relevant taxpayer considerations and existing tax-planning opportunities, nonetheless captures a number of key factors. Bearing the limitations of the methodology in mind, the results obtained can be used to infer incentives provided by the tax system for channelling savings into portfolio investment when a collective investment institution (CII) is used as a financial intermediary, and to compare the return realised by using this vehicle to the return on direct portfolio investment by individuals. For both cases, the after-tax rate of interest on bonds is taken as the standard or benchmark rate of return. The methodology employed allows to analyse both domestic and foreign portfolio investment undertaken by a resident individual. Analogously, this chapter considers a domestic CII which undertakes either domestic or foreign portfolio investment on behalf of a resident individual. The formal analysis has not been extended to the foreign CII case.

Differences in the tax treatment of income received at the personal level pose a difficult problem to all studies of incentive effects of taxation which are based on individual optimising behaviour. King-Fullerton (1984) noted in particular the difficulty in determining the required rate of return on real investment when retained earnings are used as the source of funds. The cost of capital then depends on the tax rate of the investor, yet retained earnings cannot be attributed to only one group of stockholders[1]. To reconcile this problem that both tax-exempt investors and individuals facing the highest marginal tax rates own corporate equity, King-Fullerton computed the cost of capital for retained earnings as a weighted average of the values for the cost of capital obtained for each category of investor. The share-ownership proportions of the investors were used as weights in this so called 'fixed-p case'. Having determined a common value for the cost of capital (the pre corporate-tax rate of return), King-Fullerton then estimated the real after-tax rate of return to the different categories of investors/savers.

In a second case, known as the 'fixed-r case' King-Fullerton assumed instead that arbitrage in capital markets leads to an outcome in which each (real) investment project offers the same rate of return to savers before personal tax. In the 'fixed-r' case, which has been assumed in chapters 2 – 3 and part of chapter 4 of the Report, pre-tax rates of return on real investment differ, and the after-personal-tax rate of return may differ between categories of savers as well, reflecting the variation in personal tax rates. Hence, the 'fixed-r' case assumes that the variation in personal tax rates is not eliminated by arbitrage.

To determine the tax incentives that may impact on the allocation of savings between bonds and shares, and between domestic and foreign shares, an alternative approach can also be taken: the 'fixed-s case' for the marginal shareholder. In chapter 4 of the Report it is assumed that both the pre-personal (after-corporate tax) tax rate of return to portfolio investment and the market price of shares are uniquely determined by a hypothetical marginal investor, who sets the share-prices to equate his after-tax returns on bonds and shares. The after-tax rate of return on portfolio investment undertaken by other investors may in this case differ from his after-tax return on bonds, to the extent that the tax treatment of these other investors in respect of dividend relief differs from that offered to the marginal investor.

In this respect, the approach under the 'fixed-s' case differs from the 'fixed-r'-case. Different after-tax returns obviously might cause investors to specialise in particular securities according to their tax treatment, although in practice anything remotely like complete specialisation is not observed. As the essential objective is to identify and measure the tax incentives involved, no attempt is made here to characterise the ensuing general equilibrium.

In the remainder of this Appendix , a general model is derived for measuring tax incentives that may be instrumental in channelling savings into domestic versus foreign shares, directly or via domestic Collective Investment Institutions (CII). Formal explanations of various concepts used in the Report are introduced. In section A.2, the analysis mainly deals with the most complex fixed-s case where an individual saver undertakes portfolio investment either directly in publicly marketed corporate shares, or indirectly as a shareholder/unitholder of a CII, which in turn invests in shares. The focus is on the wedge between the pre-personal (after-corporate) tax rate of return from portfolio investment, and the net-of-tax return received by the saver. Also, an effective rate of tax on portfolio investment is derived which is comparable to the rate of tax paid by the saver on his interest income. In section A.3., the general methodology is extended to represent the tax treatment of dividend income (direct or via a domestic CII) for the five countries considered in the Report: Australia, Belgium, Sweden, the U.K. and the U.S. Section A.4 summarises in tables the parameters used to represent the tax system of each representative country.

AIV.2 The general model

Consider a corporate firm that undertakes real investment. The after-corporate tax rate of return on the marginal unit of real capital employed by the company is ρ. With s denoting the after-tax real rate of return received by an individual on his savings in corporate equity (channelled into shares directly or indirectly via a CII), we obtain the marginal tax wedge, MTW, as

$$MTW = \rho - s = (\rho - r) + (r - s) \equiv MTW_I + MTW_{II} \qquad (1)$$

On the right hand side of (1), the marginal tax wedge is decomposed into two parts. The first of these, MTWI , measures the extent to which the after-corporate tax real rate of return differs from the real market interest rate, here denoted as r, which can be earned on an alternative investment available in the international market. The second tax wedge, MTWII, measures the extent to which the after-tax real return to the saver(s) differs from the real market interest rate.

When the corporation uses new issues of equity as the source of funds, MTWI will be zero under a classical system of corporate taxation, whereas a tax system which mitigates economic double taxation at the shareholder level drives MTWI below zero. Since the after-corporate tax rate of return ρ is also the company's discount rate, the magnitude of MTWI obviously is of importance to the company's pre-tax cost of capital, which in the long-run determines the seize of the real capital stock. However, by itself the wedge MTWI conveys little information. To evaluate its impact on the cost of capital, MTWI must be considered in conjunction with the full set of corporate tax rules. Conceivably, a negative MTWI in conjunction with a high statutory corporate tax rate and unfavourable rules of fiscal depreciation could combine to a higher cost of capital than obtained from a zero MTWI in combination with generous tax rules at the corporate level.

The focus of interest in this Report is therefore on the 'portfolio savings wedge', MTWII , defined as the difference between the real market rate of interest, r, and the after-tax real rate of return to portfolio investment, s. In particular, it is attempted to determine to what extent MTWII differs between direct portfolio investment (DPI) and indirect (via CII) portfolio investment. In addition, the 'portfolio savings wedge' is set against the tax wedge on the return to bonds, indicating whether the tax system diverts savings into or away from bonds. When interest income of individuals is taxed, this latter wedge is simply the tax rate times the interest rate, say mr where m is the rate of tax on savings. Also, an effective rate of tax te on portfolio investment is derived by relating the 'portfolio savings wedge', MTWII , to the market interest rate:

$$t^e = \frac{MTR_{II}}{r} \quad (2)$$

For investment in bonds, equation (2) implies that $t^e = m^2$. For portfolio investment it will be shown that depending on the tax rules t^e may equal or differ from m.

The saver's after-tax real rate of return on portfolio investment is obtained as

$$s = \frac{\delta^{net}}{X} \quad (3)$$

where δ^{net} is the after-tax dividend received by the saver and X is the cost to the saver of (directly or indirectly via a domestic CII) acquiring the entitlement to the return on a marginal unit of capital employed by the corporation. Though equation (3) takes a simple form, the complexity of the measurement problem to be considered remains in the expressions for δ^{net} and X.

Following the approach in OECD (1991), equation (3) assumes that the after-corporate tax return is distributed in full to the shareholders of the corporation. The difference between ρ, introduced above, and δnet is therefore entirely due to the tax treatment of dividends. Equation (3) may thus be re-written as

$$s = \frac{\rho\left(1 - t^f\right)}{X} \quad (3')$$

where t^f is the total rate of tax levied on the dividend paid by the corporation in which the saver invests (directly or indirectly). t^f denotes the *formal rate of tax on dividends.* For direct investment, t^f captures the combined impact of the taxes paid by the saver and any imputation credits extended as a mitigation of economic double taxation at the shareholder level. For indirect investment via a CII, t^f captures the combined impact of the taxes paid by the CII and the saver, including any imputation credits extended as a mitigation of economic double taxation. In the case of foreign portfolio investment, t^f also includes any foreign withholding taxes (and credit for foreign tax).

The after-corporate tax rate of return ρ in turn depends on the identity and tax treatment of the corporation's marginal shareholder, that is the shareholder which sets the price of the corporate shares on the stock market, and on the source of funds used by the corporation. However, the saver, whose after-tax rate of return is given by (3), may or may not be identical to the company's marginal shareholder. The cost of investment, X, likewise depends on the source of funds used by the company, and also -- in the case where the saver invests via a CII -- on the source of funds used by the intermediary to finance portfolio investment. It must be also noted that ρ, δnet and X may differ depending on whether the CII (or the shareholder) invests in domestic or foreign shares.

As a first step in unveiling the complexities of equations (3) and (3'), the after-corporate tax rate of return ρ will be derived. The fundamental assumption employed here is that the corporate firm is valued in the stock market so that the marginal investor, who invests directly in the company and is resident in the same country as the company, is indifferent between holding the shares of the firm and investing in an alternative asset yielding a pre-personal tax return of r. When the after-corporate tax rate of return is fully distributed to the shareholder, this indifference is expressed by the ('no arbitrage') equilibrium condition:

$$\rho\theta^m\left(1-m^m\right)=r\left(1-m^m\right)q^m \tag{4}$$

where q^m is the market price of the shares, per unit of real capital employed by the company. The left hand side of (4) is then the after-tax return to the marginal shareholder obtained by investing directly the amount q^m in the company's shares. This return depends on whether the tax code allows for mitigation of double taxation at the shareholder level, as captured by the tax discrimination variable θ^m (≥1)[3], and on the shareholder's marginal tax rate on capital income, m^m.[4] The right hand side of (4) is the opportunity cost of the equity investment, written as the after-tax return from investing the amount q^m in bonds, yielding a pre-tax nominal market interest rate of r+π. Equation (4) gives

$$\rho=\frac{rq^m}{6^m} \tag{5}$$

Next to be determined is the market price qm , which depends on the source of funds used by the company. For the marginal shareholders to willingly fund an addition to the company's capital stock by participating in a new share issue, the marginal unit of capital must raise the market value of the shares by one currency unit (krona, pound etc.). Hence, qm =1 when new equity is the marginal source of funds. With retained earnings as the source of funds, the expected appreciation in the market value, say qm, must be sufficient to compensate the shareholder for a foregone after-tax dividend of θm(1-mm), plus an additional liability to capital gains tax of zmqm (where zm is the (accruals) tax on capital gains). For the marginal shareholder to be indifferent between distribution and retention, the required share appreciation when the company retains one unit of after-tax earnings for new investment is therefore

$$q^m = z^m q^m + \theta^m(1-m^m)$$

or,

$$q^m=\frac{\theta^m\left(1-m^m\right)}{1-z^m} \tag{6}$$

Using qm = 1, when new equity is issued, or the specification given by equation (6), when retained earnings are used, it is straight-forward to compute the after-corporate tax rate of return ρ from equation (5). The empirical information required here is a characterisation of the company's marginal shareholder in terms of the tax parameters θm, mm and zm. This characterisation will be addressed below.

To compute the after-tax dividend δnet [the numerator of (3)] or equivalently, the formal composite tax rate tf, additional information is required on the amount of taxes paid by the CII and by the saver on a unit of dividends. As the tax treatment varies considerably between the countries included in this report, this issue is reviewed in the country sections below.

The next problem is to determine X, that is, the cost to the saver of the portfolio investment [the denominator of (3)]. In the case of direct portfolio investment, X = qm , which simply means that the saver pays the prevailing market price of shares. In the CII-case, generally X = qm Q, where Q is the owner's/unitholder's valuation of an extra currency unit in the hands of the CII. This means that X differs from qm to the extent that Q is different from unity. In the event the CII uses new capital injections from its owners to add to its portfolio of shares, Q = 1, and hence X = qm as for the case of direct portfolio investment. The saver foregoes qm to enable the CII to invest the same amount.

If the CII retains earnings on portfolio investment as a source of funds, the cost to the owner may be different. To illustrate the possibility of a different valuation, assume that retention of dividends from portfolio investment enables the shareholder/unitholder to defer taxation.[5] Each currency unit retained means that the owner foregoes the amount θpI(1-m), where θpI is the dividend-cum-credit for dividends received via a CII. For an open-ended CII, where the owner is assigned a pro-rata share of the fund's portfolio, then Q = θpI(1-m). The cost of investment (X) is hence the prevailing market price of shares, qm, multiplied by the amount foregone by the unitholder per currency unit retained with the fund. For a close-ended fund, retention of earnings will also cause the market price of the CII to rise, and force the owner to pay, say, zQ in capital gains tax. For the CII's shareholder to be indifferent to the earnings retention, the share appreciation Q must therefore be sufficient to compensate for both the capital gains tax and the foregone dividend. Formally, Q must satisfy the condition Q = zQ + θpI(1-m). Hence, for a close-ended CII, Q = θpI(1-m)/(1-z).

Summing up, the discussion above has identified four (potentially) different regimes to take into account in order to determine the marginal tax wedge for portfolio investment via a CII. These regimes are characterised by whether the corporate firm, undertaking real investment, uses new issues or retained earnings as the marginal source of funds, and by whether the CII uses injections from its owners/unitholders, or retains dividend income to finance its additional portfolio investment. Another question concerns the identity and tax treatment of the marginal shareholder of the corporate firm.

However, given the focus of this Report on the wedge between the market interest rate, and the after-tax rate of return to the saver, the analysis is less demanding. Although the after-corporate tax rate of return, ρ, and the market value of the corporation, qm, both depend on the source of funds used by the corporation to finance real investment, it is clear from (5) that the ratio r/θm, which is the pre-tax rate of return on portfolio investment, does not. Using X = qm Q and (5), the after-tax return to the saver is derived as

$$s = \frac{r\left(1-t^{f}\right)}{\theta^{m}Q} \qquad (7)$$

Equation (7) thus holds both when new equity and retained earnings are used as sources of funds for real investment. As a further simplification, set Q = 1. This may in turn be interpreted as an assumption that the CII's portfolio investment is financed by injections from its shareholders/unitholders, or as a result of specific tax rules that do not allow the shareholders/unitholders a deferral of personal tax when the CII retains dividend income.[6] In the case of Q = 1, two pieces of information are required to determine the after-tax return of the saver: *i)* the tax discrimination variable for the marginal investor, θm, (which together with the market interest rate determines the pre-tax rate of return on portfolio investment, ρ/qm = r/θm), and *ii)* the formal rate of tax on dividend income, tf.

As its main case, this Report assumes that the marginal investor in the markets where the CII undertakes portfolio investment is a fully taxable resident individual. The tax discrimination variable θm is hence chosen to reflect the host country's practice of extending dividend relief to its citizens (if any). Whether the marginal investor in practice is a resident individual or someone else is of course an empirical question, which is beyond the scope of this Report to settle. The next section is devoted to a country-by-country examination of the formal rate of tax on dividend income, tf.

AIV.3 Taxation of returns from Direct investment vs Investment through CII: Five examples

AIV.3.1 United Kingdom

This section gives a condensed description of the taxation of dividend income channelled via U.K. collective investment institutions (CII), and dividend income from direct portfolio investment. (Note that the abolition of ACT and FID from April 1999 and the reduction in the rate of tax credit would substantially alter the analysis.) U.K. tax rules are summarised by deriving analytical expressions for the formal rate of tax on dividend income, tf. Both the case of an open-ended authorised unit trust (AUT) and a closed-ended approved investment trust (AIT) are examined. Both a domestic case, where the CII receives dividends from U.K. domestic shares, and a foreign case where the CII receives dividends from foreign shares are analysed.

The following notation is used throughout this section:

τ_c = rate of corporate tax of CII

τ_{ACT} = rate of advance corporate tax (ACT)

ρ = dividend paid by corporation in which CII holds shares

δ^P = dividend distributed by CII to its shareholders/unitholders

δ^{net} = dividend received by shareholder/unitholder net of tax and imputation credits

η_u = credit rate received by shareholder/unitholder investing directly on company equities.

θ^m = $1+\eta_u$, saver's tax discrimination parameter; in case of a foreign imputation credit extended to the shareholder, use θ^{mf}

η_I = credit rate received by CII

θ_I = $1+\eta_I$, CII's tax discrimination parameter; in case of a foreign imputation credit extended to CII, use θ_I^f

η_p = credit rate received by shareholder/unitholder of CII

θ_p = $1+\eta_p$, shareholder's/unitholder's tax discrimination parameter when dividend is distributed by a CII; in case of a foreign imputation credit extended to shareholder/unitholder use, θ_p^f.

w^f = foreign withholding tax

w^{ftc} = credit for foreign withholding tax.

ACT^{Net} = (Amount of) Advance corporate tax net of ACT set off/repayment.

Portfolio investment channelled through domestic AUTs or domestic AITs

Domestic case -- franked investment income -- (the same set of rules applies for AUTs and AITs)

Assuming that the dividend income net of any tax paid at the CII level is distributed to the unitholder/shareholder:

$$\delta^P = \rho + \eta_I \rho - t_{ACT}\, \delta^P$$

or, using the above notation,

$$\delta^P = \frac{\rho\theta_I}{1+\tau_{ACT}}. \qquad (8)$$

The after tax dividend received by the unitholder/shareholder is then

$$\delta^{net} = \delta^P + \eta_p \delta^P - m(\delta^P + \eta_p \delta^P) = (1\text{-}m)\theta_p \delta^P$$

$$= \frac{\rho\theta_I}{1+\tau_{ACT}} \theta_p (1\text{-}m) \equiv \rho(1\text{-}t^f) \qquad (9)$$

The total formal tax on dividends is therefore:

$$t^f = 1 - \frac{\theta_I}{1+\tau_{ACT}} \theta_p (1-m). \qquad (10)$$

Foreign case - 'foreign source dividends'

The dividend distributed by the domestic CII to its shareholders\unitholders is:

$$\delta^P = \rho\theta_I^f - w^f \theta_I^f \rho - \tau_c \rho\theta_I^f + w^{ftc} \theta_I^f \rho - ACT^{Net},$$

$$\delta^P = \rho\theta_I^f (1 - w^f - \tau_c + w^{ftc}) - ACT^{Net} \qquad (11)$$

where the amount of the advance corporate tax net of ACT set off/repayments is:

$$ACT^{Net} = t_{ACT}\, \delta^P - (\tau_c - w^{ftc})\theta_I^f \rho \geq 0. \qquad (12)$$

Full setoff of ACT, and hence ACTNet = 0, is obtained for

$$\tau_c \geq \frac{\tau_{ACT}\left(1 - w^f + w^{ftc}\right) + w^{ftc}}{1+\tau_{ACT}} \qquad (13)$$

For wf = wftc = 0.15 and τACT =0.25, condition (13) requires that τc > 0.32. Hence, for τc < 0.32, ACTNet > 0, that is, the Advance Corporate Tax is effectively a tax on the CII and indirectly on the dividend income distributed to the shareholder/unitholder. Indeed, for

Case $ACT^{Net} > 0$ (AUT, $\tau_c = 0.2$),

the dividend distributed by the CII to its shareholders/unitholders is reduced by the factor $1+\tau_{ACT}$:

$$\delta^P = \frac{\rho\theta_I^f\left(1-w^f\right)}{1+\tau_{ACT}}$$

and

$$\delta^{net} = \frac{\rho\theta_I^f\left(1-w^f\right)}{1+\tau_{ACT}}\theta_p(1-m) \equiv r(1-t^f). \tag{14}$$

The total formal tax on dividends is therefore:

$$t^f = 1 - \frac{\theta_I^f\left(1-w^f\right)}{1+\tau_{ACT}}\theta_p(1-m). \tag{15}$$

Case $ACT^{Net} = 0$ (AIT, $\tau_c = 0.33$)

$$\delta^P = r\,\theta_I^f(1-w^f-\tau_c+w^{ftc}) \tag{16}$$

and

$$\delta^{net} = \rho\theta_I^f(1-w^f-\tau_c+w^{ftc})\,\theta_p\,(1-m) \equiv \rho(1-t^f). \tag{17}$$

The total formal tax on dividends is therefore

$$t^f = 1 - \theta_I^f(1-w^f-\tau_c+w^{ftc})\,\theta_p\,(1-m). \tag{18}$$

The numerical examples in the main text assume that wf = wftc.

Direct portfolio investment by UK individuals: domestic source dividend income

For comparison, the same computations are carried out in the case of direct portfolio investment. Including dividend relief, the after-tax dividend distributed by a resident company is:

$$\delta^{net} = \rho\theta^m(1-m) \equiv \rho(1-t^f) \tag{19}$$

for domestic investment. Hence the formal tax on dividend income from a direct portfolio investment in UK shares becomes:

$$t^f = 1 - \theta^m(1-m). \tag{20}$$

Direct portfolio investment by U.K. individual: foreign source dividend income

The after-tax dividend distributed by a non resident company is entitled to a foreign tax credit if subject to foreign taxation on distribution from the foreign company to the U.K. shareholder:

$$\delta^{net} = \rho\,(1 - w^f + w^{ftc} - m) \equiv \rho(1 - t^f). \tag{21}$$

Hence

$$t^f = 1 - \theta^{mf}\,(1 - w^f + w^{ftc} - m). \tag{22}$$

All numerical examples in the main text assume that the foreign tax credit compensates the foreign withholding tax, so: $w^f = w^{ftc}$.

AIV.3.2 The United States

In the United States, the same set of tax rules applies for open-ended and close-ended investment funds. Using the same notations as above and assuming that dividend income net of any tax paid at the CII-level is distributed to the unitholder/shareholder, the net dividend before personal taxes in the hands of a U.S. shareholder becomes:

$$\delta^P = \rho\,\theta_I^f - w^f\,\theta_I^f\,\rho = \rho\,\theta_I^f\,(1 - w^f) \tag{23}$$

where θ_I^f captures (any) foreign dividend relief extended to the U.S. CII. The net of tax dividend of the shareholder/unitholder is then

$$\delta^{net} = \delta^P - m\,(\delta^P + w^f\,\theta_I^f\,\rho) + w^{ftc}\theta_I^f\,\rho = \rho\,\theta_I^f\,(1-m) \equiv \rho(1-t^f) \tag{24}$$

assuming that wf=wftc and that the individual claims the foreign tax credit. Hence

$$t^f = 1 - \theta_I^f\,(1-m). \tag{25}$$

For domestic portfolio investment undertaken by the U.S. CII, set $\theta_I^f = 1$, and wf= wftc = 0.

In the case of direct portfolio investment by a U.S. marginal shareholder, the after-tax foreign source dividend income is

$$\delta^{net} = \rho\theta^{mf}\,(1 - w^f + w^{ftc} - m) \tag{26}$$

where, as before, θmf denotes the tax discrimination variable, capturing (any) foreign imputation credit extended to a U.S. individual direct portfolio investor. Hence

$$t^f = 1 - \theta^{mf}\,(1 - w^f + w^{ftc} - m). \tag{27}$$

All numerical examples in chapters 2 - 4 assume that wf= wftc.

For direct domestic portfolio investment, there is no integration relief for dividend income therefore by setting θmf = 1, and wf= wftc = 0 it follows that tf = m.

AIV.3.3 Belgium

Dividends received from portfolio investment in Belgium are subject to a final withholding tax. However, collective investment institutions are fully credited for the payment of withholding tax, effectively eliminating the dividend tax of the CII.

The after-tax dividend of the saver is thus:

$$\delta^{net} = \rho(1\text{-}m) \tag{28}$$

as Belgium operates a classical corporate tax system (the tax discrimination variable equals unity). The same expression applies for direct portfolio investment, though in this case the domestic withholding tax m may be either 15 or 25 percent, depending upon the 'vintage' of the shares acquired by the saver.

The after-tax dividend from foreign portfolio investment is

$$\delta^{net} = \rho(1\text{-}w^f)(1\text{-}m) \tag{29}$$

as foreign imputation credits are not extended to Belgian portfolio investors (the tax discrimination variables are all unity) and as withholding taxes levied in the (foreign) source country may not be credited against Belgian taxes. For direct foreign portfolio investment m = 0.25, whereas for investment via a CII (the distribution case), m = 0.15.

In general thus:

$$t^f = w^f + m(1\text{-}\ w^f) \tag{30}$$

for both direct portfolio investment (with m = 0.15 or 0.25) and investment via a CII in the distribution case (with m = 0.15). For domestic direct and intermediated investment $w^f = 0$.

AIV.3.4. Sweden

Dividends from portfolio investment constitute taxable income for Swedish (close-ended and open-ended) investment companies, and an imputed income corresponding to the share e (=100 per cent) of the market value of equity-related instruments is included with taxable income. As an offset to this, dividends paid to the shareholders are deductible against the base of the tax.

The classical treatment of corporate income means that the tax discrimination variable in the domestic case takes the value of unity. With τc as the statutory tax rate, the dividend paid by the CII is

$$\delta^P = \rho - \tau_c(\rho + \varepsilon q^m - \delta^P)$$

or

$$\delta^P = \rho - \frac{\tau_c \varepsilon q^m}{1-\tau_c} \tag{31}$$

taking into account the deductibility of dividends paid and the requirement to include an imputed income, equal to a fraction ε of the value of the portfolio of shares, with the tax base. Using (31) the after-tax dividend received by shareholder/unitholder equals

$$\delta^{net} = \left(\rho - \frac{\tau_c \varepsilon q^m}{1-\tau_c} \right)(1-m) \tag{32}$$

where m is the (uniform) personal tax on capital income. The formal tax on dividends channelled via a Swedish CII is therefore:

$$t^f = 1 - \frac{\delta^{net}}{\rho} = 1 - \left[1 - \frac{\frac{\tau_c \varepsilon}{1-\tau_c}}{\rho / q^m} \right](1-m). \tag{33}$$

In the case of domestic direct portfolio investment the corresponding expression is simply tf = m.

Sweden operates an exemption system to eliminate international double taxation. Neither mutual funds nor investment companies are given credit for foreign taxes paid by foreign bodies. However, full credit is (in general) given for withholding taxes, wf = wftc. Any imputation credit extended by a foreign government as part of a double taxation treaty constitutes taxable income to the Swedish CII, and to the individual shareholder in case of direct foreign portfolio investment. The following relationship can be derived:

$$t^f = 1 - \left[\theta_I^f - \frac{\frac{\tau_c \varepsilon}{1-\tau_c}}{\rho / q^m} \right](1-m) \tag{34}$$

as the formal tax on foreign source dividends. The tax discrimination variable θ_I^f captures (any) foreign dividend relief extended by the foreign government to the Swedish CII.

For foreign direct portfolio investment the formal tax becomes

$$t^f = 1-\theta^{mf}(1-m) \tag{35}$$

where θmf is the tax discrimination variable for individuals in case of direct foreign portfolio investment.

AIV.3.5 Australia

An Australian unit trust, which can be open-ended, semi-open-ended or closed-ended, is not a tax entity. A unitholder is subject to tax on his share of the income of the trust, and imputation credits and foreign tax credits flow through the trust to the unitholder. Using the same notation as in previous sections, the after-tax dividend received by the unitholder when the trust undertakes domestic portfolio investment equals

$$\delta^{net} = \rho\theta_I(1\text{-m}) \tag{36}$$

The formal tax on the dividend yield is hence

$$t^f = 1 - \theta_I (1 \text{-m}) \tag{37}$$

For foreign dividend income the after-tax dividend return is

$$\delta^{net} = \rho\theta^{mf} (1\text{-}w^f - m + w^{ftc}) \tag{38}$$

and

$$t^f = 1 - \theta^{mf} (1\text{-}w^f - m + w^{ftc}) \tag{39}$$

In the case of direct portfolio investment the corresponding equations are obtained by replacing θ_I and θ_I^f by θ_p and θ_P^f.

AIV.4 Summary

The methodology for measuring tax incentives impacting on portfolio investment outlined in the previous section for each representative country, determines *i)* the saver's/CII's pre-tax return on portfolio investment, *ii)* the formal tax on dividends, *iii)* the after-tax return on portfolio investment, *iv)* the tax wedge on portfolio investment and *v)* the effective tax rate. This section collects the equations used for each of these steps, and Table A.III summarise the input parameters used in computing the numerical results for the four countries.

i) Pre-tax return on portfolio investment:

$$\frac{\rho}{q^m} = \frac{r}{\theta^m} \tag{40}$$

where r is the real market interest rate, θ^m is the tax discrimination variable for the marginal domestic investor and q^m is the share price. Table 4.2 in chapter 4 and column (1) in Table AV.1 below show figures for the parameter ρ, under the assumption that q^m = 1, r = 10% in each representative country.

ii) Formal tax rate on dividend income, tf.

Columns (3) and (5) in Table AV.1 give a parametrical representation of formal tax rates according to country and type of investment, while columns (4) and (6) show the rates used to calculate formal tax rates in the main part of the report..

iii) After-tax return on portfolio investment, s

$$s = \rho\left(1 - t^{f}\right) \tag{41}$$

iv) Tax wedge on portfolio investment, MTWII

$$MTW_{II} = r - s = r - \rho(1 - t^{f}). \tag{42}$$

v) Effective tax rate, te

$$t^{e} = \frac{MTW_{II}}{r}. \tag{43}$$

Table AV.1 Required Pre-tax rate of return (ρ) and Formal tax on dividends (tf)1

	$\rho = rq^m/\theta^m$	Parameters assumptions	Formal Tax on *Domestic* Dividend Income	Parameters assumptions	Formal Tax on *Foreign* Dividend Income	Parameters assumptions
United Kingdom						
AUT	6.4%	$q^m=1$, $\theta^m=1.25$, r=10%.	$1 - \frac{\theta_I}{1+\tau_{ACT}}\theta_p(1-m)$	$\theta_I=1.25$, $\theta_p=1.25$, $t_{ACT}=0.25$, m=0.4	$1 - \frac{\theta_I^f(1-w^f)}{1+\tau_{ACT}}\theta_p(1-m)$	$w^f=0.15$, $\theta_p=1.25$, $t_{ACT}=0.25$, m=0.4, $\theta_I^f=1$
AIT	6.4%	See AUT	$1 - \frac{\theta_I}{1+\tau_{ACT}}\theta_p(1-m)$	see AUT	$1 - \theta_I^f(1-\tau_c)\theta_p(1-m)$	$t_c=0.33$, m=0.4, for θ_I^f, see AUT
DPI	6.4%	See AUT	$1 - \theta_p(1-m)$	$\theta^m=1.25$, m=0.4	$1 - \theta^{mf}(1-m)$	m = 0.4, $\theta^{mf}=\theta_I^f$ for AUT.
United States						
CII	10%	$q^m=1$, $\theta^m=1$, r=10%.	m	m = 0.466	$1-\theta_I^f(1-m)$	m = 0.47, UK: $\theta_I^f=1.25$, all other countries: $\theta_I^f=1$.
DPI	10%	see CII	m	m = 0.466	$1-\theta^{mf}(1-m)$	m = 0.466, $\theta^{mf}=\theta_I^f$
Belgium						
CII	10%	$q^m=1$, $\theta^m=1$, r=10%.	m	m = 0.15	$w^f + m(1-w^f)$	m = 0.15, $w^f=0.15$, UK: $w^f=0$
DPI	10%	See CII	m		$w^f + m(1-w^f)$	m = 0.25, w^f see CII
Sweden						
CII	10%	$q^m=1$, $\theta^m=1$, r=10%.	$1 - \left[1 - \frac{\frac{\tau_c\varepsilon}{1-\tau_c}}{\rho/q^m}\right](1-m)$	m = 0.3, open-end: $t_c=0.3$, ε=0.015, close-end: $\tau_c=0.28$, ε=0.02.	$1 - \left[\theta_I^f - \frac{\frac{\tau_c\varepsilon}{1-\tau_c}}{\rho/q^m}\right](1-m)$	for m, τ_c and ε, see domestic; for θ_I^f, see DPI, except open-end CII into UK, where $\theta_I^f=1$.
DPI	10%	See CII	m	m = 0.3	$1-\theta^{mf}(1-m)$	m = 0.3, for UK, $\theta^{mf}=1.25$, all other $\theta^{mf}=1$
Australia						
CII	8%	$q^m=1$, $\theta^m=1.56$, r=10%.	$1 - \theta_I(1-m)$	m = 0.485, $\theta_I=1.56$	$1 - \theta_I^f(1-m)$	m = 0.485, $\theta_I^f=1$
DPI	8%	$q^m=1$, $\theta^m=1.56$, r=10%.	$1 - \theta^m(1-m)$	m = 0.485, $\theta^m=1.56$	$1 - \theta^m(1-m)$	m=0.485, UK: $\theta^{mf}=1.25$, all other countries $\theta^{mf}=1$

1. The equations in this table are derived using wf = wftc.

NOTES

1. King and Fullerton (1984), p. 24. Hence the cost of capital for a firm financing out of retained earnings must be the same for all shareholders.

2. The effective tax rate te is a real rate of tax and the comparable tax on interest is therefore m(r + π)/r , that is the tax wedge on the return to bonds divided by the real market interest rate. Clearly m would differ from m(r + π)/r when there is a high rate of inflation, otherwise the difference may be disregarded.

3. We define, θm=1+u/(1-u) where u is the rate of imputation credit offered the (marginal) shareholder. For example u = 0.2, makes θm = 1.25.

4. It is assumed that dividend income and interest income are subject to the same statutory tax rate since most countries tax capital income in the same way at the individual level. The main result does not change under the alternative assumption under which tax rates on dividend income and interest income are different. In this case, however the pre-personal rate of return on equity would also depend on the relative size of the two rates: $\rho = \frac{(r+\pi)q^m}{\theta^m}\frac{(1-m^r)}{(1-m^m)}$, where mr is the statutory tax rate on interest income.

5. Several countries, including the United Kingdom and the United States, tax the CII's shareholders/unitholders *as if* dividend income had actually been distributed.

6. For Belgium, the transactions tax on capitalisation shares may be interpreted as implying that Q < 1. However, as shown below, this report chooses to model the transaction tax as affecting the formal tax tf.

OECD PUBLICATIONS, 2, rue André-Pascal, 75775 PARIS CEDEX 16
PRINTED IN FRANCE
(23 1999 03 1 P) ISBN 92-64-17045-6 – No. 50597 1999